D1333167

FROM DICKENS TO *DRACULA*

Ranging from the panoramic novels of Dickens to the horror of *Dracula*, Gail Turley Houston examines the ways in which the language and imagery of economics, commerce, and particularly of banking are transformed in Victorian Gothic fiction, and traces literary and uncanny elements in economic writings of the period. Houston shows how banking crises were often linked with ghosts or inexplicable non-human forces and financial panic was figured through Gothic or supernatural means. In *Little Dorrit* and *Villette* characters are literally haunted by money, while the unnameable intimations of *Dracula* and *Dr. Jekyll and Mr. Hyde* are represented alongside realist economic concerns. Houston pays particular attention to the term "panic" as it moved between its double uses as a banking term and a defining emotion in sensational and Gothic fiction. This stimulating interdisciplinary book reveals that the worlds of Victorian economics and Gothic fiction, seemingly separate, actually complemented and enriched each other.

GAIL TURLEY HOUSTON is Associate Professor of English at the University of New Mexico.

CAMBRIDGE STUDIES IN NINETEENTH-CENTURY LITERATURE AND CULTURE

Nineteenth-century British literature and culture have been rich fields for inter-disciplinary studies. Since the turn of the twentieth century, scholars and critics have tracked the intersections and tensions between Victorian literature and the visual arts, social organization, economic life, technical innovations, scientific thought – in short, culture in its broadest sense. In recent years, theoretical challenges and historiographical shifts have unsettled the assumptions of previous scholarly synthesis and called into question the terms of older debates. Whereas the tendency in much past literary critical interpretation was to use the metaphor of culture as "background," feminist, Foucauldian, and other analyses have employed more dynamic models that raise questions of power and of circulation. Such developments have reanimated the field.

This series aims to accommodate and promote the most interesting work being undertaken on the frontiers of the field of nineteenth-century literary studies: work which intersects fruitfully with other fields of study such as history, or literary theory, or the history of science. Comparative as well as interdisciplinary approaches are welcomed.

A complete list of titles published will be found at the end of the book.

FROM DICKENS TO *DRACULA*:

Gothic, Economics, and Victorian Fiction

BY

GAIL TURLEY HOUSTON

CAMBRIDGE
UNIVERSITY PRESS

CAMBRIDGE UNIVERSITY PRESS

Cambridge, New York, Melbourne, Madrid, Cape Town, Singapore, São Paulo

CAMBRIDGE UNIVERSITY PRESS

The Edinburgh Building, Cambridge CB2 2RU, UK

Published in the United States of America by Cambridge University Press, New York

www.cambridge.org
Information on this title: www.cambridge.org/9780521846776

First published 2005

Printed in the United Kingdom at the University Press, Cambridge

A catalogue record for this book is available from the British Library

ISBN-13 978-0-521-84677-6 hardback
ISBN-10 0-521-84677-3 hardback

Dedication

For Helen Turley

Epigraph

[Man] is even more spectral than the spectral. Man *makes himself fear.* He makes himself into the fear that he inspires.

(Jacques Derrida, *Specters of Marx.* Copyright 1999 from *Specters of Marx: The State of the Debt, the Work of Mourning, and the New International.* Reproduced by permission of Routledge / Taylor & Francis Books, Inc.)

Money, the great machine of trade and commerce, is, perhaps, the most valuable invention of man. But alas! like other great discoveries, it has been perverted by false laws into a horrid engine for grinding the labouring industrious classes to the dust.

(J. H. Macdonald, *The Errors and Evils of the Bank Charter Act of 1844* [London: Richardson Brothers, 1855])

[Money] contains its own lack as a nightmare always ready to surface.

(John Vernon, *Money and Fiction: Literary Realism in the Nineteenth and Early Twentieth Centuries* [Ithaca: Cornell University Press, 1984])

Contents

Illustrations

Acknowledgments

This study could not have been done without the help of many colleagues, friends, and family. Many thanks are due to Ann Dinsdale and the staff at the Brontë Parsonage Museum and Library, as well as the staff at the British Library, the University of London Library, the Huntington Library, Guildhall Library, the Beinecke Library, and the New York Public Library. The University of New Mexico Inter-Library Loan staff were always helpful with the many demands I made on their time. Joyce Bell and Rachel Decker, of the Women Studies Program at the University of New Mexico, were a godsend in the final stages of the writing. The many research grants from the University of New Mexico made research travel possible, and a year-long sabbatical, also from the University of New Mexico, was invaluable to the completion of this work. Discussions with colleagues and students must not be overlooked as providing important insights into the process of writing this book. Anne Bingham graciously helped to prepare the last draft of the study. I am also indebted to the refined sensibilities and professional guidance of Cambridge University Press literature editor Linda Bree. The insightful comments of the first and second readers also find their way into the revisions of the manuscript. My gratitude also goes to my brilliant mentor, Alexander Welsh, who, during my graduate studies and thereafter, taught me the meaning of professional scholarship and personal integrity. Minrose Gwin and Gary Harrison have provided friendship and mentoring all along the way. I thank SueAnn Schatz for her gracious support as well as Sally Mitchell for generously sharing her wealth of material, including *A Banker's Daughter*, with Victorianists everywhere. I thank, as well, Tate Schieferle for kindly allowing me to use the letters of Robert Louis Stevenson. Brandie Siegfried, Claudia Harris, and Susan Howe remain friends despite the geographical distances between us. My colleagues at the University of New Mexico also enriched my thinking and my life during the writing of this book. As always, I thank Michael, Melissa, Rory, and Kate for their unfailing patience, support, and love, especially during difficult economic times that ironically underwrote a portion of the composition of this manuscript. Margaret, Christopher, Mark, Louise, and Kent must also not be forgotten in my thanks. The four-legged muses of my household provided cheerful consolation during the solitary rewriting phase of the project.

Abbreviations

BL	British Library
BPM	Brontë Parsonage Museum
CB	Charlotte Brontë
CD	Charles Dickens
HM	Huntington Museum
RLS	Robert Louis Stevenson
UL	University of London Library

CHAPTER 1

Banking on panic: the historical record and a theoretical frame

> If we were in a more primitive state, if we lived under roofs of leaves, and kept cows and sheep and creatures, instead of banker's accounts ... well and good.[1]

> It has not been sufficiently observed how very peculiar and technical is the sense in which we now talk of "panic." It would naturally signify a general destruction of all confidence, a universal distrust, a cessation of credit in general. But a panic is now come to mean a state in which there is a confidence in the Bank of England, and in nothing but the Bank of England.[2]

When Walter Bagehot declared in 1864 that "panic" had become virtually an economic term, he articulated what Judith Halberstam refers to as "a Gothic economy," a condition in which the "logic" of capitalism transforms "even the most supernatural of images into material images of capitalism itself."[3] Many critics point out that it is no coincidence that fiction became the most popular genre at the same time that capitalism's construction of reality required that a new discourse be developed around "the economy."[4] Academic studies of nineteenth-century British economics vis-à-vis literature also assume that in the Victorian period economics fashions fictions, and fiction produces economic realities. Fashionable cultural studies chiasms, of which the previous statement is one, are themselves illustrations of a Gothic economy in which different ideological modes or ontological entities haunt their others. In this study, I argue that Gothic tropes register, manage, and assess the intense panic produced and elided by the unstable Victorian economy to which Bagehot refers in his startling statement. Concomitantly, I show that, however self-consciously scientific economic discourse becomes in the nineteenth century, it is frequently accompanied by terrifying phantom appendages.

Since panic was being described and represented in the popular Gothic literature of the time, I also test Bagehot's statement about the monolithic economic nature of panic. I specifically juxtapose nineteenth-century economic discourse with novels that refer explicitly to banking or banking crises vis-à-vis ghosts or inexplicable non-human forces as well as novels in which there are points of contact between banking panic and other forms of crisis that are figured through Gothic or supernatural means. The novels I study include two classic Victorian Gothic tales, *Dracula* and *Dr. Jekyll and Mr. Hyde,* along with two narratives that marry the realist with the Gothic mode, *Little Dorrit* and *Villette.* If *Little Dorrit* and *Villette* illustrate the mundane world of capital, economic crassness also appears quite naturally in *Dracula* and *Dr. Jekyll,* even though one does not expect to see the horrifying Gothic protagonist at the bank and certainly not fumbling for petty cash. Likewise, while *Dracula* and *Dr. Jekyll* condition the reader to the unnameable and uncanny, one cannot deny that Little Dorrit and Lucy's obsession with money represents a kind of haunting.

It might be said that *unheimlich* (meaning, of course, "unfamiliar," literally, "unhomely") is the appropriate term to describe the milieu of the texts I examine, especially when it is recalled that the word "economics" comes from the Greek term for control of the house.[5] As Linda Nicholson suggests in *Gender and History,* prior to the seventeenth century the economic was not constructed as separate from the familial domicile.[6] Indeed, as Mary Poovey reminds us, the domestic economy – the sphere in which the wife oversaw the needs of the household and managed a monetary budget as part of her duties – precedes and gives shape to the professional, masculine sphere of professional economics that increasingly concentrated on national and global finance.[7] While absolutely dependent upon the female-dominated domestic economy, the capitalist version of economics focused all but monomaniacally on the individual's economic desires vis-à-vis a global network of goods, suppressing the communal nature of former definitions of economics. Thus, though seemingly expanding its focus of study, professional economics also elided the domestic economy that had been its source.

In real ways, this elision must have made the Victorian household, in its diminished form, a place of *unheimlich* despite and because of the culture's sanctification of the home and hearth. Certainly, in the texts I examine, the former meaning of "economy" haunts the skeletal remains of "economics," just as the former reality of the "domestic economy" figures as a ghostly remainder in the industrialized Victorian period. Indeed, nineteenth-century English banking precisely illustrates Raymond Williams's concept of the simultaneous existence of emergent and residual cultural practices. While the modern notion of "the economy" itself was being established, as Edwardian economist Ellis T. Powell remarked so vividly, "It was the projection of the old conditions into the new era ... that caused much of the financial disquietude of the mid-Victorian age. They survived like the caecum in the human frame, into an era which had no use for them."[8] Powell's description adds a Gothic twist to Williams's prescient understanding of cultural changes.

With the rise of capitalism and the concomitant demise of the household as the center of the economy, the subject became fragmented and compartmentalized, a self haunted at home as well as at work. Responding to this condition, Fredric Jameson suggests that prior to the establishment of the market economy it was not necessary to create a sign system through which to understand the relationships between the economic and the social, "because on that level they were never separate from one another." At the same time, there was a horrifying merging of subjects, for the new economy also created a ghostly haunting in which, according to Jameson, "the opposing classes necessarily carr[y] the other around" and are thus traumatized by this "foreign body" that it is impossible to "exorcize."[9] But long before Jameson many Victorian writers, including Marx, knew that capitalist compartmentalization produced haunting psychic superstructures that would require the new (capitalist-produced) profession of psychology to medicate the alienated, disoriented (capitalist-produced) *homo economicus.*

If the relics of the domestic (economy) haunted Victorian capitalism, it might also be true that the domestication of the new economy and the domestic sphere it valorized were characterized by *unheimlich.* Panic, that is to say, became naturalized in the tropes used by economists and Gothic novelists alike. In this regard, it might be said that the rhetorical features of professional economics were in some ways gothicized and that the Gothic was economized. Indeed, the language of panic and crisis so elemental in the nineteenth-century Gothic novel paralleled references to the Victorian bourgeoisie as the "uneasy classes," haunted not by the Gothic novel but by the Gothic marketplace and the households it had consumed.[10] That women readers, trapped in the new domestic economy, made up the Gothic novels' majority of consumers throughout the age goes in tandem with the domestication of the Gothic novel as it moved its settings from the exotic to trivialized domestic spaces. With this in mind, one might experience a hint of *frisson* when remembering that nineteenth-century banks were referred to as "houses" and that it was common for the small family bankers' home to exist (up)on the actual premises of the banking establishment. These linguistic and physical constructions of the bank as a home ostensibly served to domesticate the inhospitable features of a nascent capitalist society. Naturalizing, that is, making banking panic at home, Victorian classical and neo-classical economic theory constructed *homo economicus* as able to tolerate recurrent crisis.

Before turning to the historical matter of Victorian economic panic, in the following section I lay out the theoretical foundations of this study, beginning with the construction of the field of economics itself. Though from William Jevons (1870s) onwards it has been *de rigueur* for professional economists to view themselves as rigorously scientific, by the 1980s some in the field had begun to deconstruct the dismal science.[11] Critiquing economic stances based on Enlightenment principles of reason, objectivity, universality, and truth, post-modern theorists question monolithic assumptions. For example, warning of the "totalizing impulse" of economics, Douglas and Amy Koritz analyze the work of Gary Becker, a Nobel Laureate in economics who suggests, as the Koritzs summarize, that all social dynamics can be described as "exchanges of owned properties culminating in a reflexive property – the individual – that has property in itself." Similarly, Martin Hollis interrogates ostensible universal rules about the market that ignore specific "time, place or stage of historical development" because such laws ignore the infinite happenstances and variables that influence economic events.[12]

Others suggest that the scientific method is hardly objective. Observing that neo-classical theory is always hypothetical – concerned with not "what will happen but of what would happen, if certain conditions were fulfilled" – Hollis points out that those conditions can only be realized based upon the successful fruition of the economist's computations. If economics as a profession disciplines what can be said about material economic conditions, Hollis argues that it is impossible to discipline or rationalize real-world economic conditions themselves. Another problem is that one can only evaluate economic theories through the rules set up by the discipline of economics: "Neo-Classical economics is the study of Rational Economic Man," that is, of a human being who "conforms to the model." Hence, economic discourse itself is always in danger of falling into circular argumentation and tautologies.[13] One such tautology occurs in David Ricardo's assumption that money is a fictional concept. Admitting that gold is just as variable in its value as any other commodity, Ricardo consciously "suppose[s]" money to be "invariable" in order to anchor his economic system.[14]

Current critiques of economics within the field focus on the assertion that economics is a "system of rhetoric" with a stylistics, poetics, history, and ideology of its own.[15] In terms of its history, asserting that economic theory was initiated in 1776 with Adam Smith's *Wealth of Nations*, Keith Tribe suggests that economic *discourse* only began in the nineteenth century, when it first became possible to construct economics through "systematic analysis of production and distribution." As Tribe explains, this new "economic agenc[y]" makes it possible to focus on the economy qua economy rather than just the larger political organization of the polity.[16] As to discursive practice, as Warren J. Samuels points out, analyzing the economy requires the use of "language to describe, interpret, and explain the economy," in other words, to use "one artifact to write about another artifact."[17] Indeed, the economist's use of analogies and appeals to authority, statistics, and economic models or paradigms relies upon metaphorical devices that assume some kind of narrative.[18] Focusing on the fictional hero *homo economicus* and the fictional economic world he inhabits, economics must be viewed, as Donald McCloskey argues, as "saturated with narration" and essential storytelling.[19]

Highlighting the connection Adam Smith makes between cause and effect in order to cover over the indeterminacies that would undermine the economist's authority, Mary Poovey describes the crucial point at which Smith turns to fictive narrative. As Smith writes: "We should never leave any chasm or Gap in the thread of the narration even though there are no remarkable events to fill up that space. The very notion of a gap makes us uneasy for what should have happened in that time." Smith, Poovey maintains, resorts to using literary tropes to solve the problem when he resolves that the "other way of keeping up the connection" between cause and effect is "the Poeticall method, which connects the different facts by some slight circumstances *which often had nothing in the bringing about the series of the events.*"[20] Astoundingly, then, the scientific method developed in the seventeenth and eighteenth centuries allows, even depends upon, fictions. Later, however, when establishing the professional status of economics in the early part of the Victorian period, economists made a point of distinguishing themselves sharply from literary critics, who, like the economists, were simultaneously establishing their own field as a profession.[21]

In a way, the "New Economic Critics" return us to Smith's concession to fiction, for they suggest that literary critics must examine the mutual relations between economic and literary discourse.[22] Indeed, Smith's assertion also must be chiastically reversed to acknowledge the way that economics comes to fill nineteenth-century fiction's fissures brought about by capitalist economics. Contending that in Victorian fiction money acts as the sign that links events and characters in the novel, John Vernon, for example, argues that the "conventions of paper money and the conventions of realistic fiction constitute a code collectively shared." Or, as Christina Crosby puts it, Victorian works of literature actively accustomed Victorians "to the imaginary relations money effects, even as literary texts are riven by the contradictions inherent in money."[23]

My academic work has increasingly become anxiously engaged in studying the economics of literature and the literature of economics, for while it is certain that the Victorian novel is informed by many panics and anxieties about race, class, gender, sexuality, and empire, these have been richly studied to great and continuing effect. In contrast, there has not been enough study of how England's economic system incorporated panic and how the economy informed and was informed by the novel and its Gothic tropes. In this study, I focus on the mid to late Victorian period, a time before banking became almost completely centralized in the early twentieth century. If, as Warren Montag notes, ideology is "the ghost of the material world," I seek to find traces of panic that are a hallmark of nineteenth-century British fiction and capitalism while also acknowledging the conundrum that economic theory is unrelated to economic reality and that economic reality can only be represented discursively.[24] Thus I add to the monstrously large body of criticism on the Gothic novel that teeters dangerously into the tendency, like Dr. Frankenstein, to create ever more "hideous progenies" of theoretical analysis as they fulfill the will to dominate the Gothic text, a tantalizing formulation conceived by Fred Botting.[25] At the same time, I endeavor to suggest new paradigms through which to engage the novels so central to criticism of the Gothic.

I am also in agreement with Rastko Močnik's statement that in capitalist systems there is no ideological position outside of that "produced within the economic sphere."[26] Nevertheless, having faith in the reality and power of individual and group agency – and confident that any theoretical position must ultimately declare its faith in something – I am persuaded that if proclamations like Močnik's can be made, then there are more possibilities for individual agency and influence on culture than such a statement might imply. I also am certain that there are material, economic realities that affect and are affected by real people. That is why it is important to study the discourses that speak through and are converted by real people who, as I suggest, bank on panic – since, as I am contending, to live in a capitalist economic system means that one is permanently in crisis. But I also believe that, whereas language may speak the self, human speakers do change language in creative, unanticipated, powerful ways. Indeed, I own up to the belief that the use of literary tropes can have the power to name the dangers of capitalism and exact a measure of responsibility and change.

Using the strategies of the New Economic Critics, I suggest that between 1850 and 1900 the Gothic – which haunts its other, realistic fiction – shares a code with the conventions of what Rondo Cameron refers to as the "'monetization' of the entire economy" and ultimately "bankerization." Jean-Joseph Goux defines bankerization as the centralization of banking and the almost complete turn to monetary exchanges that are facilitated through credit (settlement through sign) rather than gold, check, or banknote.[27] As will be noted in the following section, the dominance of banking came about through amalgamation of banks that could then centralize capital under their aegis and thus subordinate capital controlled by industries. By 1900 the unstable Victorian economy had transitioned from competitive, industrial capitalism to monopolist capitalism, a form of capitalism requiring banks to monopolize lending and other forms of monetary transactions. Though bankerization occurred when the gold standard was rescinded in 1931 in England, its traces were already apparent in the Victorian period. Marx, for example, asserts that England's banking structure was "the most artificial and most developed product turned out by the capitalist mode of production."[28] Concerned that banking was becoming the controlling middleman, he worries that banks "concentrat[e] large amounts of the loanable money capital in the bankers' hands." Likewise, he argues that, replacing individual moneylenders, bankers were able to meet their powerful industrial and commercial capitalist clients from a more powerful position as "representatives of all moneylenders." As a result, banks became the "general managers of money-capital" by concentrating "all the borrowers vis-à-vis all the lenders."[29]

The Bank Act of 1844, which will be discussed in more depth in the second half of this chapter, was a significant step in the paradigm shift towards bankerization. Gordon Bigelow asserts that the Act represents the establishment of a "modern mode of knowledge" in which all problems are considered within the "fetishized" space of "the economy."[30] Goux believes that in this fetishized economy the move away from the material standard of gold to the paper standard of the note and then credit is "homologous" to modernist literature, which ceases to posit a connection between signifiers and signifieds. In other words, signifiers are inconvertible or incapable of being converted into the signified. Causing the novel genre to lose "its confident realism," bankerization underwrites literature that becomes increasingly fragmented and cubist, according to Goux. The meaning of bankerization, then, is similar to Patrick Brantlinger's iteration that the move towards defining money "in increasingly relativizing terms" should be interpreted as "a general 'crisis of representation.'"[31]

The crisis of representation worried Lord Overstone, among others. Fearing that a credit system could not "coexist with an honest and well regulated Monetary system," Overstone referred to the "system of Credit" as "vicious and dangerous," as well as potentially "too gigantic, and too powerful to be grappled with."[32] Three decades later, Bertram W. Currie echoed Overstone's concerns. Testifying before the Royal Commission on the Recent Changes in the Relative Values of Precious Metals, he responded positively when asked if London was not "the financial centre of the world" and a "clearing house to which all debts are referred and through which they are paid." When the query was, "The gold sovereign is the *language* in which it carries on its transactions?" Mr. Currie agreed, remarking that "anything which would shake the faith of mankind in the fact that what £100 means is a certain amount of gold of a certain weight and fineness, might disturb it very materially."[33] For both Currie and Overstone, the center would not hold if the world's premier capitalist, banker, producer, consumer – London – was cut off from the language of the gold standard, which linked capitalist processes to an ostensible, knowable reality.

Others were more sanguine or at least savvy about the process of bankerization. When Bagehot comments on "the vast increase of credit" occurring in banking during the second half of the nineteenth century, he notices a form of bankerization.[34] Charles Dickens reveals a sophisticated awareness of the phenomenon in *Little Dorrit* when he has Mrs. Merdle nonchalantly remark to Mrs. Gowan that primitive societies keep cows and sheep, whereas Victorian England keeps "banker's accounts."[35] In making this comment, Mrs. Merdle recognizes intuitively what Robert Heilbronner asserts: economics "appears in history only when activities of provisioning" of human needs become considered as inhabiting an autonomous and separate sphere.[36] Noting that "money is never used in commerce now, except to pay balances of debts," H. D. Macleod extols bankerization to Parliament in 1887, saying, "the better organised and the more extensive the system of banking is the less bullion you require to carry on commerce ... All commerce is now carried on by the creation, the transfer, and the extinction of obligations."[37] A decade later, George H. Pownall calmly acknowledges that cash has come to be used only to pay wages as "nearly everything is done by clearing."[38]

With the proliferation of complex forms of paper money – including, but not limited to, bills of exchange, checks, bonds, stocks, consols, drafts, promissory notes, Exchequer bills, Treasury bills – the gold in the gold standard gradually became obsolete. Thus the question, what is cash?, is not just rhetorical. As the renowned Bagehot asserts, businessmen "are perplexed to define accurately what money is; *how* to count they know, but *what* to count they do not know."[39] In 1883 British economist Henry Sidgwick reiterated the difficulty of defining money when he declared that, "the very denotation of the term money" is "fluctuating and uncertain." Nevertheless, Sidgwick attends to the fact that "the immaterial part" of money functions as efficiently and legitimately as cash or coin and that, like gold or paper money, it is "accepted in final settlement of all debts."[40]

For banking to achieve its vast modern commercial powers, postponing payment – or to put it another way, advancing credit – had to be established on a large scale, an act of faith of grand proportions.[41] Indeed, financial credit entailed perhaps more faith in the economy than ever was required of those Victorians who experienced the religious crisis of faith in God. John Mills essentially aligned banking crisis with religious loss of belief when he concluded that, "Panic is the destruction, in the mind, of a bundle of beliefs." Marx also writes of capitalism's reliance on "faith in the prevailing mode of production and its predestined order."[42] Certainly, the use of credit as noun relies heavily on emphasizing credit as verb, as Poovey points out, for participation in capitalism amounts to faith in capital as invisible transcendental signifier.[43] Remarking upon the secular leap of faith, Thomas DiPiero suggests that though economic and linguistic systems are inconvertible – that is, not connected to material reality – they are still accepted with faith by the general population as long as they remain mystified and fetishized. What DiPiero writes about fiction can equally be said of economics, that is, that it "is realistic only when its legitimating agency is invisible and the historical traces of its past are effaced."[44]

Almost a prophet of despair in his belief in the "total bankerization of existence," Goux contends that the banking system that evolved under Victorian capitalism has now become the specter haunting the globe. Believing that "the regime of inconvertibility" has become "structural" and "ontological" in the modern period, Goux fears that this end to representation might be just a foreshadowing of absolute bankerization through a monolithic combination of financial configurations and cyberspace. It is no wonder, then, that he refers to "the hegemony of economic discourse" as "ever more crushing."[45] On the other hand, in light of Bagehot's suggestion that capital is "all-engrossing," Bigelow finds that the resulting "fantasy of a total circulation brings with it the threat of total indeterminacy."[46] The opposite totalities described by Bigelow and Goux are classic examples of how the rhetoric of crisis and panic shape and are shaped by the analysis and theorization of Gothic economies.

To recognize this puts economic and novelistic discourse under rhetorical scrutiny. If the business cycle has been described as consisting of "fluctuations in: (1) employment, (2) aggregate output, (3) prices, and (4) money value of the national product," it has tremendous repercussions on the quality of emotional, psychological, and physical life.[47] In this study, I assume that words have the power to produce biological actions and reactions in the human body. I also assume that "panic" – whether performed or felt as an unmediated essence – is a condition with dramatic biological and psychological manifestations. Thus, with the phrase "banking on panic" I assume that in the Victorian period the human body and psyche are containers of the culture's anxieties not only about capitalism but also about the transition from competitive capitalism to monopolistic capitalism. That capitalism adores risk, individualism, and the return of the repressed, then, implies that in a capitalist society there is a need for investments in panic. In such a system, the subject is motivated by the panic caused by the fact that there are no assurances that the economy will not cycle through a depression at any time and there are few safety nets if that depression occurs as one faces retirement, catastrophic illness, divorce, natural disaster, racism, sexism, or any of the other variables that enter into heightening the level of individual emotional and economic disaster experienced in a market crash. I have chosen to study *Villette, Little Dorrit, The Strange Case of Dr. Jekyll and Mr. Hyde,* and *Dracula* because they seem to have profoundly rich psychic and bodily effects upon the reader and because they register the culture's economic and other forms of panic in the most subliminal, and, therefore, powerful fashion.

In addition, I privilege the novel over other forms of discourse, including economic, because of its overdetermined[48] hybridity. I see the novel as an extraordinarily robust site for expression and change through the dialogue produced between reader and text. Flawed though it may be, in some ways the genre of the novel fulfills Jameson's suggestion that social life is a seamless web that cannot be disconnected from economic events or sign systems.[49]

If, as I assert, Victorian capitalism normalized economic panic so that it became necessary to a so-called healthy economy, what did the novel do in return? I believe that the novels I examine create potently descriptive narratives in which economic panic is a deep structure; that they model means of managing and sublimating panic in order to achieve fiscal success;

that they encourage unlimited desire while also relying upon crisis and permanent panic in order to contain that desire; and that they illustrate, as Jameson argues, that desire itself is an historically specific product of capitalism in that one cannot speak of desire unless it has been abstracted and isolated out from the seamless web of culture. Likewise, my study rests on Jameson's suggestion that psychological fragmentation is only possible after capitalist economies are established in the eighteenth and nineteenth centuries.[50] Nevertheless, while depicting fragmentation, despair, and submission to larger economic forces, the novel often produces a space for displays of unexpected dignity and strange but admirable, affirmative acts.

With John Vernon, I believe that the realistic novel is the result of a "complex evolution in the art of representation" that stretches "across all of human culture – across art, politics, dress, economics, religion."[51] Thus to view generic nineteenth-century English fiction as anything but richly complex, conflicted, and dialogical about the full range of issues confronting Victorians is hardly to understand its enormous impact. Further, I suggest that the Gothic tropes that emerge in so many Victorian novels act as (a)venues of Victorian conflict, containing and putting into dialectical exchange the hybrid languages of economics, science, the Gothic, and the psychological. When I use the term "contain," I refer to it as both noun and verb, thus drawing upon its range of ideological nuances. By adding the phrase "dialectical exchange," I include the notion that though the novel may be itself contained by capitalism and the State, its dependence on hybrid languages always creates a space for unintended and inadvertent motifs, transactions, and rhetorical features that might produce openings for revolution.

Jerrold Hogle describes classical Gothic literature, which became so popular in England at the end of the eighteenth century, as including the following narrative conventions: a setting in an "antiquated space" which contains secrets from the past that haunt the characters in psychological and physical ways through the supernatural forms of "ghosts, specters, or monsters"; these entities foreground "unresolved crimes or conflicts that can no longer be successfully buried from view." As such, this genre plays with and fluctuates between mundane reality and supernatural phenomena.[52] Maggie Kilgour reminds us of Ian Watt's important contention that the Gothic and psychoanalysis share "a sense of the mysterious and immobilising power of the past." David Punter adds that the "Gothic knows the body" and its "fragility" and "vulnerability" and thus makes available a "language" for imagining "bodies and their terrors."[53] These formal properties ensure that the Gothic is "excessive, grotesque, overspilling its own boundaries and limits" and that it has sensational effects upon the bodies of its readers.[54]

Paula R. Backscheider suggests that the study of the eighteenth-century Gothic novel must consider the popularity of this genre in light of its excesses; why, that is, was it so popular, and how does the Gothic represent the reading audience's anxieties and wishes at specific times in their history.[55] Likewise, Hogle notes that the Gothic features a "second 'unconscious' of deep-seated social and historical dilemmas." This is what Annette Kuhn refers to as the "cultural instrumentality" of a genre, that is, how it represents cultural conflicts and anxieties.[56] Such approaches are implicitly associated with what I assume in this study: that the Victorian Gothic, as it appears in the novel, illustrates supernatural responses to capitalist requirements that Victorian culture bank on panic. In other words, a culture that continually banks on panic would naturally produce overdrawn (that is, representing economic lack as well as stylistic excess) accounts, if you will, not only at the bank but in the culture's literature as well. Indeed, it is well to remember Adam Smith's turn to literature to fill gaps in the relationship between cause and effect: literature, particularly the Gothic, fills the gap that opens up in economics when that science views emotional and psychological accounts of the subject's reactions to economic panic as illegitimate data.

It is important to acknowledge, then, that, as David Punter notes, the Gothic can be understood not only as a genre specific to the period between the 1760s and 1820s but also as a term that describes broader impulses in the novel in general.[57] Julian Wolfreys outlines the suggestion that after 1820 the Gothic became a trope. Instead of being a genre, says Wolfreys, the post-Romantic Gothic is a "haunting spirit" that is as likely as not to appear in discursive "phantom fragment[s]" in other genres.[58] This approach allows that the Gothic may materialize in segments of a realist novel or in economic and other treatises as well as, more obviously, in the strictly Gothic novel. *Villette* and *Little Dorrit* are examples of such a dynamic. In these two narratives, "phantom fragments," ghostly obsessions, and frightening repetitions temporarily invade the otherwise realist narrative that is so heavily focused on economic distress. In contradistinction, the supernatural atmosphere of both *Dracula* and *Dr. Jekyll and Mr. Hyde* are invaded at times by startlingly mundane indications of the capitalist sensibilities of title characters. Thus, I intertwine my study of these novels with analysis of the Gothic features of nineteenth-century economic essays, letters, and philosophies.

To say that the Gothic is fragmented and dispersed does not lessen its power. As Wolfreys suggests, by moving the setting from the castle to the urban landscape, the Gothic "becomes more potentially terrifying because of its ability to manifest itself and variations of itself anywhere."[59] The Gothic, as I see it, is virtually anywhere in Victorian discourse as a trace of the fragmentation of language and subjectivity apparent in the increasingly bankerized Victorian period. Indeed, as Punter notes, the Gothic always illustrates a "radical decentring." When James Kincaid states, "If the gothic can be explained, it is no longer gothic," he essentially comments on the decentering at the heart of the Gothic as well as its impenetrability.[60] The impenetrability of language and subjectivity is perhaps why the Gothic features the return of the repressed, as if the compulsion towards repetitive language and actions might reinstate some kind of hoped for self-unity. Of subjectivity, the Gothic might be said to illustrate "disembodied, ghostly articulations within and against the dream of full, simple, self-evident" and "stable" speech that is the marker of realist fiction.[61] This "highly unstable genre" and its dialogical text, then, may be complicated by terrors that the Bakhtinian Marxist or Marx himself, whom I will discuss in more depth in the next chapter, cannot fully exorcise though they can name their capitalist excesses.[62]

To turn to the historical record on Victorian economic panic(s) is not to turn away from Gothic forms of speech or decentering. In 1927 Joseph A. Schumpeter informed his readers that "it is *extremely probable* that crises" are an "essential element of the capitalistic process," while in 1930, R. H. Mottram described the "terror at the back of our grandfathers'" economic panic. If, as contemporary economist D. N. McCloskey notes, "The ghosts of grasping capitalists, expropriated small farmers, and exploited factory workers still haunt economics and politics," S. G. Checkland suggested in 1964 that because panic had become fully associated with economics, in the nineteenth century there was an "immense concentration of debate on the monetary system." Charles Kindleberger's catalog of the rhetoric used to describe financial speculation includes references to "*insane land speculation,*" "financial orgies," "frenzies," and "blind passion."[63]

The said descriptions hardly distance modern economic discourse from that of the nineteenth century, for modern historians accept that current economic theories have not been able to explain adequately nor help to stabilize panics when they do occur. As will be apparent in the following overview of Victorian financial panics and the theorists who attempted to contain them, economic discourse often figured itself in terms of the Gothic.

The first modern capitalist society, with an economy that dominated the globe, Victorian England experienced extreme economic fluctuations. Albert Gallatin wrote in 1841 that "All active, enterprising, commercial countries are necessarily subject to commercial crises ... These revolutions will be more frequent and greater in proportion to the spirit of enterprise and to the extension or abuse of credit." In 1859 D. Morier Evans noted that "Within the last sixty years, at comparatively short intervals, the commercial world has been disturbed by a succession of those terrible convulsions that are now but too familiar to every ear by the expressive name, 'panic.'"[64]

The trade cycle has been defined as a "sequence of events" that display oscillation in the "aggregate economic" indicators of price and employment levels and amount and worth of the nation's output. The crucial points in the cycle are the "*peaks* and *troughs*" or the phases of boom and bust.[65] According to François Crouzet, there were eighteen cycles during the century between 1815 and 1914, with ten business cycles between 1837 and 1901, the average length being nine years. The major crises occurred in 1837, 1847, 1857, 1867, and 1878, followed thereafter by the twenty-year Great Depression. N.C. Frederickson includes 1842, 1864, 1873, 1881, 1882, 1883, 1889, 1890 as years in which the Victorians underwent significant financial calamities.[66] It should also be noted that there were many smaller crises interspersed between the major ones. For example, in 1866 in a pamphlet on the causes of panic, John Benjamin Smith states that from 1858 to 1865 there were constant "little panics" and the discount rate changed eighty-five times.[67]

Virtually every economic history of England notes, and is haunted, if you will, by the turbulence. During the Industrial Revolution, writes Cameron, fiscal difficulties "were a continual source of trouble for the nation." Peter Mathias points out that the development of industry caused increasingly potent cyclical ups and downs, and McCloskey flatly states that from 1780 to 1860 England's economy "was unpredictable because it was novel, not to say bizarre."[68] Though individual circumstances were different, the bizarreness lasted well into the 1890s. Powell finds that up to around 1850 "Banks crashed in apparently endless succession," while Checkland suggests that "[i]n the second half of the century fluctuations persisted."[69] Clearly, if the ur-*homo economicus* was firmly established in nineteenth-century Britain, part of his profile was to exist in conditions in which economic crisis was a norm.

In part, the title of this chapter, "Banking on panic," refers to the Victorian capacity for dealing with a recurrent state of economic instability at a time when banking, banking panics, and the notion of "the economy" were being defined. Indeed, at the same time that the economic cycle's volatility was considered inherent to the capitalist condition, Victorians were being trained to have faith in fiscal credit. If, to Victorians, economic panic was a nightmarish condition that augured personal bankruptcy, they kept on banking, for in increasing numbers Victorians deposited their money in the bank rather than under the proverbial mattress.[70] One study shows that in 1840 the average per person deposit into a banking account was 13 shillings; in the 1880s it was between 5 and 6 pounds; in 1885 it was 5 pounds 19 shillings and 4 pence; and it rose to 6 pounds 9 shillings 8 pence in 1888.[71] Curiously revealing an explicit connection between the Gothic and the economy, in slang terms Victorians called the sovereigns they deposited and spent "goblins."[72] Marx's theoretical framework – his superstructure – for understanding capitalism and its money fetishism, discussed in the following chapter, depends upon this merging of the supernatural and the economic.

Despite the increase in individual banking accounts, during the same period, there was a general increase of bankruptcies. Between 1800 and 1826, bankruptcies jumped from an average of 938 to 1,357 a year. There were 1,447 insolvent debtors in 1813 and 5,186 in 1830.[73] In the 1850s bankruptcies were at an average of about 1,000 a year; according to the *Annual Register*, in 1852 there were 1,222, 1,009 in 1853, and in 1857, 2,014. In 1861 the number went to 1,034, and from 1862 to 1869 bankruptcies fluctuated between 7,224 and 10,396, an increase that far exceeds the rate at which the population grew.[74] Later in the century, in a regular column entitled "Financial and Commercial Embarrassments," *The Bankers' Magazine* lists 267 failures for the week of 30 January 1883 in England and Wales, while for the week of 28 May there were 200. The "embarrassments" for 24 December were 302. The February 1885 *Bankers' Magazine* shows 11,465 bankruptcies in the year 1883 while there was a drop to 5,098 in 1884.[75] If only a percentage of Victorians went through bankruptcy, it is likely that a good portion of the population personally knew someone who went bankrupt; many, too, teetered on the verge of bankruptcy without falling into the abyss. Thus, if one can amend Gibbon Wakefield to say that throughout the nineteenth century all English people were the "uneasy classes" and that this was the normal condition of industrialized England, by the mid-century the phrase "panicked classes" could serve as well.[76]

Since the discursive study of economic cycles began because of financial crashes, one might argue that nineteenth century economists were heavily invested in panic. In fact, early treatises focused only on crises rather than on any ostensible larger economic cycle. If, as Alvin H. Hansen notes, "in the barter economy there were no business cycles," then it can be assumed with Wesley Mitchell that the business cycle is only present in cultures with a modern market form of organization.[77] McCloskey makes an excellent point when suggesting that, "If the models of business cycles could predict the future there would be no surprises, and consequently no business cycles." Nevertheless though, as Jürg Niehens points out, initially nineteenth-century economists viewed crises as haphazard occurrences, after the panics of 1825, 1836, 1847, and 1857, it was clear that one could approximate a crash to occur about every ten years, making the theory of random bubbles no longer apt.[78] Furthermore, despite the fact that by 1867 the ten-year cycle was standard in economic discourse and though there was an outpouring of discourse on the trade cycle and banking panics, economic theory was still extremely conflicted, and there were certainly no uniform plans put forward recommending procedures for eradicating crises or the cycle itself.[79]

But if, as Crouzet asserts, Victorians "hardly understood" the trade cycle, they conversed about it as though they could discover invariable laws to obtain financial stability. A. W. Coats points out that in the early nineteenth century economists attempted to make a strong distinction between experienced and amateur economists because economists themselves had not been formally trained in the new field that was establishing itself as a profession. There was not an obvious difference between amateur and professional economists because the chief economists of the day had authority by virtue not of having an academic chair – though economics became a university subject as early as 1828 at Cambridge – but by having established the Political Economy Club of London in 1821 where they discussed their fiscal theories. Thomas Malthus was one of the first of the professional economists in the making to study a specific economic crisis, while Samuel Jones Loyd, later named Lord Overstone, was one of the first to refer to a trade cycle (figure 1).[80] Writing in 1837 that the "state of trade" is "subject to various conditions" that return in "an established cycle," Overstone describes that cycle as going through the following phases: "a state of quiescence, – next improvement, – growing confidence, – prosperity, – excitement, – overtrading, – convulsion, – pressure, – stagnation, – distress, – ending again in quiescence."[81]

Overstone's famous description typifies the superciliousness of many Victorian economists. Elsewhere, the London banker and lord-to-be histor-icizes "the steps by which the human mind advances from the dark abysses of error to the pure and elevated light of truth" exhibited by economists like

Figure 1. J. Johnstone's graphic illustrates Lord Overstone's famous description of the business cycle.

himself. Remarking that previous to 1819 "self-styled practical" men "imperfectly apprehended" the economy but were "the popular oracles of the day," Overstone forcefully distinguishes between those men with "practical knowledge" and "those who are sometimes sneeringly denominated philosophers and abstract reasoners," the skilled economists of whom he counts himself one. Referring to pre-1819 as "the dark age of currency," Loyd asserts that a watershed moment occurred with the 1819 Reports of the Select Committees of both Houses of Parliament. Then, for the first time, according to Loyd, the legislature was in tune with "sound principles of currency" because of the new professional bent of economics.[82]

Despite the "sound principles" of the new discourse, economic conditions remained inconsistent, incommensurate, and intractable. Contrary to Loyd's fulsome view of Victorian economic theories about panic, they were often clumsy. When there was a recovery after a crash, economists commonly referred back to indicators apparent in earlier crises and averred that economic expansion was an appropriate response if the symptoms of that earlier smash were not present.[83] One of the most bizarre accounts of crises came from a sterling source. Father of neo-classical economics and author of *Principles of Science* (1874) and *Theory of Political Economy* (1879), which John Maynard Keynes referred to as the "first modern book in economics," William Stanley Jevons was responsible for being at the forefront of professionalizing economics in the last quarter of the century by insisting that it be a mathematical science.[84] He also crafted the peculiar "sunspot theory." Examining the economy from roughly 1710 to 1881, Jevons calculated that every 10.5 years a crisis occurred in an ostensibly classic display of the domino effect: that is, fluctuations of sunspots change the sun's rays; the sun affects agricultural crops and the harvest; the harvests affect prices; ergo, prices, of course, influence the business community's faith in the market and if prices were low this would cause economic distress.[85]

Mainstream theories of crisis were just as questionable in their acceptance of crashes as the price for an ostensibly healthy capitalist economy.[86] Certainly John Stuart Mill, the mid-century's political classical economist par excellence, accepted the cost, explaining that crises were temporary occurrences that capitalism would overcome. To Mill the "growth of all the signs of national wealth," population increase, and the improving condition of workers, confirmed that each crisis "is very far from destroying" capital. Mill went further, though, suggesting that crises actually assisted the economy. As Kyun Kim writes, Mill believed that during depressions the "economy moves from one equilibrium to another and production is redirected toward more profitable areas." Mill also contended that the intermittent destruction of fixed capital could neutralize the natural abatement of rates of profit.[87] D. Morier Evans agreed, arguing in 1859 that panics and banking failures relieved the pressures of overtrading, speculation, and exorbitant expectations. Asserting that "the commercial atmosphere [was] cleared by the explosion" of companies established on a "false basis," Evans propounded that panics exposed "wrong principles" and curbed the potential for "mischief." As late as 1900, Edward Jones calmly pointed out that "crisis simply ruptures untenable conditions and reduces valuations to their proper level." In Jones's view, crisis was "serviceable," because it enacted "a necessary work in readjusting economic forecasts to reality." Banking on panic had paid off with interest – crisis was now at home.[88]

Not to be confused with John S., Manchester banker John Mills established the periodicity of crises and noted that previous studies of the trade cycle had been haphazard. In his 1867 paper "On Credit Cycles and the Origin of Commercial Panics," Mills argues that the trade cycle needed to be studied in depth. Suggesting that governmental attempts to manage the economy were useless, he asserts that, "the malady of commercial crisis is not, in essence, a matter of the *purse* but of the *mind.*" In fact, Mills declares that fluctuations in the economy were due more to the business-man's cyclical psychological dynamics than to anything inherent in capi-talist economics.[89] As Alvin H. Hansen explains, to Mills "[f]avorable conditions breed optimism, optimism breeds recklessness, and recklessness breeds stagnation," with "trade recover[ing] from depression only when men's spirits recover."[90] Comparing this psychological cycle to the natural phases of human life, Mills finds that, like human beings, the cycle of trade begins with "infancy, growth to maturity, diseased over-growth, and death by collapse," which then leads to a renewal of energy and health. Mills concludes that increased knowledge about the cycle would help to allay its negative effects and even lengthen the time between crises.[91]

Considered a discoverer of the business cycle, Clement Juglar authored *Of Commercial Crises and Their Periodic Return in France, England and the United States* (1860). In this work he established that economic conditions were not only influenced by the harvest or by epidemics, arguing, instead, that the economy itself had a kind of intrinsic biological clock. Juglar was also the first to publish a book exclusively about the trade cycle and the first to suggest that crises must be studied in conjunction rather than as separate, distinct entities.[92] Like Mills, Juglar urged the public to under-stand that crisis was as much a part of the cycle as was prosperity and claimed that his book would "*mitigate* those terrible disasters which are called *commercial crises.*"[93] Hoping that by increasing the public's know-ledge about the trade cycle, they would feel assured that the market always recovered from crises, Juglar also wanted his readers to learn to have more moderate financial dealings and expectations, thus helping to stabilize the market and ensure longer periods between panics.

The Bank of England, of course, was at the center of intense debates about its role in producing and eradicating banking panics. In 1826, Robert Mushet referred to the Bank as "the fountainhead" and "first cause" of the fluctuating cycle of trade.[94] At the same time, George Cruikshank announced in his famous graphic "The British Beehive," that the Bank

Figure 2. "The British Beehive" by George Cruikshank.

of England was the guarantor of solidity (figure 2). Later in the century, one ex-Chancellor of the Exchequer referred to banks as a "*locus standi*," while Ellis T. Powell suggested that finance was an "undying corporate organism, which has evolved around the original nucleus represented by the Bank of England."[95] An anomalous entity from the start, the Bank of England was both the banker to the government as well as a private commercial bank, with the added responsibility of being the chief provider of the nation's financial stability. Specifically aimed at ending the disruptive crises that occurred repeatedly after the end of the war with France in 1815, the Bank Act of 1844 required that the Banking and Issue Departments become "entirely independent" entities; the one part to issue notes up to the amount of £14,000,000 and the other to act as a bank of deposits.[96] However, the two departments were to remain under the same roof – the Bank of England – and retain the integral authority of that institution. Recognizing the anomalous nature of the Bank of England after this Act was approved, Bagehot opined in 1875 that "if you started *de novo*," England would not again consider establishing such a "peculiar" system.[97] Bagehot was referring to the fact that the Act made the Bank of England an anomaly amongst other banks in England, for it was to act as the keeper of reserves as well as the lender of last resort.[98]

The Bank Act ensured that aside from becoming the sole minter of coin and paper money, the Issue Department would reinforce the gold standard according to the currency school of thought.[99] The belief was that the value of money would rise when its quantity decreased, and, concomitantly, money's value would decrease when its quantity increased.[100] According to this approach, in order to retain money's value, bank notes were tied to gold and thus, with regards to circulation, had to "fluctuate one-for-one" with changes that occurred with the Bank's gold reserve.[101] Meanwhile, under the Act the Banking Department was never to pressure the Issue Department to increase the specie in circulation during times of crisis, again, a strategy that was thought to drive down the value of money. The proponents of the Bank Act also contended that reserves of money in the Banking Department should never go below a certain predetermined level. Suggesting that since "the monetary world would become feverish and fearful if the reserve in the Banking Department went below £10,000,000," Bagehot argued that it should never fall lower than £11,000,000.[102]

The 1844 Act successfully centralized the issue of money, putting it gradually and completely into the hands of the Bank of England, but it failed in the more important task of preventing banking panics. In fact, within three years the Act's premises were shattered with the onset of the panic of 1847. Though the Bank of England never crashed, on a number of occasions it struggled desperately. In 1825, 1836, and 1839, for example, it barely escaped inconvertibility (the state in which it could not convert every client's fiduciary money into gold), almost totally smashing, while in

the years 1847, 1857, and 1866, it scarcely weathered major panics. Too
often the Bank relied on emergency devices, such as abrogating the Bank
Act itself for the period of the crisis.[103] The unseemliness of regularly
breaking the law in times of crisis led Disraeli to ask the House of
Commons in December of 1857 to answer what the effect was "of allowing
the currency of this country to be regulated by an Act which we are in a
continual state of being prepared to suspend."[104] Thus the 1844 Act became
a lightning rod, and it was revisited by Parliament throughout the rest of
the century.

As important to my study of banking crises as the Bank Act of 1844 is the
Victorian banking quandary that resulted in centralization and amalgamation. Referring to the Victorian ambivalence about market controls
and free banking, Charles Neville Ward-Perkins lays out the main concern:
should banking authorities manage and manipulate banks, credit, loans,
etc., or should they practice the precepts of laissez-faire, including the
capitalist ideals of unregulated buying, selling, and competition.[105] The
laissez-faire approach was typified in J. R. McCulloch's statement to
Overstone, in a letter dated 20 November 1857, that legislation should
not impede the actions of bankers and financiers. As he argues, "You
cannot hinder them from mismanaging their affairs, from giving improper
credits, re-discounting and so forth" because these "evils" are "inherent" in
the system, and if "the interest and unlimited liability of the partners in
such concerns will not teach them prudence nothing will."[106] Victorian
laws on banking illustrate the conflict. While enforcing rigid oversight of
bank organization, such as how many partners were permitted, the law was
more laissez-faire about such things as cash ratio and amount of reserves
and cash on hand required.[107] On one end of the spectrum, then, there is
George H. Pownall worrying that the "sensitive" British money market had
so "refined" its mechanisms that the preparation English bankers made for
times of panic often "create[d] the danger it was hoped to avert." In
contrast is Crouzet's opinion that the Bank of England seldom interceded
in a timely manner when there were panics.[108]

Inexplicable, recurrent crises increased the perceived need for what
Robert Ewen in 1898 referred to as a "revolution in banking," that is to
say, the move away from decentralization and towards amalgamation.[109]
The trend towards amalgamation was first motivated by the 1857 crisis and
reinvigorated by the Baring Crisis of 1890.[110] By the end of the century,
banking had become, according to Ellis Powell, "the most highly organised, delicate, and susceptible factor in the fabric of civilisation" through
"*financial* combination, concentration, centralisation, and unification."[111]

In 1899 George H. Pownall called London "the financial Rome of the civilised world."[112]

But for all the optimism, the efficiency of centralization had negative effects as well, including the bankerization Goux refers to and its increase of complex, abstract economic signs, a process that could not help but affect other cultural phenomena. As I study those phenomena, it must be acknowledged that centralization should not automatically lead to a view of Victorian banking as monolithic. R. S. Sayers qualifies the centralization process, suggesting that Victorian economists and bankers were probably unaware that they were in the process of producing a theoretical discourse about central banking. Rondo Cameron adds that up to the 1850s the English banking system was hardly aggressive or even directive. Rather, it fulfilled its responsibility to provide financial services but it was not interested in directly augmenting economic growth.[113] Nevertheless, any ostensible unconsciousness of the movement towards centralization does not erase its results.

It does not erase the remaining chaos either. The disorder still embedded in centralized banking is apparent when one considers what banks were not required to do during the Victorian period. Until the nineties, there was no compulsory publication of balance sheets showing separately cash on hand at the Bank of England and money at call and on short notice. Country bankers rarely published their balance sheets, and published cash ratios only started occurring after 1890, while private London banks rarely if ever published their balances.[114] Actual business practices within banks varied, and supervision of the books did not necessarily increase over the century. A report in 1880 by Chief Cashier, Chief Accountant and Secretary of the Bank of England, Mr. Hammond Chubb, reveals fluctuations in attitudes about the need for safeguards against fraudulent accounting. In his report, Chubb notes that Thomason Hankey's *Principles of Banking* (1867) assumed that the higher departments of the organization checked the accounts of the lower, the chief accountant, for example, overseeing the accounts of the chief cashier. Complaining that this understanding had "been put aside" gradually, Chubb states that until 1849 "a vast system of supervision and administrative control" was in place because the accountants used two sets of books. Chubb protests that with the elimination of the Accountant's Chancery Office in 1875 the older method of oversight had "met its death blow."[115]

Tremendous growth and amalgamation of banking resulted in byzantine transactions between banks. For example, *The Bankers' Magazine* of June 1885 includes concern from a Mr. Barnett about the "weakness" that "one bank should be cancelling cheques for very large amounts against assets consisting of cheques on other banks, which, in turn, are at the same moment being cancelled against assets of the same character." Recognizing the impossibility of stabilizing the meaning of money as it circulates through its many exchanges in differing banks, the writer notes: "The whole thing moves in a circle, steadily enough in general, but it is obvious that it might easily be otherwise ... The danger does not consist so much in the character of the transactions, or even in their magnitude, as in their interdependence, and the fact of their being dealt with in different establishments at the same time."[116] Clearly, the fictionality and bankerization upon which credit – ergo amalgamation – is based is at the heart of this all but terrifying description of the machinations brought about in banking. The fear that the fictional was debasing the coin of the realm as well as its basis in reality resonates in this statement and is reminiscent of Victorian fears about the ostensibly deleterious effects of reading the novel, let alone Gothic fiction. Anxiety about the national character (identity) being based upon fictions would follow not far behind this Gothic panic.

In the following chapter, I analyze the Gothic in specific Victorian economic texts, in particular in Bagehot, Marx, and Lord Overstone, an economist Marx reviled. In chapters 3 through 6, I focus on *Villette, Little Dorrit, The Strange Case of Dr. Jekyll and Mr. Hyde*, and *Dracula*. I argue that economic panic in *Villette* is an insistent *basso ostinato* against which moral, sexual, or mental frenzy – materializing in the form of the ghostly nun/none – appears to have more serious implications for the main character, teaching her to keep accounts of and bank on panic and constant exchange. In *Little Dorrit* fictional representations of banking transactions and crises, speculation and hysteria are parallels to and intensifiers of social, emotional, or intellectual crises metonymically expressed in the haunting of Affery. Imagining the bankerized self as a machine that constantly works to instill the duty to increase circulation, *Little Dorrit* reveals that the very energy produced by circulation leads to eventual collapse. The horrifying half-lives transacted between Jekyll and Hyde or between Dracula and his minions occur, in part, as banking crises, where to obtain credit the self must enter the voluptuous, dangerous eddies of circulation. Reconstructing the Jekyll/Hyde relationship by taking it literally to the bank, Utterson tracks down his alter ego Jekyll, who has manufactured a means of consuming and incorporating exchange, unlimited fluctuation, production, desire, and panic. In *Dracula* bankerization is all but complete when banks become "corporate personalities" and the human body is drained of personality and life-blood.

CHAPTER 2

Gothic economies in Bagehot, Marx, and Lord Overstone

While T. E. Gregory suggests that it is important to consider the rhetoric of economic statements as well as their content, Jean-Joseph Goux argues that probing the fictional aspects of economic theory reveals the "density of [economic] assumptions."[1] Victorian descriptions of speculation, financial crisis, and the Bank Act of 1844 illustrate the panicked underside of the scientific, objective language ostensibly favored by professional economists. As Charles Kindleberger has noted, his nineteenth-century counterparts did not shy away from using the language of panic, frenzy, and crisis to describe the triumphs and terrors of capitalism.[2] In this chapter, I consider explicit and subliminal Gothic tropes in the writings of Bagehot, Marx, Overstone, and other Victorians as they discuss financial panic. I argue that panicked accounts of financial disaster suggest that the objective reporting of professionalized economics elides but cannot cancel out a whole range of knowledge about the trade cycle when it excludes language that conveys emotional – and even bodily – responses to panic. Following the modern tendency to separate the economic from other areas of life, even Overstone and Bagehot cannot fully omit the emotion of panic when describing banking crises. Marx's "economic" writings often sound anything but professional to modern ears because he insists on describing capitalism's effects on the body and the psyche, as well as on the economy. Likewise, articulate emotional responses from Victorian have-nots illustrate frustration with economists who view feelings and moral responsibilities to the community as peripheral to the work of economics. In each of these writers fragments of the Gothic subliminally haunt the text, for there is always the sense that there is something irrational, monstrous, or supernatural about economic panics because no rhetoric or set of laws can contain them.

Hamer Stansfield, for one, worried that "Fluctuations and oscillations are inherent in trade, but violent fluctuations and periodical oscillations are peculiar only to our own currency system." In "Money: How the Banks

Make it Scarce and Dear!" the anonymous writer Sigma advocates the establishment of a national bank because bank managers obtain outrageously excessive profits from "the use of depositors' money and the special privileges now allowed them." Focusing on bankers, Sigma's words might equally represent the increasingly professionalized sphere of economics: bankers, he expostulates, are "narrow-minded creatures of arithmetic, subservient to figures, and incapable of understanding the words 'public benefit' or 'public interest.'" Scrappily pointing out how they project their own avarice onto the proponents of a national bank, he suggests that bankers who advocate the status quo contend that a national bank would be "grossly selfish" because, in fact, they themselves are rapacious speculators.[3]

With equal ferocity, R. Legg critiques Lord Overstone's view that it is naïve to be outraged by the ostensible fact that the economy must cycle through phases of convulsion and stagnation. In response to Overstone's famous description of the trade cycle, Legg fumes that Overstone takes for granted that the cycle is a natural law that cannot be controlled by the government or individuals. "[A] gigantic evil, acknowledged, recognised, and apparently understood as the necessary result of commercial enterprise," the cycle, Legg complains, is to be hands-off to legislation but completely given over to "untrammeled speculation." Lambasting the assumption that business takes precedence over the non-economic needs of the community, Legg reviles the economists who believe that though the 1844 Act "may bring about convulsion, pressure, stagnation, and distress," it is to be "regarded as inevitable, and no remedy is to be attempted or put in force but the purging of the court of Bankruptcy!"[4]

Like the irate Legg, J. H. Macdonald in 1855 curses the 1844 Act. Calling it a "crooked" "monster" that has "greatly aggravated one evil – a money panic," he wonders, "what in the name of Solon is the use of such an Act?" Macdonald accepts that capital is the foundation of Victorian life, gloating that money "is, perhaps, the most valuable invention of man." But that does not stop him from analyzing the invention's effects upon the lower classes. As Macdonald laments, "it has been perverted by false laws into a horrid engine for grinding the labouring industrious classes to the dust."[5] Similarly, Samuel Mountifort Longfield suggests in 1840 that if financial crisis "is like the plague," the "poorest are overwhelmed, the wealthy alone survive the shock." Meanwhile, the title of James Taylor's pamphlet *Money should be the Servant of the People Not Their Master*" implicitly resists what Gordon Bigelow refers to as the paradigm shift towards seeing everything first and foremost through the logic of "the economy." Turning

the insensible logic of economics on its head, Taylor asserts that governments must make the currency system "subservient to the *comfortable
employment of the people*," rather than that "people's *comfort*" be "*subservient
to* or *dependent upon* a supply of the precious metals." As he prophesies,
otherwise a "combination" of capitalists could temporarily stop the supply
of gold and thus wreak havoc on the nation.[6]

In the early twentieth century, R. H. Mottram suggested that it
was impossible to forego such sensational language because the modern
capitalist economy itself was not yet fully formed, theorized, or profession-
ally articulated. Asserting that bank crashes of the nineteenth century
exerted an "emotionalizing power we shall not recapture," he finds that
banking panics bore intimations of the "doom" found in the biblical phrase
"Mene, Mene, Tekel, Upharsin." Unable to cancel affect completely from
his own rhetoric, the writer assumes an objective, condescending attitude
towards the ostensibly less economically sophisticated Victorians when he
dramatically opines that, "The comparatively new and obscure force of
credit was a young and tender plant, promising much, deceiving so
tragically ... 'The Bank has Broke' chilled their hearts as 'No Water'
daunted the early explorer."[7]

Also recognizing the difficulty of finding a language that adequately
represents economic panic, Amasa Walker wrote in 1859 about the 1857
crash: "Newspapers and periodicals laboured with articles upon this all-
absorbing subject." But though "Everybody could write, for everybody felt
and suffered," Walker cannot help but wonder, "what was the nature of all
this financial literature, so to call it?"[8] To Walker the dramatic increase of
professional venues for discussing economics only highlighted the fact that
economic rhetoric itself banked on panic and the ineffectiveness of emotional and rational analysis of the economy. The implied rule of thumb,
then, was that the more that was written about economic crisis, the less did
conditions seem to be under actual control.

Referring to the Bank Act as "this monster Act of legislative unwisdom,"
J. H. Macdonald intuits the anomaly of economic theory that depends upon
hypotheses without having any necessary link to real economic conditions
and their effects on human beings. Asking, "Did Lord Overstone even
attempt to explain to himself how this wonderful process [the economic
conditions instituted by the Bank Act of 1844] took place in a purely
imaginative manner?" Macdonald contends that under the Act's strictures,
circulation was "made to burn at both ends – by the large exportation of gold
and the corresponding withdrawal of bank-notes" in contradistinction to
what Overstone had imagined. The articulately livid Macdonald also points

out the "arrant nonsense" of expecting the currency in the Issue Department of the Bank of England to be dead while the living were in distress. As he remarks, "we might as well talk of the motionless current of a river, or of an immovable revolver, as of an inconvertible currency!"[9]

As Victorians were reminded during every banking crisis, market speculation depended upon unrealistic imaginings. Illustrating the "mania for new Railways" occurring in the 1840s, in *Practical Hints for Investing Money* (1855), Francis Playford comments that frenzied speculation was "confined to no particular class," for "noblemen, gentlemen, clergymen, and even ladies of rank ran headlong with the rest into the vortex." Many attempted to describe that vortex. The penman of *The Railway Investment Guide: How to Make Money by Railway Shares* writes, "So much has been said of the thousands amassed in a few weeks by some successful speculation in Railway Shares, that the public is running mad with the idea," as they "rush headlong in the same direction" and thus risk being "trampled to misery and ruin." Likewise, J. R. McCulloch writes to Overstone during the 1857 crash that, "The more I consider the subject the more I am impressed with the conviction that our situation is becoming extremely precarious, and that we may be subjected to an universal smash."[10] The air was filled with "the miasma of extravagance" according to E. T. Freedley, because "designing men" "strike away the prop, cause a sudden affright or panic, and induce their neighbours to pull those misfortunes they apprehend upon their own heads."[11] Likewise, when referring to the rise of the discount rate from 4 to 5 percent instituted in 1863 by the Bank of England in order to deflate a potential bubble, the usually cool Lord Overstone participates in the panicked rhetoric. "Who," he histrionically asks, "was the Tyrant who marked his progress by the decapitated bodies of his subjects?" In the same year, Overstone worries that, "we are in the centre of a political cyclone" and "surrounded on every side by storms and tempests," and he agonizes that these "rage[s]" indicate that, "Commercial and Monetary affairs again outrun my capacity."[12]

Newspapers and journals also could not avoid banking on panic linguistically when it occurred economically. On 9 May 1866, for example, *The Times* raved that, "the mania of terror seems likely ... to proceed unchecked," and two days hence the newspaper described the terror that would be experienced "in the remotest corners of the Kingdom" because of the crash.[13] On 12 May 1866 the reputable newspaper featured an even starker depiction of the crisis: "The doors of the most respectable Banking Houses were besieged," and the "throngs heaving and fumbling about Lombard-street made that narrow thoroughfare impassable" as a "reign of terror" and "Panic" "swayed the City to and fro."[14] The crash of Overend, Gurney, the famous Victorian financial institution, left a strong imprint, for *The Bankers' Magazine* of December 1886 describes how "The effect on the City was as the shock of an earthquake," and that it was "impossible to describe the terror and anxiety which seized everyone's mind for many days." Likewise, a little over two decades after the Overend crash, *The Times* referred back to the events of 1866 in conjunction with the panic of 1890. Reporting on 15 November that there was "gnawing care and smothered alarm among men of business," the London newspaper asserted that, "The City has passed through a crisis verging upon panic such as has not been known since the awful Black Friday that followed the suspension of Overend, Gurney, and Co., nearly a quarter of a century ago."[15]

As pointed out earlier, Walter Bagehot, editor of *The Economist* from 1866 to 1877, defined panic as a "state in which there is a confidence in the Bank of England, and in nothing but the Bank of England." He also publicly proclaimed, "A panic grows by what it feeds on; if it devours" the "second-class men, shall we, the first class, be safe?"[16] Pertinent to these statements is the fact that during the banking panic of 1857, Bagehot was a bank manager with his father's firm. In addition, in the fall of 1857, just prior to the panic, Bagehot became engaged to Eliza, daughter of James Wilson, owner and publisher of *The Economist*.[17] Walter had met Miss Wilson when he came to discuss with her father the possibility of writing for Wilson's periodical. Alarmed about her health, Eliza traveled to Edinburgh in search of medical treatment immediately after the engagement. The couple's epistolary communications during her absence represent an emotional seesaw: indeed, I suggest that their witty, often humorous repartee is underwritten by a structure of panic.

Along with their private panic, it is important to reiterate, as Eliza's sister, Mrs. Barrington, does in her edition of the letters, that the country was financially in a "troublous condition" when "Eliza received Walter's first love-letter."[18] Bagehot's fretful relationship with his fiancée, I suggest, illustrates the extent to which the Bank of England was enmeshed with the couple's sexual and psychological panic. For one thing, the economic and domestic spheres cross-fertilize in the letters, and the dynamics produce a structure of feeling composed of supposedly hermetically sealed Victorian venues as the couple bank on panic in a number of contradictory ways. Indeed, the initial sentences of Bagehot's first epistle provide the economic context for his personal passions: "I have just rushed down here from Bristol and it appears to me that I shall rebound again to London tomorrow . . . as the panic is getting worse and requires watching." In his second letter, Walter admits that being in love is "always *fatiguing*," but in their case it is coupled with a financial "panic which is wearing, and really a trifle anxious." Likewise, early on he remarks that he would come see her in Edinburgh "If it were not for the crisis," explaining that "I must go and talk currency."[19] A few days later he reiterates the same, saying he would rush up to see her if not for the banking "panic." On 7 December, he thanks her for her letter that "snatched a moment from the turmoil of business," and in a brief note in January of 1858, Walter writes, "I am again not able to write to you" because there is "always a great bother in the Bank." In the midst of sweet nothings in yet another love note, Walter slips in the fact that the financial panic "is spreading and *widening,* but less intense at the focus in London."[20]

Bagehot's figuration of the banking crisis in the city is similar to the language he uses to describe the sexual and psychological panic masked in the letters. In his epistle to Eliza on 29 November, for example, the budding economist describes feeling "*restless,*" "agitated," and in a "state of mental *interjection*" as well as experiencing emotions that are "dreadfully exciting," a series of descriptions that limns both professional and personal anxiety.[21] He worries, too, that his "wild and wearing feelings" are a "plague" to Eliza. Admitting that "the feeling" of being in love "has been too eager not to have a good deal of pain in it, and the tension of mind has really been very great at times," Bagehot notes that "at the worst," he experiences "a wild, delicious excitement" accompanied by a "wild, burning pain." Trying to understand his volatile emotions, on another occasion Bagehot admits to "feeling a little *wild* the last day or two, but I know that this is wrong, and struggle against it."[22]

Given Bagehot's emotional susceptibility, it must be recalled that Eliza and her sister went to Edinburgh to receive medical "rubbings" from a Dr. Beveridge, ostensibly for chronic headaches that plagued the fragile sisters. Although the actual medical condition from which Eliza suffered is uncertain, her own descriptions suggest the psychosomatic "nervous" diseases so common to middle- and upper-class Victorian women. The effects of Eliza's nervous condition also should be seen in light of the mental illness Bagehot's mother experienced for most of her adult life. Having to care for his mother during her frequent and ongoing bouts of insanity, it must have been disconcerting for Bagehot to have his fiancée disappear the moment they became engaged in order to seek medical attention. Furthermore, after Bagehot told her about his mother's psychological problems, Eliza, apparently apprehensive about her own mental strength or Bagehot's, replied that she needed time to consider her answer to his proposal. That Bagehot was one of his mother's prime caretakers before the death of his father, and then the sole caretaker, possibly made Eliza think twice about her commitment to such a man, especially since she herself was delicate physically and emotionally.

To a certain extent, then, the subliminal psychological gaps in the lovers' epistolary exchange – the mundane Gothic of a mother's and fiancée's (potential) insanity – are filled and articulated by explicit alarms about the banking panic of 1857. Indeed, the lovers' panic must be contextualized in part by the Gothic (economic) construction of feminine madness. If, as I suggest, the Gothic novel and the Gothic economy serve as pre-text and context for the letters written almost daily between Eliza Wilson and her future husband during her stay in Edinburgh, it should be reiterated that the Victorian Gothic is brilliant in its understanding that insanity occupies the living rooms – and bedrooms – of Britain as well as the exotic Continent. How the mother's insanity and the fiancée's possible mental troubles might have been constructed by the Victorian sensibility cannot be known fully. However, we do know that Gothic fiction, as well as its simulacrum, the sensation novel, was filled with terrors about feminine madness and the possibility that it might be inherited. Certainly, by the Victorian period, the Gothic commonly considered every woman (mothers, wives, sisters, and daughters) as a potential madwoman in the attic.

Bagehot's own mother's insanity and his future wife's intimations of mental and physical instability are at least partially informed by this Victorian construction of the feminine. And, in fact, Eliza's scrupulous health concerns often evoke manic reactions in her future partner, who continually describes the emotional upsets he experiences as a result. Referring to Eliza's medical treatments as the "Beveridge mania," Bagehot feels it socially unseemly of Eliza to stay in Edinburgh when he is so anxious to be with her. He complains outright that the Beveridge cure is a "form of intoxication," that her problems are "somewhat in the mind," and perhaps even due to "temporary insanity."[23] Late in the correspondence, noting that she is "a little delicate," he grumbles that her "continual puttings-off worry me beyond expression" and that he is put into an unsettling emotional state because he constantly hopes to see her but is then always disappointed when she delays her return once again. How could Eliza be stable, Bagehot implies, if she could not even meet his mother. Indeed, the wait to introduce Eliza to his family caused Walter, tongue-in-cheek, to worry that they would come to think him mad, for his fiancée might seem just a figment of his imagination – a "Scotch myth," as it were.[24]

In addition, the Victorian secrecy about sexual and psychological conditions covers over a fear that madness and sexuality might merge on the wedding night – a possibility that all but defines Victorian marriage as Gothic. Classic and Victorian Gothic, that is, often seem to depend upon the derangement of identity and the grounds of meaning that might typically occur when new identities are in the process of being formed and familiar ones abandoned, such as what occurs when a woman takes a new name and individuals become a couple. Naïvely unpracticed lovers experiencing considerable anxiety constructing themselves as a couple while physically apart, the pair's representations of their states of mind are a palpable merging of economic and emotional panic. Walt W. Rostow remarks of Bagehot that, "*The Economist* was forced, in a sense, to tell its readers where they stood at any moment, in relation to the trade cycle."[25] In the love letters, Eliza and Walter are forced, if you will, to explain where they stand at any moment emotionally as their love – and the economy – cycles through excitement, anxiety, crisis, and intermittent calm. The material effects of the couple's economic and social consolidation emerge in their obsessive focus on Eliza's ostensible illness and her refusal to return to Bagehot until she feels cured. Both see their relationship as in a kind of panic – Bagehot continually referring to the fact that Dr. Beveridge gets to "rub" Eliza on a daily basis while he is incommunicado – with the wedding itself seen as bringing about the ultimate crisis.

Part of that panic for the middle- and upper-class woman, as I will discuss in more depth in the next chapter, and as depicted in the Gothic and sensation novels written by Victorian women writers, had to do with the fact that for the bride marriage presented quite graphically her all but complete material reliance on her new husband. If marriage was the Victorian middle-class woman's profession, she was entirely economically dependent upon the groom, in whom, in a horrifying metaphor, she would become legally submerged according to the law of coverture. If the capitalist economic cycle was never stable for anyone, it presented the Victorian wife – who became legally non-existent upon marriage – with potentially terrifying economic (in)security. To be sure, marrying in the midst of economic crisis produced some anxiety on Bagehot's part. Though stating that he is not worried that his own bank will crash, nevertheless, Bagehot admits that it is "not pleasant" to depend upon this belief "just when all business opinion is disturbed." In generic terms, he acknowledges that, "when any bank goes the minds of men are disturbed and they are apt not to bear in mind with accuracy which bank it is." He adds, too, that in personal terms, "in practical things I have rather an anxious disposition," a disturbing trait for one dealing with the panic of his bank's customers.[26] Such tremors would have been compounded for the wife whose job it was to live without economic job skills while also providing succor to the husband, her source of economic security, whose career might be endangered by such drastic economic fluctuations.

I suggest that the new arrangement or derangement Eliza Wilson and Walter Bagehot confront as they stand on the brink of marriage is intensified by the economic crisis within which they prepare for the frightening – in Victorian terms – secret, sexual rites performed on the wedding night. In the Gothic tradition, the said rites held the seeds of future economic and social consolidation as well as possible future madness. In a similar vein, banking crises had come to be viewed as "fevers" necessarily recycling through the period at ten-year intervals that brought madness and, ostensibly, eventual catharsis and stability. Clearly, sexual panic and economic consolidation underwrite the letters between the lovers. Not yet "mentally ready," Eliza remarks, for instance, that Walter's "pleasure in the anticipation" of marriage makes her "a little nervous." At one point in response to such fears, he humorously points out that though marrying him may constitute an "ordeal," in the past "ordeals" always involved physical pain, such as being branded by "red-hot ploughshares." Thus, he reasons that though she "may be nervous, and feeling leaving home a *wrench*," she should not be upset because marriage to him will not involve being "hurt horribly" physically.[27] Bagehot's inappropriate joke would probably not have done much to erase his fiancée's psychological anxiety nor the virgin's subliminal concerns about the precipitate sexual duties of marriage.

Implicitly referring to those sexual duties, Eliza calls the planning of the wedding "a dreadful ordeal" and worries about backing out at the last minute. At one point writing that "every now and then I get a nervous feeling about it which makes me feel quite *faint* – a real physical faintness," in another letter Eliza inquires, "Does not the marriage seem really *awfully* near?"[28] Late in the correspondence, she is still saying things such as "at times a tremulousness comes over my mind which is not compatible with its peace." Responding to such qualms, Walter at one point says that he will "*hurry*" her along "as an antidote to nervous faintness." Perhaps worried that her trepidation might be serious, Bagehot admits that, "the nearer the time seems to come" the more anxious he is "as to something preventing" the marriage.[29] Of the actual wedding itself, there is little said, but the rhetoric relies inordinately upon the term "crisis." Cheerful throughout his letter, nevertheless, Bagehot describes the wedding breakfast as a "moment of confusion" and remarks upon "the crisis" in their attempts to "banish all nervousness." Likewise, in a letter to his mother after the wedding, he notes that Eliza was "anxious at the crisis" and "is a trifle tired by the crisis."[30]

If the sexual, Gothic, and economic climax in the letters is not realized in the description of the wedding, it does occur in a curiously Victorian rite, repeated at least three times during the correspondence. In response to Eliza's request that he "kiss" her "letters in private," Bagehot writes back in one letter that before reading her epistle he actually kissed it "in the bank." Later, composing a note to her from the bank, though he confesses that it is "not a place where one can write metaphysics," Walter essentially implies that their marriage relies on the credit and panics of banking. Attempting to prove that their love is the signifying center of their letters, on another occasion Bagehot exclaims, "when I have really read [your letter] I will thank you for it, but it seems too *delicious* to dwell on in public and business places."[31] The fact that the lovers implicitly seek to proclaim their love at the bank suggests that the discursive field of banking has set the terms of their correspondence and desire, and, at some inchoate level, that their marriage absolutely depends upon the bank's cycle of trade, including occurrences of banking panics. When Bagehot kisses Eliza's letter in the bank, it is as though the financial institution bestows credit and sexual legitimacy on the couple's relationship. Thus, it is appropriate to the structure of the love letters that emotional and banking panic reached a denouement at the same time, for the banking panic of 1857 resolved itself when Eliza was finally ready to return to England in April 1858.

More than any other nineteenth-century figure, Karl Marx speaks with a voice of prophecy fueled by profound panic. Indeed, to read Marx, one might conjecture that as long as capitalism exists there will always be reincarnations of the Gothic, for despite the West's triumphant exclamations about Communism's burial in the 1990s, Marx's specter has not vanished from the intellectual terrain. Writing in the same time period as the novels I examine, Marx suggests that capitalism is a fiction-making entity that creates the brilliant but mad conditions within which its subjects exist. To read Marx suggests that the Gothic was invented, in part, as a prism through which to represent capitalism's ceaseless haunting of its subjects. Illustrating the collective code used by economics and literature, Marx is at once a master teller of ghost stories – the thing we often forget about the much-maligned Marxism's originator – and a brilliant, if often flawed, analyst of classical economics. Notwithstanding the problematic nature of Derrida's late turn to "*a spirit of Marxism*" in his 1994 *Specters of Marx*, the deconstructionist's focus on the haunted Marx is shrewd.[32]

Derrida highlights the fact that the German term "Geist," which Marx uses throughout his oeuvre, means "ghost" as well as "spirit." This is important because Marx explicitly sees the ideological difference between the two meanings as crucial to his materialism, "spirit" being an abstract, Platonic ideal unencumbered by material embodiment, and the "ghost" being a liminal pseudo body and spirit that haunts a real embodied entity. This double meaning is lost to a great extent in English translation, though the "ghostly" meaning haunts, as it were, the more dominant spiritual definition of "Geist." Given the fact that Marx so often uses the rhetoric of the supernatural, Derrida suggests that *German Ideology* is an "inexhaustible gloss on" ghosts.[33]

Attempting to describe nothing less than the phenomenology of capitalism, Marx repeatedly uses Gothic tropes to capture what Derrida calls the "[h]aunting [that] belongs to the structure of every hegemony." To Derrida, Marx's *Capital* explains how modern money "produces a *remainder,*" the ghostly traces of capitalist ideology.[34] As noted earlier in this study, Fredric Jameson suggests that the ghostly effect is an ideologeme in that "the opposing" class necessarily carries "the other around in its head and is internally torn and conflicted by a foreign body it cannot exorcize."[35] Essentially, when Marx proclaims that "the spectre of communism" haunts Europe, he seems to imagine the supernatural mutual haunting of Communism and capitalism on a spectacularly global scale. But it is capitalism's specter, not Communism's, that captures Marx's imagination and tests his rhetorical, intellectual, and psychological powers, for his is a colossal endeavor to wrestle with what Georg Lukács calls the "phantom objectivity," shape-shifting, conjuring, panic-inducing, Gothic monstrosity of capital.[36]

Kurt Heinzelman argues that for Marx capitalist ideology has a material "*ex-istence*" that "literally stands outside us 'as a real object.'"[37] Heinzelman is referring to Marx's statement that, "The difference between effective demand based on money and ineffective demand based on my need, my passion, my wish, etc., is the difference between *being* and *thinking,* between the idea which merely *exists* within me and the idea which exists as a *real object* outside of me."[38] In this observation, Marx indicates that the ineffective person exists only internally (that is, only to himself) while the effective individual exists both internally and externally (is believed to be a self both by himself and others) because he has money's power to fulfill his desires. Since the arbiter of the distinction between effective and ineffective beings is money itself, money becomes the decisive judge of what is human. Thus, if Walter Benn Michaels queries, "But can economies be subjects?" it is exactly the transformation of things like economies into subjects and human beings into things that Marx's extravagant rhetoric attempts to depict.[39]

Struggling to capture the effects of the Industrial Revolution, Marx develops a hybrid language, similar to Thomas Carlyle's in its intensity, strangeness, and mix of well-established and new generic forms as well as chiastic constructions.[40] Analogous to Carlyle's metaphor of the world as "clothed" with sacred knowledge that needs periodic retailoring, Marx's materialist imagery makes the reader sensually understand the way that capitalism retailors, constricts, and disfigures humanity. Marx links demonic possession to economic possession, imagining capitalism as having a black magic that haunts, deceives, and seduces those who live under its sway. Marx's intense tone suggests that he believes he must make his readers feel the traces of the protean specter of capitalism before they are concealed by the mundane veil with which capitalism envelops reality. Lukács describes this reality as "frozen" while also "caught up in an unremitting, ghostly movement."[41] Combining Gothic narrative, jeremiad, satire, melodrama, mathematical symbolization, and his own quasi-scientific economic formulae, Marx creates a monstrous conceptual body of work that is Frankensteinian in its conglomeration of disparate linguistic materials.

Marx and Engels, of course, resist the sanguine view of crises put forth by classical economists, suggesting that capitalism produces "a society that has conjured up such gigantic means of production and of exchange" that it is analogous to a "sorcerer who is no longer able to control the powers of the nether world whom he has summoned by his spells." As Marx warns, distorting human imagination, consciousness, social relations, and language, the new economic system radically splits the human subject, the monetary sign, and the commodity, making them simultaneously haunted and haunting. Thus, in "the enchanted, perverted, topsy-turvy" capitalist world, the character of "Mister Capital" and "Mistress Land" perform "their goblin tricks."[42] The industrialist is also a ghoul whose demand for the worker's vital fluids is insatiable when Marx dramatically asserts that "Capital is dead labour," that "vampire-like, only lives by sucking living labour, and lives the more, the more labour it sucks."[43] In "The Trinitarian Formula," a chapter on the relations between capital, land, and labor, Marx also remarks that labor, "the third party in this conspiracy," is a "ghost" or a "mere abstraction."[44]

Referring to the commodity as "a very queer thing, abounding in metaphysical subtleties," Marx explains the operations of contorted fetishism that cause the commodity to become demonically possessed.[45]

Conceding the difficulty of describing the commodity, he turns to pagan religious myth in which "the productions of the human brain appear as independent beings endowed with life, and entering into relation both with one another and the human race."[46] This appeal to religion's mystic animism of the world helps to explain Marx's bizarre description of a table, which, when it becomes a commodity, suddenly stands up, walks, and showily displays itself like a vaudeville stripper. At the beginning of "The Fetishism of Commodities and the Secret Thereof," Marx describes this supernatural transformation from wood to table to commodity:

The form of wood ... is altered, by making a table out of it. Yet, for all that the table continues to be that common, every-day thing, wood. But, so soon as it steps forth as a commodity, it is changed into something transcendent. It not only stands with its feet on the ground, but, in relation to all other commodities, it stands on its head, and evolves out of its wooden brain grotesque ideas, far more wonderful than "table-turning" ever was.[47]

The unflappable Derrida is positively entranced by this "table-turning" commodity, describing it as a "sensuously supersensible" thing when it parades itself in a kind of "spiritualist séance." Similarly, Fredric Jameson contends that Marx's dramatic representation of the table captures the commodity's "power to act and cause in ways more complex and undecipherable than the individual human mind or intention."[48]

The startling image also encapsulates the condition in a market economy that makes the very material tableness of the table secondary, even inconsequential, compared to its monetary value. In Marx's system, transfused with the life of the worker it has drained, reified, and economized, the commodity turns everything around it into "mere ghost[s]."[49] Indeed, in Marx's spectral imagery, the human body is haunted by its own productions as well as being the carcass drained of its life-blood by the vampiric capital it produces. As a result of these supernatural transformations, human subjectivity must always be understood in relation to money. "By possessing the *property* of buying everything," says Marx, "*money* is thus the *object* of eminent possession" and is completely "omnipoten[t]."[50] In the capitalist scenario, then, desire is achingly unlimited, all-consuming, and ultimately insatiable, for it does not rest upon the notion that labor can attain the desired object but, as Heinzelman notes, that "the mediative fluency of money alone" is the defining dynamic.[51] Alienation and fragmentation are the natural results, but the exponential increase of possession of commodities and the excess accumulation of capital are represented as the means through which to suture the void created between human beings and within the reified self.

The commodity's magical capacity to multiply also provokes the first Marxist, who suggests that capital seems to be "a mysterious and self-creating source" a "thing increasing itself."[52] Capitalism, in other words, exists solely and ideally for the unceasing creation and augmentation of capital through unlimited circulation, or, as Marx writes, "The restless never-ending process of profit-making alone is what" the capitalist "aims at."[53] In Marx's famous pseudo-scientific jargon, formula C-M-C, circulation ends as soon as the consumer receives money for his commodity (labor) and then spends that money on commodities that fulfill a need, such as, food, transportation, or housing. In contrast, in the formula M-C-Ḿ, the capitalist uses money to buy commodities that he then sells for a higher price in order to increase his capital. The more times this transaction takes place the more capital he accrues. At the same time, however, this artificial and extended "chain of payments" creates the conditions for monetary crisis.[54] As Marx contends, in the M-C-Ḿ transaction, the consumer's goal is not to use the commodity to fulfill a need, but rather to increase his capital. In this paradigm the increase of capital (M-Ḿ) subordinates the commodity (C) because capital "comes out of circulation, enters into it again, preserves and multiplies itself within its own circuit, comes back out of it with expanded bulk, and begins the same round ever fresh."[55]

Walter Weisskopf asserts that the prime in the M-C-Ḿ formula is a phallic symbol indicating the worker's castration under capitalism.[56] I suggest that in a way the diacritical accent mark above the M visually exhibits the ghost in Marx's representation of circulation. As Marx asserts, the "M-C-M, or the circulation of capital," becomes "an independent substance, endowed with a motion of its own, passing through a life-process of its own, in which money and commodities are mere forms which it assumes and casts off in turn." Hence, "instead of simply representing the relations of commodities, it enters now, so to say, into private relations with itself."[57] In other words, the circulation of money creates – *ex nihilo* – more money, read as M-Ḿ. Itself ambiguous, the diacritical mark might be an apostrophe (indicating possession, lack, elision, fragmentation); an accent (indicating distortion or emphasis); or, the mathematical symbol of the small prime (indicating increase, return, repetition). In Marx's formula, the diacritical mark carries all of these meanings and is a ghostly linguistic rem(a)inder of the material relation Marx tries to describe but which it is impossible to represent because it is only a hanging/haunting mark. Both overdetermined and a representation of overdetermination (it literally hangs above the linguistic marker "M," magnifying, distorting and eliding its meaning), the diacritical mark has, like the ghost of capital, a life of its own. It illustrates, for example, not only capitalism's love affair with financial return but with the return of repressed horrors; it also represents Marx's willingness psychically to immerse himself in the nightmare of capitalism.

Disdaining J. B. Say's suggestion that supply always remained even with demand, Engels and Marx were firm believers in the ten-year trade cycle and its punctuating crises. In *Principles of Communism*, they assert that the Industrial Revolution incurred upsetting, even dramatic, oscillations between prosperous times and periods of stagnation and calamity, with a crisis occurring after five- to seven-year cycles. Concluding that "big industry" could only be maintained "at the cost of general chaos every seven years," Marx rejected the concept that such crises were cathartic.[58] Instead, he describes banking crises as "violent storms" that transpire when the sorcerer loses control and he asserts that every new panic would be worse than the last and ultimately lead to the collapse of capitalism.

Hardly systematic in his explanations of crises, Marx contends that they are "always but momentary and forcible solutions of the existing contradictions" for they only temporarily restore a semblance of order.[59] Not only viewing panic as intrinsic to capitalism, Marx believes that, as a result of its contradictions, capitalism is "in permanent crisis."[60] He sees the central contradiction of capitalism as between capital's natural tendency to create unlimited supply and the opposing need to increase profit by limiting production. As Barbara Herrnstein Smith writes, the market serves as the "arena for the negotiation, transformation, and redistribution of value."[61] In the illogical view of classical economists, crisis necessarily limits the expectations of those who live in a capitalist society at the same time that capitalism's very essence is unlimited production. Severely restricted in its consuming powers, the laboring class experienced a double whammy because the capitalist's inexorable drive "to develop the productive forces in such a way, that only the absolute power of consumption of the entire society would be their limit" inevitably produced the crises that were most difficult for the poor.[62] Labor, in other words, could never afford the commodities it manufactured. As Henryk Grossman explains, "To suppose that capital can expand without limits is to suppose that surplus value can likewise expand without limits, and thus independently of the size of the working population."[63]

Marx and Engels repeatedly lampooned the Bank Act as an instrument of panic. Writing in *Capital* that the Act of 1844 makes the Bank of England the world's largest hoarder, Marx argues that though "the credit of the notes of the Bank of England is considered impregnable by all experts," the "Bank Act absolutely ties up nine to ten millions in gold for the convertibility of these notes," making the "sacredness and inviolability" of the bank's reserves much more excessive than that expressed by "hoard makers of olden times." Deriding John Stuart Mill's belief in the Act, Marx states: "Happily this wise man spoke on June 12, 1857. Four months later the crisis had broken out," at which point Mill "literally congratulate[d] the 'bank directors and the commercial public in general' on the fact that they 'understand the nature of a commercial crisis far better than formerly, and the very great injury which they inflict upon themselves and the public by promoting overspeculation.'"[64]

Marx and Engels were particularly scathing in their remarks about one of the fathers of the Bank Act, Lord Overstone. Citing a small banker named Twells who spoke before the Parliamentary Commission in 1857, Marx highlights his response to question 4488, "How do you think that the Act of 1844 has operated?" Twells answered, in part, "Should I answer you as a banker, I would say that it has operated splendidly, for it has furnished to the bankers and [money-] capitalists of all sorts a rich harvest ... It has made the lending of money a very profitable business." To reinforce his interpretation that the Bank Act benefits bankers, he repeats Lord Overstone's glowing report to the same Bank Committee. Said the banker/Lord, "consider the wealth and prosperity of all classes of society." In an aside just after this rose-colored evaluation, Engels derides Overstone, reporting on the crisis that occurred just six months later: "To this song of praise, which Overstone emitted before the Committee on July 14, replied the song of defiance on November 12, of the same year, in the shape of the letter to the management of the Bank, in which the government suspended the miracle-working law of 1844 in order to save what could still be saved."[65]

Marx brutally satirizes Overstone's defense of the Bank Act, pointing out his hypocrisy, indeed, suggesting that he is essentially a Dr. Jekyll/ Mr. Hyde *avant la lettre*. Analyzing his appearance before the Parliamentary Banking Commission in 1840, Marx derides Overstone's complete self-interest. He notes, for example, how Overstone and "other Currency prophets" have "always [stood] the bad conscience, which makes them aware that they are trying to make capital of the mere medium of circulation by the artificial method of legislative interference and to raise the rate of interest." In parenthetical comments throughout his citation of Overstone's testimony, Marx's analysis is withering. When Overstone asserts that the variations in the interest rate are inconsequential, Marx explodes, "What a wonderful mixture of words on the part of our logician of usury!," contending further that the circumstances serve to enrich bankers like Overstone. Likewise, at one point, Overstone angrily reacts to complaints that the increased interest rate destroys the "two things [increase in trade and profits], which were its own cause," noting that such "is a logical absurdity, which one does not know how to characterise." Marx in Dickensian mode redounds, "The wiseacre! The idiocy of the present bourgeois world cannot be characterized more markedly than by the respect, which the 'logic' of the millionaire, of this dung-hill aristocrat, commanded in all England."[66]

In a critique that intrinsically explodes the notion that the economic can be separated out from other aspects of living, Marx is cynical about Overstone's contention that the Banking Department and the Department of Issue do not have any connection with each other. Like a professor ridiculing the class idiot, Marx cuts him off: "There is an intimate connection between them." As Marx points out later, the partition into the two separate departments ended the "directors' power of free disposal of their entire available means at decisive moments." Thus, inanely, the Banking Department might be confronted with complete bankruptcy at the same time that the Issue Department retained large reserves of gold and securities. The Bank Act, Marx fumes, thus "directly provokes the entire world of commerce into meeting the outbreak of a crisis" by setting aside the reserve notes at exactly the moment they are needed. These actions only "intensif[y]" the crisis "to a point at which either the entire world of industry has to collapse, or else the Bank Act."[67]

The Times obituary article on Lord Overstone of 20 November 1883 praised him for developing a "severely scientific analysis" with which to examine the banking system.[68] Despite this tribute, many Victorians aside from Marx detested Lord Overstone's inability to admit that the Bank Act of 1844, his brainchild, was a nightmare for the economy. In a letter to Henry Brookes, Loyd, later Lord Overstone, provides his ostensibly "severely scientific" description of the financial cycle: "Prosperity," he says,

will generate excess, over-trading and over-production will cause a fall of prices, accompanied by temporary depression and despondency; this fall of prices will, in turn, check production, increase consumption, augment the exports, cause the precious metals to return to the country, the quantity of money will be thus increased, prices will again rise, and the country will in the end find itself very far removed from the verge of utter bankruptcy. Such is the "constant rotation of the unwearied wheel that Nature rides upon."

This response to J. Horsley Palmer reiterates Overstone's claims that the "state of trade" is "an established cycle" beginning "in a state of quiescence, – next improvement, – growing confidence, – prosperity, – excitement, – overtrading, – convulsion, – pressure, – stagnation, – distress, – ending again in quiescence."[69]

What so many found intolerable was Overstone's facile acceptance of the panic phases of the trade cycle he helped to define. As noted previously, Overstone writes indignantly that people who imagine that it is possible to have a perfectly managed economy that would provide "perpetual ease and undisturbed steadiness in commercial affairs, are like the alchymists in search of their mysterious secret; and the discovery, if made, would prove equally useless." Rather, he rails, "Storms and tempests are not more certain and inevitable in the material world, than are the periodical convulsions of commercial affairs; and they both answer similarly useful purposes."[70] Like Marx, Henry Brookes, Secretary to the Bank Act and Currency Committee, despised Overstone's arrogant economic claims that fiscal terrorism was helpful to the economy. In the fall of 1861, over a period of one month, Overstone and Brookes corresponded about how to manage banking crises. Brookes became increasingly dismayed by what he viewed as Overstone's insensitivity to the people who were ruined by the market. As the correspondence proceeds, the tone of Brookes's letters becomes more confrontational and sarcastic while Overstone maintains a strained politeness, condescension, and rigidity of thought. For his part, Brookes complains that panic and pressure are chronic parts of the cycle of trade that must be ended by repealing the Bank Act of 1844, whereas Overstone adamantly refuses to consider the possibility that the law he helped to establish might be flawed or based on an amateur understanding of the economy. Despite their opposing points of view, both correspondents resort to fiction and Gothic tropes to support their economic claims.

In his first letter on 28 September 1861, Overstone explains avuncularly to his correspondent that panic and crisis "are the inevitable accompaniments of a progressive state of national prosperity" that are the "necessary result of that enterprise and competition which makes this country prosperous and powerful as it is." He complains not about the panics but about the way that the public so ignorantly responds to them: economic "convulsions," he remarks, "cannot occur without causing temporary inconvenience and distress, the extent and intensity of which is seriously increased when the calm sense of the public gives way to unreasoning alarm and panic: new and unnecessary causes of confusion and embarrassment are thus introduced." Overstone's haughty condescension underwrites his refusal to consider seriously the possibility that he might be wrong, at the same time that he provides few specific proofs of his theory. With a tin ear,

Overstone fills the gaps in his economic theory with a fictional anecdote. He asserts that to revile natural market convulsions is the same as resisting the medical doctor's prescriptions for cure. "Who but the maniac," says a glib Overstone, "tears away those bandages, or breaks loose from those temporary restraints, sacrificing permanent health and life for immediate relief from a painful, but salutary, discipline!"[71] Thus, according to him, those who experience panic in a market economy are already maniacs who are responsible for their panicked response to seemingly frightening exterior conditions.

In his reply on 7 October 1861, Brookes agrees that the market obviously will have fluctuations. But he denies "emphatically, that there is any natural or inevitable necessity for these periodical monetary panics." Overstone's reply reiterates his theory about the cycle of trade. He concludes that "Such is the 'constant rotation of the unwearied wheel that Nature rides upon'; it is for man to take care that he does not disturb the movements of the machinery by artificial and ignorant interference." Proposing that crises are just temporary blips that ensure "a healthy and vigorous constitution," Overstone argues that they are not "the chronic disease which indicates something essentially unsound, and leads by slow but sure steps to destruction." Repeatedly resorting to analogy to cover over the limitations of his theory, he suggests that those who grumble about panic and crisis are like "the uninstructed savage when he first meets the thunderstorm" and believes that it is the result of "a malignant spirit" that will destroy the world. Stupidly, this savage "is unable to appreciate the causes" or "beneficial results which it is destined to effect." Overstone writes that, in contrast, the civilized, rational man understands the situation from a logical perspective.[72] Indeed, to Overstone, the most natural condition for the subject of capitalism is to be so conditioned to crisis that panicked responses are considered uncivilized.

Overstone further patronizes Brookes, stating that the hysterical masses are incapable of understanding the crisis "phenomena" and if "persons as weak and uninformed as themselves assure them that the country is on the verge of utter bankruptcy, they give ready credence to the tale. So strangely will imagination assist belief in the wildest absurdities." The *coup de grâce* is his statement that "I have lived through several of these panics. I speak of what I know and have seen." Stung by Overstone's smugness and inability to accept critique, Brookes sent a furious reply on 17 October 1861, averring that Overstone seemed "to welcome a panic, with all its fearful concomitants, as a kindred spirit would welcome a brother in some great and spirit-moving enterprise."[73]

What is so interesting about his final letter is the Gothic analogy Brookes uses to articulate the flaws in Overstone's economic argument. He tells a ghost story as the "as if" by which to defeat Overstone's economic analogies. A "Little Miss Panic," daughter of "Old Ignorance," has nightmares about a ghost, named "Mr. Bank Act," who stands in her doorway and haunts her with a list of "ruins," "bankruptcies," "suspensions," and other "technicals," "abnormals," and "ghosts." When a minister is called in to exorcise the ghost that possesses the girl, he realizes that there really is a Mr. Bank Act and decides that the best means of ridding the ghost would be to hang him. The minister hangs Mr. Bank Act, and, relieved of terror, Little Miss Panic immediately and quietly goes to bed. The justices of the court release the minister accused of murder because the jury concludes that the crime is a justifiable homicide, for the Act was, in fact, harming the community.[74] As Albert Einstein so presciently understood, not all things that can be counted are worth counting and not all things that cannot be counted should be considered worthless. In this case, Brookes resists Overstone's ostensibly rational, realistic narrative with a Gothic tale that upends his silly objectivity, showing that if supposedly rational, "natural" economic acts produce supernatural horrors, then they are, in fact, panic-inducing ghost stories.

If, as Derrida suggests, Marx was a haunted author/other, this chapter has examined the nature and effects of his haunted rhetoric in comparison with the tropes used by other Victorian economists, particularly Walter Bagehot and Lord Overstone, to manage the economic specters haunting England. Turning now to the Gothic economics of Victorian fiction, I end this chapter by briefly pointing up Gothic tropes describing the novelist's profession, beginning with Walter Besant's statement in 1903 that every trade possesses "its own phantom." He explains that the "spectre of the literary man" is "that of a creature wholly incapable of conducting business of any kind," for the writer is a person "who allows himself to be plundered and robbed" of his rightful earnings.[75] Entrenched in the ivory tower syndrome, the author, according to Besant, is so immersed in the aesthetic task that he is a bumbler when it comes to negotiating economic remuneration for his work.

Eerily using the same imagery, Nietzsche claims that artists are "not men of great passion" because a "vampire, their talent," usually prevents them from spending their energy on passions. Thus the gifted man "lives under the vampirism of his talent." Grounded in the economic and the Gothic, Nietzsche's disgust for the philistine "herds" produces his call for an "economy of the future" and his "*economic* justification of virtue" for a new race of man – the Superman – who would avoid "economic waste."

Seeking an "economic valuation" of the idealism of the past, the German philosopher resists what he calls the "*economic* optimism" of the times, which sacrifices all men – the weak, and the Superman – to massification and streamlined labor. As Nietzsche argues, "It is *necessary* to show *that a counter-movement is inevitably associated* with any increasingly economical consumption of men and mankind."[76]

The authors of *Villette, Little Dorrit, Dr. Jekyll and Mr. Hyde,* and *Dracula* might have been the prototypes of the literary man haunted by the economic specter to which Besant refers. With a dissolute brother and a father who received a minimal cleric's salary, Charlotte Brontë knew that she and her sisters had to fend for themselves while also coddling the two most important men in their lives. For Charlotte, Branwell's spiral into alcoholism especially pointed up the fragility of the woman's economic position. With contempt and helplessness she writes to Ellen Nussey that, "Branwell offers no prospect of hope – he professes to be too ill to think of seeking for employment – he makes comfort scant at home."[77] On 14 April 1846, the distressed older sister refers to her brother's pathetic condition and intimates how it affects the siblings' financial stability. She explains that the railroad was willing to hire Branwell again "if he would behave more steadily but he refuses to make an effort, he will not work." As a result, she sees Branwell as "at home ... a drain on every resource – an impediment to all happiness," clearly in both financial and personal terms.[78] When the law appears on the Brontë doorstep, Charlotte cracks that the good sheriff "invit[ed]" Branwell "either to pay his debts or to take a trip to York." Fatalistic but also exhibiting a desire to remain respectable, she intones, "Of course his debts had to be paid – it is not agreeable to lose money time after time in this way but it is ten times worse – to witness the shabbiness of his behaviour on such occasions."[79]

Often alluding to his insolvency, Robert Louis Stevenson was matter-of-fact about the hegemony of money. In a letter to Edmund Gosse on 2 January 1886, the year he authored *Dr. Jekyll and Mr. Hyde,* Stevenson claimed that,

As for the art that we profess and try to practise ... We should be paid, if we give the pleasure we pretend to give; but why should we be honoured? We are whores, some of us pretty whores, some of us not, but all whores: whores of the mind, selling to the public the amusements of our fireside as the whore sells the pleasures of her bed.[80]

As will be explored in chapter 5, being on the brink of bankruptcy while writing *Dr. Jekyll and Mr. Hyde,* Stevenson mischievously wondered if his

authorial skills were bankrupt while he also quite literally capitalized on
that bankruptcy and the Gothic bankerization of Victorian identity itself.

As manager of the Lyceum Theatre and frustrated writer, Bram Stoker
often experienced economic panic. Despite Stoker's long-time success at
managing Henry Irving's books, the author of *Dracula* was hardly masterful in the fiscal accounts of his own chosen profession, writing. Stating that
"the ambitious artist *must* be his own manager," he, like Besant, asserts that
"only those strong enough to be both artist and man of business can win
through."[81] Stoker was certainly not both artist and man of business when
it came to his own writing. What with his ineffective contract with the
publisher and inadvertent errors regarding copyright in the United States,
he earned a pittance from *Dracula* and was constantly in debt in the 1890s
and early 1900s. After Irving died, Stoker attempted to focus completely on
his writing as his vocation and sole source of income, but his yearly
royalties were less than £100. So distraught did he become that in 1911 he
lobbied the Royal Literary Fund for a pension and was granted £100.[82]

The superman of the group of novelists I analyze, Dickens was incisive
about the relationship between literature and banking. In an article entitled
"A Review of a Popular Publication," he and W. H. Wills describe the
Bank of England, the *Bildungsroman* of the currency, and its demise when
it is no longer current. The hook of the article is that the currency is
described as though it is a novel:

Few can rise from a critical examination of the literary contents of this narrow
sheet, without being forcibly struck with the power, combined with the exquisite
fineness of the writing. It strikes conviction at once. It dispels all doubts, and
relieves all objections. There is a pithy terseness in the construction of the
sentences; a downright, direct, straightforward, coming to the point, which
would be wisely imitated in much of the contemporaneous literature that constantly obtains currency (though not as much).

The Inimitable explicitly notes the way that "literary men" imitate this
"work," for they use "Notes and Queries" as a "medium of intercommunication" in the same way that "commercial men" use money as a "medium
of intercommunication."[83]

In a similar article entitled "The Old Lady in Threadneedle Street,"
Wills and Dickens remark that the Bank of England's "publication department" is "admirably conducted" and marvel at the extent to which the
Bank monitors its money. Astonishingly, "with few exceptions" each "impres-
sion" of paper money that gets minted eventually returns to the Bank and
is "kept for ten years, and then burnt." Dickens archly concludes the
article by analogizing the circulation of currency with the circulation of

novels: the Bank of England, he quips, is filled with "this Great Woman's literature" (the Old Lady of Threadneedle, that is) and is thus just a "huge circulating library."[84] Recognizing that every piece of paper or page in a novel has a history – the one it records fictionally and the one it engenders as a record of the novel's relationship with each individual reader – Dickens implicitly wonders if the paper pages of novels circulate much longer than does paper money.

As Victor Hugo wrote, the writer is like a sovereign who proves he is sovereign by minting sovereigns: "Every great writer stamps his prose with his own effigy," says Hugo. The French Dickens also remarks that *"Poets are like kings. They must mint money. Their effigy must remain upon the ideas they put into circulation."*[85] As Goux explains, in the same way that economists view money as *"neutral,"* the novelist does not interrogate the "linguistic *medium* he uses, but considers it transparent" because reality seems to be presented "directly through language in an operation of equivalence (exchange) that equates the word with the thing."[86]

But of course the novelistic craft, as Dickens and his colleagues well knew, is caught in the web of circulation, which means, in other words, that money's circulation makes the novel possible. There is a connection, then, to Bagehot composing a love letter to his future wife in the bank, for both Dickens and Bagehot understand that the Bank of England underwrites their professional credit at the same time that it hangs panic over their heads. As Dickens's article on the Bank of England indicates, he knew what Mark Osteen regards as James Joyce's legacy, that is, that, "The linguistic economy is incomplete unless words are subjected to historical circulation and permitted to collect interest."[87] Indeed, Osteen's commentary on the economics of modern literary writing precisely reiterates Dickens's pert and pertinent essay, for Osteen argues that "the 'treasure-house' of language cannot be merely a storehouse." It also must be an "emporium," or site where the canon is subject to "exchanges with the marketplace tradition." By staying in literary and financial circulation, as do *Villette, Little Dorrit, Dr. Jekyll and Mr. Hyde*, and *Dracula*, what Osteen calls the "verbal currency" of the work of literature can capitalize upon reader interest and achieve "full value" economically and aesthetically.[88] Just as crisis is inherent to both modern capitalist market traditions and the literary tradition of the novel (its plot always depending upon excitation, conflict, crisis, denouement, and quiescence), so both always will feature an element of banking on panic. But lest the marketplace tradition assume a privileged position over the linguistic tradition, it should be remembered that Marx's use of the diacritical mark as indicator of the capitalization of money (Ḿ) cannot help but also represent the code of its diverse, even contradictory linguistic meaning.

The novels I study exist under the sign of that diacritical mark. The ordinary heroes and heroines of *Villette* and *Little Dorrit* struggle to distinguish themselves from the philistine herds that are thoroughly subjected to the bankerized world Mrs. Merdle describes. Created by the "treasure-house" of literary language, these characters are subject to both linguistic and market exchanges. Haunted by the diacritical mark that hangs above and overdetermines capital, they must keep accurate accounts and perpetually circulate linguistically and commercially without exhausting their own energy or the energy money ostensibly creates. In a real way, Mr. Hyde and Dracula act as Supermen whose monomaniacal wills seem to rise above the crass economic condition of modernity that collapses the specter and the speculator as well as the corporation and the human personality. The compound economic investments and interests of their foes, Mr. Utterson and Van Helsing and his cohorts, resolutely secure the containment of the would-be Supermen, ensuring that they, too, acquiesce to a world in which the subject banks on panic.

CHAPTER 3

The ghost and the accountant: investing in panic in Villette

The decade leading up to the writing and publication of *Villette* in 1853 saw drastic economic oscillations. The years 1842–43 were probably the most economically catastrophic of the century.[1] A recovery occurred through 1845, during which time there was an increase in the building of railroads, a buildup in the iron and coal industries, expansion in the textile trades, and a rise in employment and real wages. Because of cheap lending rates, there was, as Charles Neville Ward-Perkins notes, "an orgy of speculative activity," particularly with the explosion of railway building.[2] The Bank Act of 1844 was instituted in part as a corrective to railway speculation, but within three years of its passing, Parliament had 1,035 railway schemes to consider authorizing, for, as Ward-Perkins argues, the financial "disturbances" of 1847 resulted from "an incredibly heavy programme of capital investment in the form of railways" and capital expenditures increased on railways by more than £221,000,000. This caused one Governor of the Bank of England to write that "Speculations were never carried to such an enormous Extent as in 1846 and the Beginning of 1847."[3]

Advocates of the currency school of economics, including Lord Overstone, George W. Norman, and Robert Torrens, believed that the Bank Act of 1844 would stabilize the economy and obviate crises. They could not have been more wrong. Bad harvests (including the Irish famine) and over-speculation in railways and corn caused the 1847 bank crash.[4] On the last day of September the Bank of England resolved that it would stop providing advances on stock and Exchequer bills, a decision that "forthwith gave birth to universal panic."[5] The reserves in the Bank of England went down to £9.3 million from £13.4 million between January and April of that year. 16–23 October 1847, known as the "week of terror," saw reserves in the Bank of England fall from "£2,376,000 on Friday (22 October)" down to £1,194,000 the next day.[6] George Norman, one of the Bank of England's board members, wrote of that week that, "Prices of stocks and commodities tumbled" dramatically and that "Every man seemed to be afraid of his neighbour."[7] To allay the panic, the Bank Act was suspended on 25 October, and the Bank of England produced £400,000 in new notes and drew on their own hoarded reserves in order to meet the needs of commercial enterprises and citizen demand.[8]

As a result of the 1847 panic, the House of Commons realized that the Act of 1844 was not the panacea it had seemed. Evidence given by the Governor and Deputy Governor of the Bank of England to a House Committee on Commercial Distress in March 1848 indicates that bankers seemed to have all but given up controlling crises. "It is in the nature of panic to exhaust itself," they lamely observed. The Report of the Secret Committee of the House of Lords on the Commercial Distress (28 July 1848) opined that the Act could not "effectually prevent a Recurrence of Cycles of Commercial Excitement and Depression" nor could it be "relied on as a Security against violent Fluctuations in the Value of Money." Indeed, as the Committee learned, thirty-three large businesses in London worth "the Amount of £8,129.000" failed in 1847.[9]

The early 1850s brought financial equilibrium as Britain "justly laid claim to the title 'workshop of the world.'"[10] There are many reasons for these glory years: the repeal of the Corn Laws in 1846 allowed more overseas trade; what with mechanization and new inventions, the real cost of production decreased, causing industrial production and consumption to accelerate; and gold was discovered in California, helping to fill a shortage of the metal that served as the currency standard. Advancements in industry, business, and transport produced a burgeoning export trade carrying "British-made goods all over the globe."[11] Nonetheless, despite the seeming placidity, in 1852, a year before *Villette*'s publication, William John Lawson describes looking forward to the day when the government and bankers will be able to control banking crises so that "the conceived hobgoblins, frightful monsters, and horrid spectres called Panics, shall vanish, cease, and be no more."[12] In this regard, as Alison Milbank notes, Charlotte Brontë was like many of her contemporaries in that she used "phantasmagor[ic]," apocalyptic imagery to describe the economic disturbances of the 1840s.[13]

In statistical terms *The Annual Register* records that there were 1,222 bankruptcies in England, Scotland, and Ireland in 1852.[14] Bankruptcies brought the need for more accountants. In addition, the railway boom helped to make accountancy a thriving profession as Parliament took increasing responsibility for regulating this heretofore limited field of endeavor. Noting that professional accounting increased dramatically in the 1850s, Nicholas Stacey writes that during this time there were substantive efforts to professionalize the field. For one thing, the Companies Act of 1844 legislated that companies were required to provide auditors and strict maintenance of fiscal records. In addition, as the government steadily increased its control of economic and social planning, the need for accurate records required the use of professional accountants in the public as well as private business sectors. As a result, in London between 1850 and 1883 the number of accountants grew dramatically from 264 to 840.[15]

At the same time, banks were in the process of training their customers to keep accounts as Victorians of all stripes learned to order their finances in the form of passbooks and ledgers. As the "Barclays [Bank] Fact Sheet" records, in the eighteenth century there was only one copy of the customer's balance and that was kept on bank ledgers, which the customer signed to indicate agreement with the bank's recorded balance. In the nineteenth century, however, banks distributed passbooks to their customers that were duplicates of their account record at the bank. Sent to the bank from time to time for updating, these passbooks were ineffectual if the bank and the customer did not regularly check and update the client's fiscal records. Though clumsy, the process was necessary to keep accurate records of credits and debits.[16] *A Banker's Daughter* (1864), a guide for women with bank accounts, is precise in its instructions. Explaining that "In the course of three or four years, and not till then, you will learn what is necessary to keep and what is not," *A Banker's Daughter* warns the reader to "Keep all papers, letters & c. relating to money and business transactions. Never burn any letter or paper on business; much trouble and loss is often occasioned by inexperienced persons doing this." "Arrange your Papers under a few heads," says the cool financier's progeny or her ghostwriter, and "Fold them up neatly of a size, and docket them; that is, write outside what they are, and the date of receiving them." Constructing the bank client as essentially an accountant who retains many forms of official paper, the narrator admonishes the female bank patron to be meticulous and retain "all receipted Bills six years" by folding them up "lengthways." Then, at the end of the fiscal year, all the bills "are quickly arranged alphabetically and tied up," thus making "no trouble in referring to a Bill." The writer reiterates that though "All this seems irksome," it is "wonderful how natural it becomes to fold them of one size and docket them before putting them away in your drawer."[17]

In a letter to William Smith Williams about his "description of the Model Man of Business," Charlotte Brontë remarked that in the "World to come ... conscientious effort and patient pain will meet their reward." Worried that too many have to "labour" past "almost what nature can bear," she nevertheless accepts the cycle of trade, commenting that, "when the evil of Competition passes a certain limit – must it not in time work its own cure? I suppose it will – but then through some convulsive crisis – shattering all round it like an earthquake."[18] Banking on panic, Charlotte acknowledges the need for "limit[s]" and in doing so also concedes a space for the "convulsive crisis" that is the "cure." The romance in Charlotte's novels depends upon the linkage between "Competition" and its limitations and passionate "convulsive crisis." Indeed, in her fiction Brontë was unsparing about how economic crisis affected the domestic sphere and produced panic in middle-class women as the culture confronted them with impossible expectations: they must marry but not be husband-hunters; they must rely on husbands, fathers, and brothers for economic support but not understand money.

Charlotte certainly understood the role of money in the cramped lives of Victorian women. Commiserating with Ellen Nussey (Nell) because she had been friendly to a young man whom she believed was married, Charlotte unflinchingly assesses her friend's situation: "I know that if women wish to escape the stigma of husband-seeking they must act & look like marble or clay – cold – expressionless, bloodless – for every appearance of feeling of joy – sorrow – friendliness, antipathy, admiration – disgust are alike construed by the world into an attempt to hook in a husband."[19] Charlotte also realistically acknowledges the position money plays in romantic affairs. In a letter to Nell dated 24 April 1845, she remarks of her sister's flirtation with a young man as follows: "whether it will ever come to a match is another thing – *Money* [underlined three times] would decide that point as it does most others of that nature." Similarly, she quips about a mutual friend that, "his wife elect has a handsome fortune – not that I advocate marrying for money in general – but I think in many cases (and this is one) money is a very desirable contingent of matrimony."[20]

The cunning future novelist, who seemed always to feel the need to pinch pennies, also contends that "cash" makes all the difference in a romantic relationship: "Who holds the purse will wish to be master," she asserts to Ellen, adding that "whether Man or woman," the partner "Who provides the cash will now and then value himself (or herself) . . . and even in the case of ordinary Minds, reproach the less wealthy partner." In a bid for equal rights, she concludes strongly that, "no husband ought to be an object of charity to his wife – as no wife to her husband."[21] Always resistant to condescension, Charlotte also feels constrained to sound out the price of things. On one occasion when Ellen asks her to visit, she starkly queries: "Can you give me a notion of the cost?"[22] Ever money-conscious, in another instance Charlotte rather crassly sends Ellen cash instead of a "present" because "I know myself how trying it is to be without a shilling of pocket-money."²³

Whether or not a dissipated brother is the reason Charlotte's Lucy Snowe is exasperatingly vague about what events made her an indigent orphan, she is constantly limited by "Competition" and in search of a "convulsive crisis" as the "cure." Fatalistically, she banks on panic while also investing in banking procedures that represent the limits of her condition. Certainly a deep structure of *Villette* is that of investing and bookkeeping vis-à-vis ineluctable financial and emotional panic figured through the image of the ghost.²⁴ Indeed, it is surprising how much the fiscal background haunts the novel's social foreground. Lucy is like an invisible ghost (and ghostwriter) who keeps accounts of everything she sees; and as an accountant she is haunted by the return of her repressed economic condition. In terms of actual fiscal crises, the main characters in the story, including the Brettons, M. Paul, the Walravens, and the Fanshawes are monetarily compromised by banking failures, bad investments, or poor handling of money. Mrs. Bretton, the "guardian" of a "handsome property" for her son has invested it in "some joint-stock [bank] undertaking," and as a result it "had melted" to a "fraction of its original amount."²⁵ Thus her son Graham has to work for a living. As a young man, M. Paul's father was a "rich banker" who "had failed, died, and left behind him only debts and destitution" (485). Likewise, Justine Marie's father has "some financial transactions which entailed exposure and ruinous fines" (485). Meanwhile, Mme. Walravens owns an estate in the West Indies that was "received in dower on her husband's failure." Even Polly's prosperous father, M. de Bassompierre, is a profligate who once "had thrown away all his money" (559, 115).

In addition, *Villette* figures drastic events as part of a business cycle in the Overstone vein: there are phases of serenity, quiet, and dull stability disrupted by climactic moments of anxiety and crisis. The terms "crisis" (106, 110, 541, 562, 580), "panic" (176, 342, 477), "dread" (564, 596), "terror" (596), "fever" (105, 230, 231, 239, 244, 254, 259, 280, 554), "frenzy" (113, 554) and "peril" (109, 117, 119, 128), Victorian terms used to refer to negative phases of the economic cycle, occur repeatedly throughout the text and become a structuring device for the dramatic fluctuations in the plot. If *Villette's* times of crisis are interspersed with periods of deadly torpor and self-denial, Lucy's description of the loss of her family is exemplary: hers is "a bark slumbering through halcyon weather, in a harbour still as glass"; then a "storm" and "wreck" occur accompanied by a period of "cold, of dangers, of contention," as well as "shocks and repulses … humiliations and desolations" (94, 93).

This cycle recurs after her employer Miss Marchmont dies without making good on a promise to will Lucy a monetary bequest. Realizing that she is a "placeless person in debt," and "loathing" her "desolate existence," Lucy faces the "crisis" and goes to Belgium in search of a job (103, 110). When the ship docks, she bemoans the fact that her "resting-time" is over and her "stringent difficulties" begin again as "the necessity for exertion more urgent, the peril (or destitution) nearer, the conflict (for existence)" becomes "more severe" (118, 119). That crisis structures her mental life is indicated when, a few pages later, Lucy remarks "the secret but ceaseless consciousness of anxiety lying in wait on enjoyment, like a tiger crouched in a jungle" (122).

As with other Victorian novels, in *Villette* the middle-class heroine's marriage prospects are also her economic prospects. Of course this responsibility was complicated because women could not appear actively to pursue a marriage partner and because, for the many "superfluous" women who could not find a partner, the culture's answer seemed to be that marriage was the only way it was willing to support middle-class women. For an unattractive woman without family or inheritance, like Lucy, the economic circumstances are frighteningly unstable. As Margit Stange notes of the domestic novel and the marriage plot, "Domestic ideology and market culture come together" in the "discourse of the exchange of woman."[26] Likewise, Jan Cohn remarks of the contradictions inherent in Victorian marriage, that romance fiction is a reaction to the condition of women who are "doubly enjoined against seeking their own economic success: first by the strictures of bourgeois society in relation to work and the marketplace, and second by the values of romantic love as they affected marriage."[27] Hence, as Lucy repeatedly experiences monetary and emotional crisis with intermittent times of deadly inanition, in response, she rigorously limits her desires when they seem to be excessive (541). When it is clear that Dr. John is not attracted to her as a marriage partner, Lucy attempts to "swallow" and "lock up" her emotions (348). The feeling behind her self-deprivation is anything but ascetic, for when she seems to face the same rejection from M. Paul, she emotes, "something tore me so cruelly under my shawl, something so dug into my side, a vulture so strong in beak and talon, I must be alone to grapple with it" (566–67).

In a pamphlet chastising Lord Overstone for dealing with banking panic by restricting the issue of money in times of crisis, James Robinson uses similar psychological and physical images of illness to describe an economy in panic. Indeed, Robinson's economic images hauntingly illustrate the emotional panic and self-deprivation Lucy so often exhibits and to which Charlotte alludes in her letter to Williams. "A panic," Robinson says, "has always had its commencement with the restriction of the currency" and leads "towards loss and ruin." Disparaging the editor of the *Leeds Mercury* for "recommending the national bank to restrain its issues" to the "least possible amount" because "the nation is plunged into all the horrors of PANIC," Robinson argues that by stringently curbing funds "every banker in the kingdom becomes more or less needy." This creates a "hopeless and melancholy" environment and the "mind sickens at the prospect." Likewise, Robinson declares that such restriction brings "a whole train of ills, which may be summed up in one sentence – universal want and commercial depression – and shakes the social fabric to its very centre!"[28]

An incarnation of Robinson's description of panic resulting from excessive restriction, Lucy believes she can survive in this culture only if her emotional economy is restricted to the lowest possible level. She also essentially lives with the "horrors of PANIC" on a regular basis. We have seen how classical economics – and Charlotte Brontë – positively viewed banking crises as a means of destroying an overly heated economy, thus limiting the speculator's unrealistic expectations; at the same time, said Marx, capitalism inherently sought infinite production and consumption. Lucy's states of quiescence and panic illustrate this contradiction. In regard to her sexual desires – which are always already economic desires – Lucy simultaneously craves extravagant fulfillment and severely restricts her longing. Invested in the capitalist economy as she is, her own bodily economics mirror capitalism, for she experiences the Gothic conditions of terror, anxiety, and a "sickening to the mind" that are the price to pay for supposed economic stability.

Having observed and participated in the country's feverish speculations in railways in the 1840s, in part because of the sisters' pressing financial situation aggravated by Branwell's alcoholic decline, Charlotte Brontë knew first hand about the panic induced by the market's inculcation of unlimited desire and simultaneous repression. In a letter to Margaret Wooler on 23 April 1845, Brontë explains that "terms for female lives" on annuities is a "low" rate of "$4^{1}/_{2}$ per cent" at the age of twenty-five and "5 per cent for those purchased at 30" and that "an annuity purchased at 30 – and deferred twelve years – would produce 10 per-cent." She notes that the sisters' railway investments were not "threatened with immediate danger" and explains that since none of the siblings was thirty years of age yet (she was the only one to pass that age) the sisters decided to stay in railways for a year while they considered their options. Believing that it would be a "risk" to try the ten-year option, Charlotte thinks it best to put the money in the bank and make up the difference in the interest over ten years. She adds in passing that she and her sisters have had a "degree of success" with their "small capital" though they know that "there is nothing so uncertain as rail-roads; the price of shares varies continually – and any day a small share-holder may find his funds shrunk to their original dimensions."[29] Nine months later, Brontë informs Wooler that despite the "Railway Panic" their "small capital is as yet undiminished." Asserting that "the very best lines" cannot "continue for many years at their present premiums," she feels "most anxious for us to sell our shares ere it be too late." To "secure the proceeds in some safer if, for the present, less profitable–, investment" would be, she maintains, the wisest course.[30]

In March 1846, Charlotte writes to Eliza Jane Kingston, dismissing the need to pull out of railway stocks even though she has been warned of the risks. "Have you sold the shares you intended to dispose of?" she asks Eliza, and then explains that "we are still frequently advised to get out of the Railroads before it is too late – but really the Y&N Midland – as yet seems to present no signs of falling off to warrant selling out." Instead, she rather gleefully reports, "on the contrary it appears full as prosperous as ever."[31] By 8 May 1846 Charlotte's letter to Miss Kingston states that she is "sorry to hear that our Mining Shares have only a *nominal* value" but that "as they yield a small dividend we cannot regard them as wholly worthless." Then the little speculator muses, "The new 'railway' Shares are rising and on that account do you not think it would be better to sell an old share and retain them? I am not at all certain on this point therefore I only ask the question."[32] Proud that she and her sisters "have abstained from all gambling, all 'mere' speculative buying-in & selling-out," she reflects that, "we have got on very decently."[33]

Of course within a year and a half of these letters, the speculative railway bubble burst and many investors were left bankrupt. In 1849, Charlotte wrote to George Smith that

the little railway property I possessed, according to original prices – formed already a small competency for one with my views and habits, now – scarcely any portion of it can with security be calculated on ... Some of the local papers strenuously advise against selling just now; they affirm that the market is far more depressed than it otherwise would be, by the fact of shareholders hurrying to sell, in a panic.[34]

But aside from indicating that there were women besides herself and her sisters who were speculating in railway shares, these letters reveal that the Brontës were interested in, and, to a degree, more aggressive and acute in their fiscal sensibilities than most women of the time. The chapter entitled "Investments for Women" in *Beeton's Guide to Investing* suggests that, "investments should be chosen for women as are most simple," with a stable price and interest "easily received." *Beeton's* also asserts that especially "for spinsters and widows, who may have no other means, great care should be taken to select a perfectly safe security."[35] Charlotte's comments show that the sisters seemed willing to put up with a degree of risk far higher than *Beeton's* suggests for women. And though the Brontë sisters did seek masculine guidance on fiscal matters – they had to, given that the law severely restricted women's financial rights – apparently they also felt perfectly comfortable learning as much as they could about the stock market to make sure they themselves could manage their stocks.

Charlotte's reference to Emily's fiscal prowess – she "has made herself mistress of the necessary degree of knowledge for conducting the matter, by dint of carefully reading every paragraph & every advertisement in the news-papers that related to rail-roads" – implies that at least one of the sisters avidly read economic articles in the newspapers and journals that were so abundantly available in their father's home. The *Railway Magazine* was established in 1835 and the *Railway Almanac* in 1846, both supplying information about dividends and stockbrokers.[36] Emily also might have consulted the *Railway Times*, which circulated around 27,000 in 1842, a journal providing exhaustive details on many companies in such a way that the reader could easily compare share prices and dividends. Similarly, *The Economist* offered a special section on railways starting in 1845 so that, as Paddy Ireland remarks, by mid-century discussions about railway shares had become normalized "in the study and the drawing room," as news-papers increasingly provided daily information about share prices.[37]

Investment guides from the period illustrate the high risks that the Brontës and other speculators took to fulfill grand economic goals. For example, *The Railway Investment Guide: How to Make Money by Railway Shares* begins none too sanguinely that though many are "thrown into ecstacies of hope, if not of envy or jealousy, by hearing that one among them has suddenly realized a fortune," yet nevertheless, there is "an immense danger of the pressure carrying down hundreds," particularly since there is "no *vade mecum*" that would steer investors away from "disappointment, ruin, and beggary of entire families." Promising to "rescue the public from this chaos of bewilderment, confusion," and "RUIN!" the pamphlet employs dramatic, anecdotal rhetoric rather than scientific formula to illustrate the risks.[38]

Likewise, in a pamphlet entitled *Theory of Investment in Railway Companies*, Hyde Clarke remarks that people speculating in railways "have found themselves baffled and left behind in the gigantic march of events." In a melodramatic turn, Clarke warns: "Bankers found themselves threatened by a monster, which, in its cravings, seemed ready to swallow up the capital and resources of the country, or to turn it into unwonted channels." The writer concludes that "When a man sees an alligator opening a tremendous mouth directly opposite his head, he does not set to work to count the vertebrae ... but he looks to his own immediate safety; and thus it has been with the railway system, and those engaged in it." With these outlandish images, Clarke intimates that using statistics to describe financial crises cannot do representational justice to the speculating phenomena nor restore stable financial conditions. "In political economy," he acerbically writes, through "vain research" people "attempt to define in figures the distribution of capital as they would attempt to do the thickness of a line, or the diameter of a point."[39] Clarke is unwilling, then, to delete melodramatic, almost supernatural, narrative from the ostensible science of economics. Nonetheless, as Mary Poovey argues, bookkeeping was used "to manage or contain excess" and risk, as well as to elide narrative "allusions to what no rules of writing could control: shipwrecks, storms at sea, and the wild fluctuations in currency rates that characterized the early modern economy."[40]

A Banker's Daughter illustrates this argument, calmly promising to eliminate economic panic by encouraging women to believe that they have some power to control the bumpy economic fluctuations they face by keeping meticulous individual account books. Advising its readers to "Set up a neat tin box," or, a "fire-proof box," to "hold your Deeds, Scrip, Bonds, Receipts, and Papers of all kinds connected with business," the guide instructs women to "Keep this locked up in a safe place, or it may be deposited with your Bankers for safe custody during absences from home, or for longer periods if necessary."[41]

The account books kept by Patrick and Charlotte Brontë illustrate the ideological uses of accounting as well as its uneven development. If one judges from Patrick's bookkeeping, it was a hybrid affair, mixing check stub style information with narrative explanations of expenditures. One of the Reverend's account books also repeatedly inculcates the accountant mind set, as though the absentminded cleric needed such reinforcement. For example, on the inside front cover of the small (3" × 6") leather account book he writes numerous reminders to himself to be a conscientious accountant. One entry states, "[N.] B. Keep *every* page of this book for the sake of reference," while another exhorts, "Always, when necessary, get a receipt." Still another reminds him to "keep the last & that only – or lay before witnesses, & make a memorandum." In addition, the front cover reiterates twice that when he is done with this account book he needs to save it in his trunk and "procure a new memorandum Book."[42]

However, for all his attempts to be a mathematical bookkeeper, in one section of the account book, Patrick pens the statement, "I will never write" in "the margins of this book." He also declares, "I will not write in this anything of much consequence" but "what is in some way connected with [financial?] matters & very necessary – lest, as formerly, it should become very troublesome and inconvenient."[43] Clearly, the Yorkshire clergyman has difficulty keeping an account book that is merely a numerical notation of his financial doings; it seems that his ledger inevitably becomes a place for narrative as well as moralistic injunctions to be a good accountant, inscriptions that disrupt the accounting process itself, turning it into a mish-mash. That he has to write in the margins an injunction against writing in the margins further suggests his confused anxiety about book-keeping. Indeed, it seems that the Reverend simply cannot refrain from narrative excess in his bookkeeping even when insisting that the account be virtually a numerical text.

Furthermore, Patrick's accounts are not necessarily in chronological order nor are they neatly laid out. He follows the odd course of lining out the narrative and numerical information once he has taken care of a transaction. He even records in some entries that he has chosen *not* to buy something because he has thought better of doing so; in one case, for instance, he decided not to "flag the garden walks" because it would "be more slippery in frost – require washing & produce weeds between the joinings." Likewise, Mr. Brontë notes having "given up all thoughts of breaching the gables, in order to improve the chimney vents – as the expense and trouble would be too great." Thus the ledger juxtaposes debits, credits, and nixed desires in a jumble almost of stream-of-consciousness recording. Likewise, there is no organizing principle to his accounts that would separate, say, valuations of his house (in 1851 the "house was valued" at "£10-13-0-") and the signature of a painter to acknowledge that he has "receivd money on 19 July 1852 of 1 pound for painting all his windows etc. from John Hudson."[44]

The size of a small wallet ($2^1/_2$" × $2^1/_2$"), one of Charlotte's account books, in the Brontë Parsonage Library holdings, is more carefully laid out than her father's muddled book. On one page, Charlotte refers to a list of things "To be bought," including "bonnet, dress, gloves, ribbons for need" and other items. Below this list are the figures £1.8s.1d, the total price for these items. On the next leaf she very neatly catalogs "Expenses" for train tickets to Leeds and York, as well as the cost of purchases of bonnets, cocoa, oranges, and coffee. Another sheet registers "Expenses of Journey July 7th 1848." Here Charlotte carefully itemizes in columns the amount for a carriage, train tickets, porter, cab fare to Euston station, gloves, parasols, books, port, and boots. Then there are pages with columns of figures but no description of what each represents, the numerical figures crying out for a narrative.[45]

Given Patrick's propensity to narrate and overwrite/ride his purchases and Charlotte's sparer numerical bookkeeping, it might be said that she had a better head for political economy than her father, at least when it came to keeping financial records. *A Banker's Daughter* illustrates why it was important for a young lady to be "methodical" in keeping accounts, noting that "unscrupulous tradespeople" will no longer "send in a Bill twice" when they know that their customer records each transaction scrupulously.[46] Keeping fastidious accounts was not a Victorian birthright. Given that the Victorian period was the first time that masses of individuals held bank accounts, the process of learning how to keep accounts was more complicated than at first might appear, especially considering the differences between Charlotte's and her father's accounts. Given the care with which *A Banker's Daughter* explains how to keep accounts, as indicated above, one can infer that keeping detailed fiscal records was a whole new cultural enterprise and not just for women. Clearly, too, facing few laws and other means of oversight, Victorian businesses could and would cheat customers regularly if they knew that recording was not going on.

Let it be conjectured that accounting turns humans into bookkeepers and that, given Patrick's all but hysterical efforts to avoid messy accounting, panic is the underside of bookkeeping. It might also be stated that where Charlotte seems to have accepted the absolute displacement of narrative from the financial account, Patrick intuitively recognizes the textual gaps presented by mere numbers when recording financial transactions. As Patrick's record shows, numbers cannot account for the myriad psychic, intellectual, and emotional ruminations and consequences that compel and result from financial exchanges; nor can they record the commodities or services one gives up in order to opt for other commodities or services. In addition, they do not represent the emotional or other values placed upon the item or service bought, or changes in those valuations over time. Neither can they embody the state of mind of the owner of the account when a financial transaction occurs, whether that person is in a state of pecuniary and psychic ease or panic. Ultimately, because the accountant's record is virtually completely mathematical, the accountant becomes a textual entity who is nameless, objective, accurate to a pence, and always au fait – the accountant is, in other words, ostensibly omniscient and omnipresent.

In *Villette* the underside of this all-seeing, invisible positionality is the spectral. If, as Marx suggests, capitalist culture is in permanent crisis, the self constantly must be in the position of accountant in order to survive. But as Jameson suggests of the haunting Marx describes, the ghost and the accountant carry their counterpart in the subconscious. Jameson's point that the modern age actually changes the structure of the mind by "autonomizing" the senses goes back to capitalism's breakdown of the body/mind and its organs into autonomous parts.[47] Though it seems as though Lucy's keeping of accounts is the reason she has conquered panic, the necessity to keep financial records – which generates psychological accounts on a similar model – produces panic, while panic produces the need to keep financial, psychological records. Thus, keeping accounts always presumes a consciousness that expects to desire excess while also relying upon extreme self-limitation, on somebody's part, as a counterbalance. In Lucy and her narrative, the ghost and the accountant uncannily articulate the speechless, psychically intense and ceaseless narrative traces of the self's desires that demand a narrative but which cannot be named or instituted fully within a capitalist mode of accounting that absolutely compartmentalizes financial bookkeeping and emotional accounting.

Keeping accounts in order to "check" herself against desiring too much, Lucy hopes not to feel so desperately attached to the Brettons. Hence, she calls on "Reason" to "check" her passions and help her to desire with "moderate expectation" (251). "Reason" responds to her desperate appeal "But if I feel, may I *never* express," with the firm injunction, "'*Never!*'" (307) much in the same vein that Patrick lectures himself never to include narrative marginalia in his accounting. Every time Lucy "pour[s] out" in letters her feelings for Dr. John, "when two sheets were covered with the language of a strongly-adherent affection," then "Reason," "vigorous and revengeful," would "snatch the full sheets, read, sneer, erase, tear up, re-write, fold, seal, direct, and send a terse, curt missive of a page" (335). The long list of verbs describing the actions of "Reason," the accountant, illustrate that at the same time that Lucy stifles her desire, it is also excessively, luxuriously narrated and taken account of. There is also an element of masochistic self-exposure when M. Paul reminds Lucy that she "want[s] so much checking, regulating, and keeping down" (452). "Checking" is still part of her consciousness when she finally tells M. Paul of her love for him, saying, "as I narrated, instead of checking," he "incited me to proceed" (591).

Lucy's accounting is present from the very beginning of her story as are the ghosts in accounting's consciousness. Because she has no choice but constantly to take insecure jobs, she is a "mere looker-on at life" (211). She "stores up ... piece[s] of casual information, as careful housewives store seemingly worthless shreds and fragments for which their prescient minds anticipate a possible use some day" (105). Lucy's reference to the housewife brilliantly merges the domestic and political economies: if, as Brontë is well aware, the term "economics" originally referred to the domestic sphere, her characterization of Lucy limns a single woman who uses the meticulous accounting skills of the housewife. Keeping track of financial and familial accounts, the housewife cares for the psychological and social needs of the household members and manages to do so within the monetary budget she oversees. In contrast, while absolutely dependent upon the female-dominated domestic/economic sphere, the capitalist version of economics focuses all but monomaniacally on the individual's economic needs, eliding the communal nature of former definitions of economics.

Certainly Lucy's economic condition illustrates what Linda Nicholson suggests, that previous to the seventeenth century areas of life now considered separate – such as the economic, the familial, and the political – were overlapping realms.[48] As Alison Milbank argues, Brontë's story is a "*reinstatement*" of the eighteenth-century Gothic novel's concern with "the terrorizing system" that endangered women.[49] In other words, it captures the economic deep structure feminist economists challenge, including the focus of capitalist economics on individualism, rational choice, and Rational Economic Man, or *homo economicus,* to the detriment of discussions about women as economic subjects, the group and economics, and the rich range of influences upon economic decision-making other than the so-called rational. Likewise, *Villette* challenges Victorian and contemporary economic theories that illogically argue that in the public sphere humans are self-interested, but that in the private sphere – the feminine domain – people somehow suddenly become completely altruistic. The appeal to altruism, of course, covers over the bowdlerized meaning of "economics." Moving away from giving priority to provisioning, the new economics, "'Economistic' beliefs," as Ann Jennings calls them, gives priority to laissez-faire market forces. Further, *Villette* questions what Nancy Folbre and Heidi Hartmann call the "traditional boundaries between self-interest and altruism" as well as between "facts and values, public and private, reason and emotion, male and female."[50]

Charlotte's prescient narrative strongly implies that the confusion of emergent and residual economies binds and focuses her heroine's desires.

Scrupulously aware of the "signs and tokens" of the complicated world in which she dwells, Miss Snowe juggles a range of economic, social, and personal needs by "tak[ing] notice" (62, 65). Being precisely aware not only of her own desires but everybody else's is a kind of accounting that also helps her to stay afloat in a financially unstable class and gender position. Conscious that when she first meets Dr. John she is like "unobtrusive articles of furniture" to him, Lucy almost gloats that in contrast, "He laid himself open to my observation" (162). One cannot help but think of Marx's sentient table ogling the obtuse human consumer; Lucy even figures herself as a piece of furniture. Admiring Madame Beck's surveillance skills because they contribute to her school's success as well as the madame's financial independence, Lucy seems even to approve when Madame Beck inspects Lucy's belongings, including "count[ing] the money in" her purse and opening her account book to "coolly peruse its contents" (131). That Lucy surveils Madame Beck's surveillance puts the lowly Miss Snowe into a position of potency over this powerful woman.

The ending of *Villette* highlights the power the heroine gains from keeping such exact accounts. When M. Paul presents Lucy with her own apartment and attached classroom before he leaves for the West Indies, she responds, "I promised to work hard and willingly." Pledging that, "I will be your faithful steward," like a good employee, Lucy promises that, "I trust at your coming the account will be ready" (587). Given that Paul Emanuel's bequest raises Lucy out of the penury and insecurity of working for others, it is no wonder, then, that the heroine vociferously exclaims of her feelings for M. Paul that "[I]n *this* Love I had a vested interest" (567). With the specifically economic twist to M. Paul's and Lucy Snowe's relationship at the end of the novel, the reader must view all that precedes it as an economic as well as emotional account. In this account we learn that Lucy has overcome regular bouts of intense financial and emotional panic and thus is able to offer a good account of herself to the reader and M. Paul. Writing of the three years M. Paul is gone, she claims, "I worked – I worked hard. I deemed myself the steward of his property, and determined, God willing, to render a good account" (6). As though intended for a job performance review, Lucy's stuttering iteration of "worked hard" magnifies her superb employee skills.

Likewise, when she unexpectedly receives one hundred pounds from Mrs. Marchmont's estate after M. Paul buys her the school, the financially acute Lucy Snowe admits in a tone worthy of a modern corporate executive, "I asked no questions, but took the cash and made it useful" (593). With this money she expands her franchise, turning her *externat* into a *pensionnat* "that also prospered" (594). It is not surprising that Terry

Eagleton has called Lucy an "enterprising individualist," for she is certainly aware of what those terms mean as well as the difference between "workers" and "capitalists" (395).[51] Blunt about financial matters and working "for the sake of the money," she looks down on the other teachers at Madame Beck's, despising both the colleague who hoards her money as well as the teacher who is "prodigal and profligate" and who is always "in debt" (369, 194, 195). Lucy's first complaint about the Cleopatra portrait, too, is that the reclining beauty "appeared in hearty health, strong enough to do the work of two plain cooks" and therefore "had no business to lounge away the noon on a sofa" (275).

Furthermore, when she goes to London, Lucy is impressed by the "city," which "seems so much more in earnest" than the West End because it is about "business" and "serious things." In contrast, while "The city is getting its living," the "West-end" merely "enjoy[s] its pleasure" (109). Here the narrative echoes Charlotte's own sentiments. While in London in 1853, she exults: "Being allowed to have my own choice of sights this time – I selected rather the *real* than the *decorative* side of Life." Besides visiting Newgate and Pentonville Prisons, she also chose to spend time at the Bank of England and the Exchange, the redoubtable sites of masculine finance.[52] We know, too, that Lucy has an aggressive career "plan" modeled on Madame Beck's "flourishing establishment." Closely considering "'Living costs" and "House-rent," she calculates that once she has saved her money she will be able to afford "a tenement with one large room, and two or three smaller ones." The ambitious Miss Snowe conjectures, also, that, "With self-denial and economy now, and steady exertion" her "labour for independence" may have rich rewards (450).

It is perhaps mean-spirited to judge Lucy, as Eagleton does, according to a masculinist economics that elides the impossible position to which Victorian working middle- and lower-class women were subjected, something like the attitude displayed towards "welfare mothers," who are berated for staying home with their children (and vampirically bleeding the nation's budget) but who are provided no childcare assistance when legislators demand that they go to work full time for a pittance of a salary. Indeed, as David Punter notes, the Gothic always considers the "law of the orphan"; that is, in some way, the Gothic figures the law as "the soul of injustice and untruth" and focuses on the orphan who seeks to "find a way of inserting oneself into a world in some other way than 'merely' as a 'foreign body' to the other."[53] In Lucy's case, the logic seems to be that she must starve physically and emotionally in order to prove that her economic intentions are purely altruistic and thus becoming to a woman. She must, in other words, absolutely separate the private and the public, a regulation detrimental to so many Victorian women like Lucy. One of the results of this imperative to keep a strict ledger of her economies (self-suppressions) are the ghosts that linger at the margins of Lucy's accounts and that ultimately refuse to be marginalized.

The ghost is a richly correspondent, overdetermined antithesis to the accountant in Brontë's narrative. *Villette* features many characters described as being ghosts, including Lucy, Polly, Dr. John, M. Paul, Madame Beck, and Mrs. Walravens (69, 92, 127, 136, 180, 431). Among other things, the text associates ghostliness with Lucy's shadowy invisibility to others; her body a spectral burial ground of her own aborted desires, it is also a body that is consistently discounted or buried by those around her because she is a cipher economically and sexually (226, 403, 175). The narrative also explicitly figures the obsessive surveillance of Madame Beck and the meticulous observations of the "ghost-seer" Lucy as supernatural spectral activities (353). In addition, monomaniacal emotional longings explicitly turn Polly and Lucy into ghostly wraiths (69, 353, 238, 353), and, as mentioned earlier, Lucy describes her fraught economic condition in supernatural terms (107, 112). Indeed, in *Villette* the ghost motif indicates that the real conditions brought about by capitalist economics are more to be feared than any paranormal events.

Right after Lucy sees the nun for the first time, Dr. John remarks that it is a "spectral illusion ... resulting from long-continued mental conflict" (330). As I have suggested, the deep structures of accounting and haunting organize the novel's repetitive economic cycle that reels from the mental conflict between extreme yearning and intermittent but regular panicked limitation of the self's desires. In other words, every time Lucy experiences psychic trances or sees the nun it is when she is having trouble moderating her willfully expansive desires. The nun also seems to act as the accountant who confronts Lucy with her emotional debits – Lucy has "nun" when it comes to financial security, which, because she is a woman, depends completely on her erotic income. There seems no middle ground for her in an economy that puts single, less attractive women without family into desperate circumstances. That economic dread is magnified because the ghosts themselves require the keeping of meticulous accounts of their transactions with Miss Snowe, as though her painstaking emotional inter-est will somehow engender or compound economic interest.

During the long vacation, Lucy sees capitalist economics unveiled in a manner similar to Marx's uncanny account of the animated table. Learning that capitalist economics deletes the "domestic" from the original meaning of economics, she sees that in contrast to an "economics" that constructs a household in which the woman oversees both the financial and personal needs of its inhabitants, capitalism expands and limits the meaning of economics – expanding it to refer to the whole nation and limiting it by focusing only on the financial. No longer are the financial and personal needs of the subject understood as inseparable from the political, for the communal economics of the domestic household is replaced by aggressive individualism. Lucy feels the brutal effects when she is left to care for a cretin, while her colleagues and students go off for a long vacation. Devastatingly lonely, she remarks that "menial and distasteful" as was the job of caring for the cretin, when the cretin leaves, her mental condition grows worse as she has no one to care for, only her own dependent economic condition (229).

Succumbing to a "fever of the nerves and blood," Lucy hallucinates a communal economics peopled by the ghosts of her long dead family members (229, 230, 231). As though that is not enough to illustrate her bankrupt condition, on top of seeing her dead progenitors she also psychically reproduces a whole communal beehive of spectral traces of her students and colleagues when "the ghastly white beds" of the dormitory turn "into spectres – the coronal of each" becoming a "death's head, huge and sun-bleached" that has "dead dreams of an elder world and mightier race" that are "frozen in their wide gaping eye-holes" (232). Spiraling into delirium, Lucy imagines an excessive domestic economy in which she feels responsible for the personal ghosts that haunt her as well as the ghosts that haunt her ghosts. In a spectacular exhibition of taking on the burdens of the world, Lucy also envisions universalized ghosts of the whole race of man who also seem to demand her personal attention, that is, her panicked reaction. The terrifying hallucination demands, then, that she keep track of all the personal and public fears and desires of this counterfeit and emotionally demanding community of ghosts.

Both reining in and giving a lead to her panic, Lucy achieves some kind of control of the experience by keeping detailed descriptions of the specters that multiply before her eyes. Ultimately this compulsive accounting causes Lucy to find a place to confess her haunting in order to begin a clean page of bookkeeping, as it were. Confessing in the Catholic church is like bookkeeping, for Lucy records that "the mere pouring out of some portion of long calculating, long pent-up pain into a vessel when it could not be again diffused – had done me good" (234). To Lucy the "calculating" is not serviceable unless it can be erased without being voided. That is, the traces of her accounting must be preserved in a centralized, authoritative location that provides a seal of closure – showing that the accounts have been settled – but also assurance that the data will be preserved (as are

Lucy's letters under the nun's tree, and, for that matter, old bank notes at the Bank of England).

Leaving the cathedral, the deranged heroine faints, "pitch[ing] headlong down an abyss" (236). As Lucy wakes from the "swoon," her "consciousness revived in fear," and she is so "appalled" that she "should have understood what we call a ghost, as well as I did the commonest object," for everything she sees is "spectral." Gradually, she is restored to normality as the "life-machine presently resumed its wonted and regular working" (237). Lucy scrupulously describes her (un)familiar surroundings, the furniture being well-known, the room completely strange. The accountant and ghost collude when she notes of the furniture, "Of all these things I could have told the peculiarities, numbered the flaws or cracks, like any *clairvoyante*" (239). As she gazes at the uncanny scene, she herself becomes a "life-machine" again. At the same time that she thinks of herself as a machine, she refers to the pieces of furniture as though they are living beings with which she has had an emotional relationship. Noting that, "all these objects were of past days, and of a distant country," she memorializes them: "Ten years ago I bade them good-by," and "since my fourteenth year they and I had never met" (239).

Her subjectivity previously put into question by mental collapse and then by the uncanny surroundings to which she awakes, Lucy "gasp[s]" out loud, "Where am I?" (239). Fixating on the familiar furniture and knick-knacks in the unfamiliar setting, she gives life to the furnishings, concluding that they are the "ghosts" of the real fittings she remembers (241). Then she feels "compelled to recognize and to hail" the furniture (241). In this case, the sofas and tables have not only stood up and moved as living beings before Lucy's eyes, they also demand that their superiority be acknowledged by her, the mere "life-machine." Althusser, of course, uses the term "interpellation" to describe the way capitalist ideology "hails" or addresses the subject. Though the subject believes he has agency, in reality, ideology hails the individual to hold the belief system that corresponds with his class, gender, and race position. Informing the subject of what he can achieve economically, hailing also trains the subject's desires.[54] Putting Lucy in her place, the Brettons' furniture reminds her that she is an orphan without financial resources who must rely upon herself and the undependable, rare kindnesses of people like the Brettons.

The furniture also hails Lucy to remain in the cycle of unlimited desire and destruction of desire as well as to keep and be haunted by meticulous accounts. Thus in the strangely familiar Bretton home, Lucy's desire for Graham becomes unmanageable and intense, even as she struggles desperately to repress her feelings. It is not coincidental that Lucy's first encounter with the nun occurs with the first letter she receives from Graham. Reading the epistle in the unused garret of Madame Beck's school, Lucy cannot resist cherishing fantastic hopes that Graham might reciprocate her sexual longings for him, with marriage to an established professional doctor like Graham diminishing her economic instability immediately (325). In the midst of reading Dr. John's letter, Lucy sees the phantom nun appear in the "ghostly chamber," and in the panicked proceedings she loses her letter right when Dr. John and others respond to her screams (325). Her screams are as much about losing her letter as they are about seeing a ghost. Graham's brutal trick – he does not reveal immediately that he has found the letter – begins the agonizing destruction of Lucy's (capital) interest in the doctor.

The climactic encounter with the ghostly nun occurs before M. Paul leaves for the West Indies, when Lucy breaks out of the *pensionnat* to see her lover one last time. "[D]rugged to the brink of frenzy" because Madame Beck has tried to stop her from seeing M. Paul before his voyage to the West Indies, Lucy walks to the phantasmagoric nighttime festival in the square (554). Repeating the economic cycle she is so used to but which never ceases to produce panic, Lucy experiences a frenzy of erotic desire while the traces of its destruction haunt her consciousness. During this hallucinatory night, Lucy moves ghostlike through the festival, keeping keen accounts of what she sees. On the verge of madness, she merges nuns, exclaiming when the young Justine Marie, her arch-rival, is about to appear: "The moment and the nun are come. The crisis and the revelation are passed by" (562). At this crisis, Lucy "held in the cry," "devoured the ejaculation," "forbade the start," as she "stirred no more than a stone" (563). Merging onanism and asceticism, the will to express linguistically and the determination to cancel out textuality, this passage ends in a similar climax of expression and rhetorical annulment: "The 'Antigua' was gone, and there stood Paul Emanuel" (563).

But perceiving that Paul Emanuel has not left does not reduce Lucy's panic, for when she observes him with the would-be nun, Justine Marie, she assumes that they are betrothed. In a brutally graphic image, she describes her response: "I invoked Conviction to nail upon me the certainty, abhorred while embraced, to fix it with the strongest spikes her strongest strokes could drive; and when the iron had entered well my soul, I stood up, as I thought renovated" (566). But as Lucy's long account of the hallucinatory night indicates, her expansive desire is not so easily canceled. Acknowledging the "outrage" that M. Paul and Justine Marie may be engaged, she razes that convent-ional relationship with her own radical insistence on continuing her illicit desire:

another love, venturing diffidently into life after long acquaintance, furnace-tried by pain, stamped by constancy consolidated by affection's pure and durable alloy, submitted by intellect to intellect's own tests, and finally wrought up, by his own process, to his own unflawed completeness, this Love that laughed at Passion, his fast frenzies and his hot and hurried extinction, in *this* Love I had a vested interest, and whatever tended either to its culture or its destruction, I could not view impassibly. (567)

Here Lucy describes her love for M. Paul as an investment that has become a material "durable alloy," because of her consolidation of emotional funds, as it were.

Finally admitting her investment in illicit desire in bodily and psychic terms, Lucy feels peace looking at the moon; but she describes the lunar spectacle through the lens of an accountant, saying, "with pencil-ray she wrote on heaven and on earth records for archives everlasting" (567). Hence, what turns out to be most important is not the love itself but the keeping of an account of that love. Indeed, Lucy's description of the moon suggests that, as John Kucich points out, it is the crisis of passion contending with the disproportionate will to annihilate such desire that is more significant than actually engaging in a relationship with M. Paul or Graham.[55] In other words, Lucy has a more passionate relationship with the condition of being the ghost and the accountant, at once severely passionate and lavishly austere, than she does with Graham or M. Paul. If, as Jan Cohn asserts, romance fiction "doubly enjoined" women against pursuing economic success for themselves, in Lucy's case the double bookkeeping that occurs is the love affair with accounting and the accounting of the love affair.

When Lucy returns to find the nun's vestments on her bed, "[t]empered" by her recent phantasmatic experience, she finds that, "my nerves disdained hysteria" and "I defied spectra" (569). Asserting that on her bed "nothing *ought* to have lain: I had left it void, and void should have found it," instead, she finds the "old phantom – the NUN." But this time "nothing leaped out, or sprang, or stirred" from the "haunted couch." Hysterically, Lucy exclaims that "all the movement was mine, so was all the life, the reality, the substance, the force," almost as though the garments that have been so spectacularly animated now transfer their life to her, the human who is "void" and who has none/nun (569). In a way, of course, this transference does occur: as the reader learns, the dandy de Hamal has used the nun's robes and the legend about the nun so that he can move about freely in the girl's school in order to have trysts with his lover, Ginevra Fanshawe, after which he "bequeaths" the nun's "wardrobe" to the lovelorn Lucy (569).

However, this rational explanation of the ghostly nun does not cancel the canny capital interests of Miss Snowe from the uncanny decapitated (in)vestments of the nun. Indeed, *Villette* simultaneously associates the ghostly nun with uncontrollable desire (Ginevra and de Hamal) and excessive self-control (Lucy); with the dead nun whose sin is most likely her sexual passion that erased her virgin vows; and with both Justine Maries, one, Paul Emanuel's deceased love, and, the other, his ostensible nubile fiancée. These overdetermined lineaments transfer to Lucy when de Hamal leaves her the vestal attire. Effectively putting on these garments, Lucy becomes the altruistic nun who also guards her economic self-interest. Replacing M. Paul's beloved nun, Justine Marie the first, Lucy Snowe awaits his return as vestal virgin in charge of his accounts. She will administer and enlarge his investment in her, and when he dies, she will be his altruistic, economically astute beneficiary. In the flux that is the end of the novel, "delight of joy" and "great terror," "rescue" and "peril," "reprieve" and "dread" seesaw extravagantly, leaving the reader and protagonist at sea, with no closure but the promise of being continually accountable for the fluctuations of political and emotional economy (596). But Lucy has found fiscal comfort, for this romantic text has always been explicit (through the representation of the mutual consciousnesses inhabiting the haunting nun and the bookkeeper) about finding economic security, about who holds the purse and who has power over money, as Charlotte had so tellingly written to Ellen Nussey. Intimately aware of the fact that there is no border between personal and economic security, Brontë refuses to characterize Lucy's desires as "unfeminine."

CHAPTER 4

"The Whole Duty of Man": circulating circulation in Dickens's Little Dorrit

> There is no more striking symbol of the completely dynamic character of the world than that of money ... When money stands still, it is no longer money according to its specific value and significance.[1]

> If we were in a more primitive state, if we lived under roofs of leaves, and kept cows and sheep and creatures, instead of banker's accounts ... well and good.[2]

Written and published between May 1855 and May 1857, just preceding by six months the crash of 1857, *Little Dorrit*, a novel about debtors' prison, a banking crash, and the circumlocutionary ineptitude of government as agent of business, portrays the rough cycle of trade. As pointed out in the last chapter, the early to mid-1850s were the proverbial years of financial equilibrium: the Victorians' burgeoning export trade sent "British-made goods all over the globe."[3] With the speeding up of life through the massive production of railways all over England, concomitantly there was a need for the speeding up of the circulation of capital to keep railway and train production in gear, as it were. Banks also had to find better means of keeping up with the economic needs of industry. To give a sense of the sharp increase in industrial and banking transactions, Charles Kindleberger notes that between 1852 and 1857 the deposits in a set of five London banks grew from £17.7 million to £40 million and the typical amount of bills of exchange that were in circulation increased to 200 million from just 66 million.[4]

As a result of expanding trade during the boom, new firms were established, many of which made poor speculative investments, and individual investors followed suit. The crisis came in 1857 as a result of the dramatic and hasty increases in extending credit and establishing new bank facilities occurring in the 1850s.[5] America's money panic helped to fuel the collapse, causing many British merchants and banks to fail.[6] As *The Annual Register* for the year 1857 notes, the Bank of England raised the discount rate from $5\frac{1}{2}$ percent to 6 percent on 8 October because of a drain of the bullion. On 19 October the discount rate was raised to 8 percent. On 27 October the Bank of Liverpool failed, on 4 November the discount rate was raised to the "unprecedented" rate of 9 percent and just five days later to an unheard of 10 percent.[7] Probably the first global crisis, the banking panic began on 12 November 1857.[8] Immediately thereafter the Bank Act of 1844 was suspended and the Issue Department issued £2 million above the legal amount to the Bank Department.[9] On 13 November the reserves in the Bank of England were down to an astonishing £975,000, a nominal figure for the banker to the world.[10] Overall, at least fifty-five private firms collapsed. The Bank of Liverpool, the Banks of Wolverhampton, Western of Scotland, Northumberland and Durham, and Glasgow also failed.[11]

When the crash occurred, virtually no amateur or professional economist could retain objectivity, although the terse description by one board member of the Bank of England comes brutally close: "The plot thickens – It seems that the Western Bk [*sic*] is in extremis."[12] G. C. Lewis remarked the hysteria in a letter to Lord Overstone, saying that, "the state of mens [*sic*] minds, as to mutual confidence, during a commercial panic is as different from their ordinary state, as the state of the country when it is disturbed is different from its state when it is quiet and orderly."[13] Worrying that "we may be subjected to an universal smash," J. R. McCulloch writes during the hard times of 1857 that, "our situation is becoming extremely precarious" and he feels helpless to "interfere" with "evils inherent in the system."[14] Some of those evils had to do with bank fraud of scandalous proportions. Condemning the way "wickedness and commerce" were so "intimately allied," D. Morier Evans remarked that it was not until the panic of 1857 "that the utter rottenness of a commercial system, as carried on in Scotland, Liverpool, and London, was revealed to its full extent."[15]

An article in Dickens's *Household Words* entitled "Banking," which appeared during the time that *Little Dorrit* was written and published, illustrates the simplistic trust Victorians may have had in their bankers as well as a foreshadowing of bankers' amoral potential. In this article, Edmund Saul Dixon praises banking because when bankers loan money it "increases the productive capital of the nation." Published in 1855, Dixon's optimistic attitude about bankers illustrates the kind of thinking that created an environment for rampant fraud on the part of many bankers that only came to light in the crash of 1857. To wit, Dixon asserts that, "banking exercises a powerful influence upon the morals of society," producing "integrity and punctuality in pecuniary engagements." Dixon's assessment is that banking generates capital (by saving time and thus increasing velocity of circulation) and further increases the circulation of capital through monetary loans. He is also untroubled by the fact that bankers circulate amongst themselves their clients' reputations, suggesting that banks and bankers are the most important facilitators of the circulation of capital as well as the capitalist subject's identity. Dixon believes that bankers not only provide their customers a "credit[able]" reputation but that bankers themselves act as the touchstone of duty within the community.[16]

But the essayist certainly is no fool. He begins the article with a question that would have done much to decrease the number of banking scams occurring in the 1850s if it had been posed before Victorian culture invested so much confidence in banks and banking. Dixon, that is, wonders why there are no laws, as there are for other professions, to require men going into banking to be apprentices for a specified period of time in order to establish their legitimacy. Instead, Dixon explains sardonically, to be a banker all one has to do is be someone who is willing to accept other people's money, a character trait for which Mr. Merdle (and Mr. Dorrit) are in a class by themselves.[17]

In 1855 the *Theory and Practice of Banking* by professor of political economy Henry Dunning Macleod contributed to the ongoing question, what is money and how does banking best prop up the currency? In this text Macleod dramatically asserts that "Capital" is the "POWER" that makes commerce move "from one person to another." Like Marx, Macleod declares that capital's primary meaning is not in material commodities per se but in its dynamism. But instead of seeing capitalism as having almost demonic, supernatural powers – as Marx suggests so vividly – Macleod circulates the nineteenth-century view of currency as a kind of incorporeal energy, like steam, water, or electrical power. Thus, in contrast to the seventeenth-century mercantilist objective of hoarding (gold) money, Macleod views unused capital – "[m]oney lying locked up in a box" – as like an idle steam engine. To quantify money's power, Macleod suggests that just as "the produce of the mill is measured by the quantity of the motion of the engine," currency's utility should be determined by the degree of its "*circulation*" as well as the amount of "industry it generates." Therefore the mathematical formula or "sole test" of money's usefulness "is the product of its amount multiplied into the velocity of its circulation."[18]

Its *raison d'être* "to set industry in motion," currency, Macleod emphasizes, must also increase the speed of its circulation. Macleod accentuates the benefits of increasing the movement of money rather than increasing the amount of currency itself. Weighing in on the hotly contested debates about whether banks should circulate more money when the economy confronts a downturn, when faced with a situation in which a limited degree of business is possible, the Scotsman argues that "the quantity of currency" should be "diminish[ed]" in order to "increas[e] its rapidity of circulation." Extending the metaphor, Macleod believes that if money is the steam, the bank is "the most potent engine for the increase of the moving power of any given quantity of actual capital" because it is able to house a high quantity of money and circulates it at a higher velocity than any other institution.[19] His compatriot Robert Ewen held much the same opinion, writing in 1897 that, while "Money is the life-blood of trade," bankers are "the prime movers in trade circles," and their chief business is to "send out the money and keep it circulating through all the arteries of trade and commerce; as fast as it comes in it should be sent out again."[20]

In a rhetorical tour de force, scantly relying upon scientific terminology and mathematics, Macleod ingeniously merges two seemingly disparate totems of Victorian life, the steam engine and duty. As he suggests, "Engineers usually call the quantity of motion of the engine its *duty,* so we may call the circulation of the currency its duty."[21] Macleod's inventive shoptalk packs a wallop because it rhetorically does double duty, as it were. Defining "duty" as the obligation of currency to circulate, Macleod blurs the meaning of duty across the powerful Victorian ideological sites of industrialism, science, and Christianity. Here Macleod personifies currency and the engine, making the individual's corresponding duty both mechanically automatic and personally autonomous. Undoubtedly assuming that the reader invests in capitalism as affording the best of all political economies, the self-confident economist implies that the individual's investment in capitalism fulfills moral obligations. With the turn of phrase, Macleod, then, makes *homo economicus* the site of ethical duty. Hence, like Dugald Stewart, Macleod moves political science in the direction of, as Mary Poovey describes it, "dignify[ing] the modern obsession with wealth" by suggesting that acquisitiveness could be rationalized as part "of a larger, divine plan that was unfolding in time."[22] If invisible but immanent steam was the real power/duty of the subordinate material engine, the capitalist subject could imagine his own material avarice as fulfilling the need to fuel the higher cause of a stable, progressive society run with machine-like precision.

As M. Neil Browne and J. Kevin Quinn point out, the machine metaphor has long been popular in economics, for it provides economists "a meta-metaphor" of economic thought that typifies "the core modernist principles of foundationalism, objectivism, and control."[23] One of the many problems with the meta-metaphor, though, is that it cannot control its own economic dependencies. For one thing, Macleod's image of the machine and its duty boosts the velocity of other infrastructures besides currency: swelling the power of economics to structure Victorian life, Macleod increases the velocity of the worker's labor. At the same time, he fails to generate ways for the dutiful capitalist subject to handle psychosomatic traumas brought about by the amplified mechanization of life. Nor does he offer strategies for dealing with the inevitable vortex that seemed regularly to whirl the Victorian economy and the Victorian subject into crisis.

A theoretical maverick who disagreed with much of neo-classical economics, Macleod was one of a number of Victorian practitioners of the dismal science who consulted models of energy studied in nineteenth-century physics to bolster the new field's claim to authority.[24] As Philip Mirowski points out, the increased interest nineteenth-century physics paid to energetics formed a foundation for the establishment of neo-classical economic theory, by "providing the metaphor, the mathematical techniques, and the new attitudes toward theory construction."[25] Not only did neo-classical economic theory scavenge nineteenth-century physics, Mirowski argues that most of these economists "misrepresented" or misunderstood the theory of energy and essentially ignored principles of conservation.[26] That is, they overlooked the fact that nineteenth-century physicists studying energy were discovering and coming to terms with the second law of thermodynamics, the frightening notion that energy is not infinite but tends towards conservation. Mayer, Joule, and Helmholtz are credited with establishing the first law of thermodynamics in the early 1800s; simply put, that law asserts that the universe is made of energy that remains symmetrical or the same despite all its myriad transformations. The second law, discovered in the 1830s and 1840s by R. Clausius, William Thomson (Lord Kelvin), and Sadi Carnot, asserts that the law of entropy overrides the first law. In other words, because the universe is intrinsically dynamic, when energy is distributed and creates disequilibrium – a thermodynamic "force," also inherent in the universe – naturally acts to decrease the disequilibrium.[27]

One Victorian economist's uncritical extrapolation of the first law illustrates the naïveté behind the assumption that there was unlimited energy. Noting in 1855 that the reduction of circulation is economically absurd, J. H. Macdonald asserts, "Why diminish the number of engines, when the same, if not a greater, amount of work is required to be done? Who are the parties that benefit by this contraction? Those who hire out these engines, to be sure!" Pointing out that the previous winter had seen "how a contraction of the powers of circulating coals raised the freight or hire of the engines of circulation, and benefited all who had colliers to hire at the expense of the public," by using the second law, Macdonald essentially argues for getting more (labor/energy) for one's money.[28] But as Mirowski shows, "The maximisation of utility," along with the ominous speculation that England's coal supply was being reduced precipitately, as well as the conventional wisdom that economic crises occurred because of unstable energy dynamics external to the social dynamics of economic structures, are all "direct extrapolations from the energetic movement of the mid-nineteenth century."[29]

One of Marx's major concerns about nineteenth-century capitalism seems intuitively based on the second law of thermodynamics. As Engels asserts in *The Principles of Communism*, the Industrial Revolution and the creation of the machine produced the possibility of "endlessly expanding industrial production, speeding it up, and cutting its costs." As a result, competition assumed "the most extreme forms" as "capitalists invaded industry, and, in a short while, more was produced than was needed." According to Engels, this cycle repeats itself endlessly, causing the condition of industry to fluctuate constantly between periods of prosperity and crisis, as "nearly every five to seven years a fresh crisis has intervened, always with the greatest hardship for workers, and always accompanied by general revolutionary stirrings and the direct peril to the whole existing order of things."[30] Marx's hope for the collapse of capitalism resulting from the repetitions of the trade cycle is, in a way, a hope that capitalism's imbalanced use of energy would result in swifter entropy.

Macleod left it for Victorian novelists and thinkers to sort out the panic educed in human beings as a result of believing that the individual's duty was to increase the velocity of circulation and increasingly circulate velocity. Considering Macleod's singular, even idiosyncratic, representation of the "duty" of money to create circulation, one cannot help but wonder if Dickens and Macleod were reading each other during the publication of *Little Dorrit* since Macleod's work came out in the same year *Little Dorrit* began its serial run. The fictional Pancks's own business philosophy uncannily mimics Macleod's description of circulation and duty:

What else do you suppose I think I am made for? Nothing. Rattle me out of bed early, set me going, give me as short a time as you like to bolt my meals in, and keep me at it. Keep me always at it, I'll keep you always at it, you keep somebody else always at it. There you are, with the Whole *Duty* of Man in a commercial country. (154; emphasis added)

In Pancks's straightforward fiscal creed, the "Duty of Man" is the obligation to keep people going, or "at it." Ideally, it seems, this philosophy would cause a chain reaction of going at it amongst other men, thus causing "duty" to recur dynamically among the members of the "whole" economic system. One assumes that when Pancks refers to "it" he is referring to work. But, in fact, in both Macleod and Pancks's schemes, participating in circulation is not enough to do one's duty; one must also circulate circulation itself by making other people do their "duty" in a whirlpool of hyperactive human energy.

Dickens's image captures the frenzied (e)motion of human automatons dutifully impelling those around them to go at it at ever higher rates of speed. The "Man" described by this kind of "Duty" cannot be a stable entity, for he must be in nauseating double motion, rotating individually like a planet that also revolves in the orbit of the whole mechanized culture. But the simultaneity of revolution and rotation the capitalist subject experiences is constantly intensified by the duty to increase circulation. Obviously, if increased velocity, intensity, and duration of circulation are the desired outcome, economic power at some point will produce turbulence, hysteria, and spikes of chaos, as trade cycle theorists such as Mills, Overstone, and Juglar opined. Indeed, as Pancks's credo hints, economic panic might be the definitive form of circulation. That is, the duty to empower constant circulation – going at it – might become no longer just the means to a vibrant economy but also its human end. Becoming motion exponentially multiplied, circulation turns into crisis – the point at which motion is so intense it appears to be pure cessation of movement.[31] Leave it to Dickens to intuit the second law of thermodynamics.

Dickens's epistolary references to banking illustrate a man who was meticulously aware of his finances and often anxious that the velocity of outflow of currency outpaced the inflow. One senses that he also spoke about his finances to friends and associates with less circumspection than one might expect from more reserved Englishmen. Likewise, for all his pecuniary sophistication, Dickens, at times, seems to have made hasty financial decisions or to have been ill prepared for the economic burdens of travel.[32] During the time of writing *Little Dorrit*, he often refers to his bank, the venerable Coutts, requesting, for example, appointments to see his account book or get letters of credit.[33] He expresses disgust, too, when his publishers belatedly remit his pay for novel installments because it causes him to be overdrawn at the bank.[34] Lamentable it is to see the

Inimitable advise his wife not to spend too much money in France because he is concerned about overdrawing his account.[35] Certainly it is bittersweet, as well, to read of Dickens's concern about the circulation numbers of his work as he calculates the economic return he can expect as a result, this at the same time that he seems literally to be grinding out articles, speeches, and readings, as well as fiction.[36]

When Henry James famously referred to the nineteenth-century novel as a "loose, baggy monster," he obviously had Dickens in mind. James's characterization refers to the Victorian novel's outlandish hybridity and rejection of stylistic leanness and integrity of focus as well as point of view. I suggest that the hybridity includes the frightening presentation of the self as multiple and exchangeable in a monstrous trade cycle of its own in the vast coincidental web of, say, a Dickens novel. James's formalist aesthetic also might represent authorial terror. That is, the scene of production of the extravagant, profligate, speedily written novels by many Victorian writers responds to alarming demands made by readers, publishers, and capitalism itself for ever more consumer goods. James's own fiction might be the ultimate fulfillment of the panic-stricken Victorian novel, as the novels by this master teller of ghost stories illustrate a radically increased obsession with articulating minutely and repetitively the expansions in production and consumption of desire. Certainly, James's description of the Victorian novel also typifies the work of Trollope, who famously wrote in his *Autobiography* that "I had long since convinced myself that in such work as mine the great secret consisted in acknowledging myself to be bound to rules of labour similar to those which an artisan or a mechanic is forced to obey."[37] As Christina Crosby shows, Victorian novelists were at the mercy of tremendous changes in publishing: increased demand occurred through advertising; actual production of the book itself became industrialized; serialization, circulating libraries, and cheaply produced novels for consumption by railway passengers also expanded demand. Meanwhile, publishing houses were capitalized as they started to provide stock offerings.[38]

Unlike Trollope, who revels in the "pleasurable quality of [producing] quantity,"[39] Dickens often complains in his letters during the publication of *Little Dorrit* that his writing schedule is brutal. To Miss Burdett Coutts, 26 September 1856, he complains, "I am falling behind-hand with that reserve of Little Dorrit which has kept me busy during its progress, and to lose which would be a serious thing. All the week I have been hard at it with a view to tomorrow."[40] He also explicitly refers to feeling imprisoned by the necessity to write. For example, on 10 January 1856 he informs Miss

Burdett Coutts, "I shall try to force myself to write a No. of Little Dorrit first ... and that will hold me prisoner, if I submit, until early in next Month."[41] Meanwhile, Hans Christian Andersen received a letter dated 5 July 1856 from the novelist saying that he was "hard at work at Little Dorrit, and She will hold me prisoner for another nine or ten months."[42]

On an artistic treadmill, Dickens describes the extremes of feeling cooped up and inactive in his writing quarters, and, when done writing for the day, spending hours anxiously in motion, obsessively tramping the streets. To Leigh Hunt, on 4 May 1855 he grumbles that he is in a "disjointed state" during writing because he is "turning upon the same wheel round and round over and over again until it may begin to roll me towards my end."[43] "[A]m in a state of restlessness not to be described or imagined," he writes on 21 May 1855 in a letter to Mrs. Watson. He adds a prolonged description of himself in literal circulation during the act of writing: "walking about the country by day – prowling about into the strangest places in London by night – sitting down to do an immensity – getting up after doing nothing – walking about my room on particular bits of all the flowers in the carpet – tearing my hair."[44] On 24 May 1855, Dickens tells Miss Burdett Coutts that his "condition of restlessness" regarding *Little Dorrit* is "not improved."[45] Nine months later, on 19 February 1856, again to Miss Burdett Coutts, he names "unsettlement" a common companion while writing *Little Dorrit*; then he describes "Prowling about the rooms, sitting down, getting up, stirring the fire, looking out of window, tearing my hair, sitting down to write, writing nothing, writing something and tearing it up, going out, coming in, a Monster to my family, a dread Phenomonon [*sic*] to myself, &c &c &c."[46] Turning into a loose, baggy monster, the seeming automaton author grouses to W. C. Macready that he has "been hammering away in that strenuous manner at my book." It is no wonder that he feels like "conduct[ing] myself in a frenzied manner for the relief that only exercise gives me."[47]

Little Dorrit incorporates the anxiety apparent in Dickens's letters and engendered when "duty" is interpreted as constantly increasing one's output while simultaneously (im)pressing spurs upon others to do the same. Participating in the obligation to stay in motion at constantly spiraling velocities, *Little Dorrit* also struggles with the bleak outcome, attempting, like other novels by Dickens, to find moral authority in small social networks whose humanity has more potency than any economic system fueled by energy. But, approaching this economic system from the perspective of fiction, Dickens himself is caught in the very necessity for increased circulation of his own industry. A novel that shows how economic and moral duty are inextricably entangled in Victorian life, *Little Dorrit* depicts the appalling social circuits and networks amongst which the modern subject circulates in order to do his/her duty. It is also a novel that collapses, like the House of Clennam, under the weight of the requirement of circulation. Indeed, the Circumlocution Office spirals into maddening sterility and entropy, much on the same lines that economist Edward Jones describes in 1900: in the capitalist market, he warns, the "machinery of industry" is very "liable" to "become deranged."[48]

Constructed and deconstructed by circulation, *Little Dorrit* represents a modern understanding not present in Macleod, that the motion of money institutes social networks and socializes individuals in those networks. At the end of the nineteenth century, Georg Simmel states just that when he writes that economic "exchange is a form of socialization" by which "a number of individuals become a social group." Jean-Joseph Goux argues similarly, asserting that the money form creates sites of "connection, linkage, relation."[49] One might merge these theories with John Guillory's concept of "objective structuration" to study *Little Dorrit*. Analyzing the dynamic abstractions and fluctuations art incorporates, Guillory argues that rather than a replication of the self or society, "the work of art" represents the interrelations "between subjects, or the relations between groups."[50]

Written around the time that the use of bank accounts was becoming a norm rather than an anomaly, *Little Dorrit*, I propose, has an objective structuration that is in the bank, as it were. The idea that Victorian life was increasingly indebted to banking and all its permutations, including banking crises, as the source of social networks, certainly affects Dickens's common pattern of creating a worldwide system in which everyone is related coincidentally. In *Little Dorrit* that economic machinery includes the Clennam's private bank spanning from London to China, Meagles's thirty-five-year career as a banking clerk, Merdle's role as the "extraordinary phenomenon in Buying and Banking," and Casby's function as banker on "confidential agency business" for Miss Wade, coupled with the informal usury he practices with Pancks, loaning him money at 20 percent (487, 523). Mrs. Merdle, of course, takes for granted that having a bank account is a kind of cultural and moral duty. Likewise, each character in the book carries a psychological image of that fortress of negated circulation, the debtors' prison, as the end of the road for those who do not do their ethi-conomic duty.

Dickens's alter ego, Daniel Doyce the engineer, perfectly exhibits the economic and moral duty to increase the circulation of the economy's engine. When Doyce shows Arthur his firm's books, the accounts reveal that his engineering and personal ethics are one and the same: "[H]onest, rugged" Doyce presents the figures in their "genuine working dress" in order to increase their quick perusal. After examining the "straight to the purpose" figures, "[i]t occurred to Arthur that a far more elaborate and taking show of business" would be ineffective "as being meant to be far less intelligible" (259). Clearly, Doyce keeps the "Machinery in Motion" as Dickens so aptly titles the chapter in which his business skills are laid out. Nevertheless, the villain Rigaud is as straightforward about his business and personal ethics as Doyce, averring that he follows the same duties as the "men of the Exchange." Intently accepting and following the capitalist credo that "Society sells itself and sells me: and I sell Society," Rigaud constantly seeks ways to expand the circulation of capital, and he pressures others to do so as well (730). When he applies for money from Mrs. Clennam's bank, Rigaud initiates this capitalist ethic, and he is then socialized into the group of Clennam, Dorrit, Gowan, Wade, and Meagles in ways that Doyce cannot match.

Throughout the novel, Meagles is metonymically associated with the "pair of brass scales for weighing gold, and a scoop for shoveling out money" (189). After decades of working at the bank, Meagles carries with him everywhere the "arithmetical solidity belonging to the scales and scoop" as though these financial tools are part of his body and personhood (193). Like Mrs. Merdle, who understands that modern life is structured around bank accounts, Mrs. Gowan is quite aware that Meagles not only "belonged to a Bank" but that he was a good banker; as she remarks, "It ought to have been a very profitable Bank, if he had much to do with its management" (309). Ultimately, she and her son dispense with the inconsequential part of their duty to Meagles, informing him that they will no longer associate with him socially. In doing so, the expectation is that he will keep the truly significant economic aspect of the relationship in circulation – bankrolling his ineffectual son-in-law. As Dickens writes in his notes for book two, chapter XXXII, Mrs. Gowan's "submission to her son's marriage" is in essence "to his having his debts paid" (816).

If, as the notes for chapter XXI reveal, "People like the houses they Inhabit," meaning that his characters resemble their homes, Henry Gowan's abode in Venice is an objective structuration of his absolute economic dependence upon Meagles (812). Dickens also intuits the strange interchange between domestic economy and the bank "house," mentioned in the introduction to this study. Gowan and Pet live in an apartment above an Italian bank that appears to have the same ability as his father-in-law to keep money in motion. In this bank house, "two spare clerks" seem "merely" to dip "their hands out of sight," to "produce exhaustless mounds of five-franc pieces" (474). Thus Dickens critiques Gowan's façade of nonchalant naïveté about the source of his own providence and his skewed sense of fiscal duty. Nevertheless, like Marx and Macleod, the novelist is also fascinated by the animistic, supernatural energies inhabiting money and generated by bank[er]s who have the duty of circulating capital. The narrator at this point is comically floored by what Crosby calls the pleasure of quantity itself and its ability to multiply, seemingly by the laying on of bankers' "hands," if you will.[51]

When Miss Wade, Gowan's former lover and nemesis, threatens Gowan, Pet, and the Meagles, she participates in Macleodian duty. "In our course through life," says the scorned lover, "we shall meet the people who are coming to meet *us*, from many strange places and by many strange roads," and "what it is set to us to do to them, and what it is set to them to do to us, will all be done" (24). Miss Wade's philosophy is built upon the monomaniacal belief that her own class rage and sexual frustration can individually generate powerful retribution when the socio-economic lives of her enemies converge and ricochet. In its loathing for the lesbian Miss Wade, *Little Dorrit* is terrified of the intensity, velocity, and duration of Miss Wade's unstoppable (e)motional e/affects that circulate ominously throughout the novel. When Miss Wade makes Arthur Clennam the recipient of her remarkable apologia and life story, she expands the circle of people who are affected by her deregulated passion, causing him to be included in the crisis and breakdown of the Meagles' emotional economy. Though he ostensibly seeks to avoid the fluctuations of the crass market and the resulting emotional seesaw, Clennam is one of those to whom Miss Wade refers in her foreboding statement at Marseilles. Attempting to break his own links to the banking network, he tumbles towards certain economic crisis and collapse as "what is set" to be done to him "will be done" through his network of relationships based on the economy. One thinks chiefly of his increasing friendship with Pancks, whose investment advice determines Clennam's one-way track to the debtors' prison in a kind of fulfillment of the second law of thermodynamics.

The hero of the novel also cannot fully escape the shrewdness that is a banker's duty. For example, when Arthur informs his mother that he is giving up his partnership in the Clennam bank, he explains that the "dealings" of the House of Clennam "have been progressively on the decline," that "the track we have kept is not the track of the time," and that as bankers they "have been left far behind." He notes that in his father's time the firm was "really a place of business," but now it "is a mere anomaly and incongruity here, out of date and out of purpose" (44–45). Apparently, then, Clennam's actual reason for quitting is not because of the acquisitive nature of the banking business itself. In fact, he is more than happy to become Doyce's accountant and money manager when he resigns from Clennam & Clennam, and he obviously enjoys speculating with Doyce's money on the Exchange, for he chooses to follow Pancks's advice to do "your duty" and "[b]e as rich as you can" (567).

No, Clennam's reason for leaving his mother's employ is that her business is not thriving as it had earlier. Out of step with the new financial practices of the times – the move away from private banking to joint-stock banking – her firm is not as lucrative an organization as it had been in former times, and Clennam is well aware of this fact. One of the most important processes in banking during the nineteenth century was the decline of the private banker and the rise of joint-stock banking (the precursor of modern banks), which, with limited liability, increased the amount of money that could be circulated. More importantly, the rise of the joint-stock bank increased the velocity and expansion of circulation.

Like the father-in-law he will replace as father figure to Amy, Arthur moves from a business partnership straight to the Marshalsea Prison. The touchstone of debtors and debt, William Dorrit, like Arthur, invested in "a partnership" that had immersed him in "legal matters of assignment and settlement, conveyance here and conveyance there, suspicion of unlawful preference of creditors in this direction, and of mysterious spiriting away of property." Probably hoodwinked by fraudulent associates, Dorrit ends up in "insolvency and bankruptcy" for twenty odd years, though he figures out an ingenious way to compensate himself for the trouble by assuming the position of "Father of the Marshalsea" who aggressively keeps his minions circulating currency (60). When Little Dorrit wonders if her father must pay off his remaining debt after he has spent so many years making recompense by being imprisoned, Clennam insists that it is Dorrit's obligation. Here again, humans and money must keep doubling their duty and the circulation of money in the economic system they inhabit.

Since the debtors' prison defeats the purpose of a market economy's need for the circulation of currency, Dorrit, the debtors, and their visitors instinctively seem to know how to do their duty to keep money exchanging hands in the place erected to punish those who can no longer make those exchanges. Dorrit, a seeming financial idiot-savant, becomes a center of banking in the Marshalsea, where visitors and fellow debtors alike exhibit their credit-worthiness by how much they deposit into his hands. These "Testimonials" establish social exchanges and widen the social group of which he is a part to include Arthur, Plornish, Pancks, and Rugg and thus compound the sources from which he can receive further such investments. Dorrit's stutter and the dashes that represent it might be said to perform his fluctuating economic subjectivity while also serving as links in the chain of meaning produced between him and those who offer him testimonials. The rhythms of his stilted speech when he is accepting money also suggest the paradigm of the cycle of trade, for Dorrit loses control of his words as the need to press others to go "at it" – in their charitable donations to him – increases and he verges on stuttering panic.

Dorrit first meets Mr. Merdle because they must conclude the financial transactions that establish the marriage of their children to each other. Aside from discussion of the dowry, the narrative quips that "[t]he drafts of Mr. Dorrit" for the wedding party "almost constituted a run on the Torlonia Bank" (589). But Dorrit is triply socialized through circulation when he asks Merdle for his help in investing the Father of the Marshalsea's newly acquired wealth. This meeting ends when Merdle lets Dorrit experience the perks of monetary circulation, taking him to the City in his elaborate carriage to literally circulate among the hoi polloi "Fawners" (596). Dorrit is exhilarated because he is "set aloft" in Merdle's "public car of triumph, making a magnificent progress to that befitting destination, the golden Street of the Lombards" (596). At the absolute center of financial circulation, power, and his own eventual financial debacle that subliminally informs his death, Dorrit is positively ecstatic.

This passage highlights the idea that, as Macleod and others suggest, money changes from being linked literally with physical entities like precious metals and instead becomes a dynamic, invisible energy or credit being exchanged between people. While at "the golden Street of the Lombards," Merdle circulates among his creditors and debtors to exhibit and increase the velocity at which the power of his capital swells. Though his is a "world-wide commercial enterprise," with "gigantic combinations of skill and capital" nobody "knew with the least precision what Mr. Merdle's business was" though he is said to be "in everything good, from banking to building" with speculations that are "sound and successful" (386, 241). Meanwhile, the savvy Mrs. Merdle worries that her husband neglects his duty to circulate among society in order to make his wealth duplicate itself through that sphere of influence. Merdle himself worries that his own internal machinery is not circulating properly because he has poor digestion. When economic distress leads to his physical demise, it is as though the crash of his financial empire metonymically forces his body and the body politic to grind to a halt, for the banker's circulation of circulation comes to a deathly standstill as the second law of thermodynamics seems to take its course. Dickens's titles for the chapters representing Merdle's fall, the banking crash, and Arthur's bankruptcy – "Going," "Going!" "Gone" – also register the demise of energy through constant going "at it."

The heroine cannot be left out of the economic equation, for she is the novel's explicit paradigm of duty. When Meagles chastens Tattycoram after her return to the domestic fold, he exhorts her to consider Little Dorrit as an example because she always does her "Duty" (788). Amy, who has learned in childhood to keep an account book for her whole family's needs, desires to stay in a world in which she is always dutiful; as she has learned so well, in order to be useful she must inhabit a system always already in constant economic fluctuation and on the precipice of panic. When in impoverished circumstances her duties include handling the family's account books, locating jobs for her siblings and herself, and acting as head of the household by deciding how to use any scant incoming funds. For Amy this is economic independence. In contrast, she becomes economically dependent and thus stagnant – without (e)motion – when her family inherits wealth and she no longer has any means to exhibit her economic duty through her social relationships. How much is Amy invested in capitalism? She, it should be remembered, proudly refers to her friend Maggie as being "as trustworthy as the Bank of England" (96). It is difficult to say whether the narrative's tone at this point is ironic, but whether ironic or solemn, the statement acknowledges the centrality of banking even to the character most indifferent to money.

If the good characters Amy, Arthur, and Daniel Doyce are immersed in a double-edged rendition of "duty," the ghost story is one of the modes through which the narrative expresses this anomaly. As we know, at the same time that *Little Dorrit* was written and published Marx was writing *Capital,* which also uses the supernatural as an objective structuration of capitalism. So immersed is Marx's rhetoric in the Gothic that Derrida in *Specters of Marx* creates a neologism for Marx's ontology, transforming it into "hauntology." Marx argues that in a market economy a ghostly web of simulacra of relationships, exchanges, and circulation hovers over the whole system, indicating that people have had their humanity drained out of them by capitalism and that they are left as ghostly shells. "[M]an," says Derrida, is the most "'*unheimlich*' of all ghosts" because as the "most familiar" (*heimlich*) to himself, he becomes "most disquieting," "mak[ing] himself into the fear that he inspires." If, as Derrida suggests, "Speculation always speculates on some specter . . . It believes in what it believes it sees: in representations," then in materialist terms, the terms Marx would be interested in, the financial speculators of the Victorian period are most haunted by the chief representation in a capitalist society, capital.[52]

As Georg Lukács suggests, capitalist culture produces entities haunted by alienated beings – themselves – and disoriented by "the essence of commodity-structure."[53] Like Marx's "hauntology," Dickens imagines a ghostly web of energies and structures that mimic and overshadow mechanical economic circulations. These ghosts in the (Macleodian) machine enact both the duty to increase the velocity of circulation as well as the ultimate outcome of such increased energies, the collapse of energy in fulfillment of the second law of thermodynamics. As Alison Milbank asserts, *Little Dorrit* impels the Gothic "into the metaphysical."[54] The haunting Affery experiences in the Clennam banking house analogically simulates the circulation into frenzy and panic that occurs in a world for which banking and circulation of currency have become the foundation of meaning. We know the haunting motif is important because throughout the *Little Dorrit* number plans – the formal scaffolding of the novel – Dickens reminds himself to foreshadow the actual crash of the House of Clennam through the noises that haunt Mistress Affery (807, 811, 814, 823, 827).

Affery's haunting begins when she first sees Flintwinch's brother in the house, and then every time Rigaud enters the house she hears the same inexplicable noises. Finally, she seems to go mad from the inexplicable rappings. The representation of the house as a monotonous but "vitiated" machine accompanies those noises. As the narrator states at one point, "The house in the city preserved its heavy dullness through all" of its "transactions." The narrator then describes the tedium of the "unvarying round" of Mrs. Clennam's life, as "the same sequences of machinery" occur there in rote succession (333). Like Macleod in picturing the bank as a machine whose energy and motion are generated by the increased circulation of money through its gears, Dickens represents the banking House of Clennam as losing its clientele and thus its economic force. The "sound[s] of rustling" Affery hears are the physical evidence of the banking house's past circulations that seem to haunt the inhabitants if they do not continue in the economic "duty" to circulate capital (173). The private Clennam bank is like the dead banks that vampirize living banks and live through their previous manifestations described by Edmund Saul Dixon in his essay.[55]

When Dickens uses the extended metaphor of the haunted house to represent the bank's impending economic collapse, he brilliantly imagines the overdetermined effects of the economy that is ultimately controlled by the second law of thermodynamics. The psyche, he shows, is in danger of collapse from being structured to match the infinite physical but invisible energies of matter and money. Monomaniacally magnifying the very reflections of the house's inhabitants, the narrative pictures Affery reeling into madness. Aside from the noises, in chapter XV the narrative portends Rigaud's sinister arrival by a strange image of a magic lantern and the repetition of Miss Wade's mantra of travelers "coming and going" to "meet and to act and re-act on one another" as they go continually "at it." One particular scene graphically illustrates the domestic house's haunting of and by the attached banking house. Given the overdetermined nature of Dickens's writing, it is perhaps best to cite the scene in full to capture the Gothic effect:

The varying light of fire and candle in Mrs. Clennam's room made the greatest change that ever broke the dead monotony of the spot. In her two narrow windows, the fire shone sullenly all day, and sullenly all night. On rare occasions, it flashed up passionately, as she did; but for the most part it was suppressed, like her, and preyed upon itself evenly and slowly. During many hours of the short winter days, however, when it was dusk there early in the afternoon, changing distortions of herself in her wheeled chair, of Mr. Flintwinch with his wry neck, of Mistress Affery coming and going, would be thrown upon the house wall that was over the gateway, and would hover there like shadows from a great magic lantern. As the room-ridden invalid settled for the night, these would gradually disappear: Mistress Affery's magnified shadow always flitting about, last, until it finally glided away into the air, as though she were off upon a witch-excursion. Then the solitary light would burn unchangingly, until it burned pale before the dawn, and at last died under the breath of Mistress Affery, as her shadow descended on it from the witch-region of sleep.

Strange, if the little sick-room fire were in effect a beacon fire, summoning some one, and that the most unlikely some one in the world, to the spot that *must* be come to. Strange, if the little sick-room light were in effect a watch-light, burning in that place every night until an appointed event should be watched out! Which of the vast multitude of travellers, under the sun and the stars, climbing the dusty hills and toiling along the weary plains, journeying by land and journeying by sea, coming and going so strangely, to meet and to act and re-act on one another, which of the host may, with no suspicion of the journey's end, be travelling surely hither? (172–73)

In this seemingly "dull" scene, the firelight fluctuates, creating super-natural "changing distortions" of Mrs. Clennam, Flintwinch, and Affery, particularly highlighting Affery's "coming and going." The firelight throws its reflections "upon the house wall that was over the gateway, and would hover there like shadows from a great magic lantern" with the reflections of Mrs. Clennam diminishing as she sleeps. But while Mrs. Clennam sleeps,

Affery's "magnified shadow" "flit[s] about," until the very energy she
expends induces her into a twilight "witch-excursion," a state of tenuous
hold on physical reality. Mistress Affery's impending entropy figures in the
candle dying by her breath "as her shadow descended on it from the witch-
region of sleep."

In the eerie setting, the firelight goes "at it," as it were, impelling a vortex
of reflections that also interact with the human occupants of the house,
who appear to be in constant physical or mental motion. As the velocity of
light reflections grows, Affery, the chief contributor to visible circulation,
can only be described in increasingly supernatural terms. The circulation of
ghost-like after-images of the threesome's going "at it" institutes the
association with the worldwide circulation of a "vast multitude of travellers" who might meet and exchange with the bank of Clennam's denizens
to create more economic ripples through the sinister banking establishment. Indeed, the narrative account of the flitting, along with the hypothetical desire for future customers ("travellers") to come and meet and go "at
it" seems like a supernatural ritualization of the never-ending circulation
process.

Immediately after the description of Mrs. Clennam's house as the vortex
of a ghost story that alludes to Miss Wade's menacing desire for people to
come and go ("at it"), the narrator describes one of Affery's waking dreams.
In it the house makes "a sudden noise" of "a mysterious kind" that gives
Affery such a "shock or tremble" that she thought the "house was haunted"
(173). Affery looks out the window to comfort herself by observing "living
things beyond and outside the haunted house." Instead, in Dickensian
horror, she perceives on the "wall over the gateway" outside the "shadows
of the two clever ones in conversation above" (Mrs. Clennam and
Flintwinch), a telling reiteration of the house's magic lantern effects
(173). The objective structuration of the setting of Mrs. Clennam's room
and Affery's mimicking "dream" of it – the double circulation of circulation itself – is what is important about this bizarre, and seemingly superfluous, Dickensian elaboration. Depicting how the immaterial, abstract
dynamics of the economic world exceed, haunt, and hover above the
material, human world, this moment of panic exhibits how shadowy
human simulations structure culture.

Seeking a talisman to protect her from the horrific shadows of
Flintwinch and Mrs. Clennam going "at it," Affery scuttles upstairs and
stands outside Mrs. Clennam's door, "to be near the clever ones as a match
for most ghosts" (174). It is a strange moment, for she seems to seek
assurance by being in closer proximity to the very source of the horror

that terrifies her. But what is even more terrifying is that at this point the real Flintwinch and Mrs. Clennam *have* become mere shadows of the horrendous economic machinery they keep in motion, the template of which are the supernatural, diacritical (M-C-M̂) shadows of themselves projected on a wall outside the Clennam premises.[56] More afraid of the ghostly simulation of monetary transaction than the human transactors, Affery can no longer make distinctions between the economic machine and its supernatural after-effects. The mechanization of the supernatural and the paranormalization of economic circulation produce a subject in permanent panic and motion. Thereafter, until the actual crash of the house arouses Affery out of her state of shock, she remains in a "haunted state of mind." She experiences "ghostly apprehensions," and "wild speculations and suspicions respecting her mistress, and her husband, and the noises in the house" (182).

When Arthur asks Affery what secret transactions are going on between Mrs. Clennam and the sinister Rigaud, he maintains that, "I want to know what is amiss here; I want some light thrown on the secrets of this house" (669). Affery cryptically responds. "[N]oises is the secrets," she says, "rustlings and stealings about, tremblings, treads overhead and treads underneath" (669). From Affery's description, it is almost as though the house's physical structure has become its economic function, circulation. Concomitant with Affery's haunting by the skittering noises of the house, Flintwinch continues his daily round of dutiful banking motions, "receiv[ing] letters, and comers, and keep[ing] books, and correspond[ence]" as well as visiting the "counting-houses," the "Custom House," and the "Change" (333). In continual economic motion from its daily business and the nightly ghosts – which are physical reverberations of that business – the banking house has doubled its duty. Until, that is, its velocity of circulation reels into panic mode when "the wonderful Bank [of Merdle]" crashes and Affery's ghost story that frames the entire narrative finally culminates in the actual physical collapse of the Clennam bank (690).

If the actual architecture in *Little Dorrit* merges with the architectonics of the novel, exhibiting the strange circulation between the Gothic and the market engine, Clennam is haunted by the house where he was raised. In particular he is haunted by the banking transactions that seem to float about it like the half-life of energy. When he goes to visit his mother on one occasion, the narrator describes the banking district around her house as full of "dim streets" that "seemed all depositories of oppressive secrets." Containing "secrets" in the "books and papers locked up in chests and safes," the "deserted counting-houses" and "banking-houses" have "secrets" in "strong rooms and wells," which are "the secrets of all the dispersed grinders in the vast mill" (526). The interior of the Clennam household mimics this banking structure. Searching through the house, Clennam finds his father's "strong room stored with old ledgers" that smell as if "they were regularly balanced, in the dead small hours, by a nightly resurrection of old book-keepers" (54, 57). This imagery directly links the intimate emotions of domestic life with the political economy of the financial public sphere. Further, in these distressed descriptions, capital has the power to keep even the dead at the duty of going "at it," much in the same way that ghosts haunt the ghosts of poor Lucy Snowe. As Dickens so brilliantly shows, the capitalist engine demands that the supernatural become the norm as the ghostly second law of thermodynamics registers the fact that all is "Going," "Going!" "Gone."

Going "at it" characterizes Dickens's sense of self while writing *Little Dorrit*, and, of course, it also characterizes the novel's structure as he imagines a society that is constantly – even in its dreams – banking on the unlimited increase of velocity of economic circulation (going "at it") and concomitant panic and collapse. Because of the Macleodian "duty" of economics, in the modern age, banks themselves must be solipsistically always open. Indeed, in one form or other, they must constantly generate, increase, and distribute capital, thus always also already generating the ghosts of capital and the ghosts in the machine that haunt the self who can only be as creditworthy as the Bank of England dictates. Haunted by his own psychic specters, Dickens also exhibits the anxiety intrinsic in what Derrida refers to as "hauntology." Dickens is well aware subliminally and consciously that the bank, as Edmund Saul Dixon points out, requires that in order to have a socially authorized identity in a culture of capital, the subject must bank on the panic that fuels the subject's acceptance of unlimited circulation and concomitant collapse. *Little Dorrit* is, perhaps, the Inimitable's definitive inscription of that knowledge.

CHAPTER 5

"Bankruptcy at my heels": Dr. Jekyll, Mr. Hyde, and the bankerization of identity

Dr. Jekyll may float us a wee.

> (RLS to W. E. Henley May 1887)

The world is too much with us; and coin it grows so sparsely on the tree! . . . I am pouring forth a penny (12 penny) dreadful . . . they call it Dr. Jekyll.

> (RLS to Sidney Colvin September/October 1885)

I have as you know been off work this considerable time, and hunger was in the bank account.

> (RLS to Andrew Chatto, 7 November 1885)

I drive on with *Jekyll*, bankruptcy at my heels.

> (RLS to his wife, 20 October 1885)[1]

The Strange Case of Dr. Jekyll and Mr. Hyde was written and published during what was known as the Great Depression, for by 1873 the periods of successive nine- to twelve-year business cycles ceased and the Great Depression, lasting for over twenty years, took place. During this time dramatic "cyclical peaks" became "flattened" and the economy stagnated.[2] Such as they were, fiscal peaks occurred in 1882 and 1890, while the "troughs" took place in 1879, 1886, and 1893. Prices and wages sank, and there were six bad harvests starting in 1873. Between 1875 and 1879 the depression grew worse as factories failed and the rate of unemployment increased. In addition, agricultural land values dropped dramatically, accompanied by the fall of incomes from farming.[3] The long economic doldrums indicated England's entropy. As C. P. Hill writes, the depression occurring between 1875 and 1879, as well as the "slump" during the middle 1880s indicated that, "the age of British economic supremacy was over." S. G. Checkland also suggests that "the golden age of British agriculture" ended in the 1870s.[4]

Through the 1870s, as Henry Warren argues, the banking system had still not learned by its mistakes.[5] Dieter Ziegler believes that the crisis of 1878 resulted in "a turning point" in the relations between industrial entities and the English banking system.[6] Similarly, despite arguments that the banking crisis of 1878 was mild compared with those of 1837, 1847, 1857, and 1866, Michael Collins agrees with Ziegler, arguing that the crisis of 1878 was acute. He suggests that key parts of banking organization and custom were still very problematic in the 1870s and that these conditions, coupled with the long depression, were enough to create a keen "contraction" in the economy.[7] When, to everyone's shock, the City of Glasgow Bank failed in 1878, it became grossly clear how easy it was for banks to lead a double life because they were not required to publish their balance sheets. Even then the balance sheets often were cooked. The City of Glasgow Bank was a model of such misconduct: for years its auditors and directors had authorized and certified false balance sheets.[8]

The 1880s brought continuing unemployment, low prices, and depleted profits as the period of industrial growth and railway expansion crested and leveled off. Testifying before Parliament on 14 November 1887, J. C. Fieldes described the "panics and depressions" in England over the course of the century, saying, "We have had bad times, when we have been perhaps worse than at any point, during this depression, but we have generally recovered in a year or two; but we have been going on for 12 years, and we are just about as bad as ever, and likely to continue so."[9] So used to having the world's premier economy and with no stable recovery in sight, the British began to question themselves. Checkland writes that "A sense of structural derangement" affected the British as they came to terms with the fact that their claim to being the world's supreme economic engine was increasingly tenuous.[10] It did not help that America and Germany had become strong economic competitors. Thus while London remained the "clearing house" to the world because "Wherever there is an exchange of any sort there is an exchange upon London," as the British Empire expanded, its economy decelerated.[11]

Just a year after the publication of Stevenson's Gothic tale, in evidence given to Parliament, H. D. Macleod argued that the more highly developed the banking system became "the more transactions are settled by the transfers of credit, and not by bullion at all." Indeed, Macleod associates bankerization with cultural enlightenment, asserting that in less civilized nations "all the credit or money is made of some material substance," whereas the more civilized a nation becomes the more it relies upon abstract means of exchange. Testifying that modern credit can be used with "most perfect facility," Macleod positively gloats that, "The whole mass of these rights or debts, whether written down on paper or not, are a vast mass of exchangeable property, they are wealth for exactly the same reason that gold is, they affect prices exactly like an equal mass of gold, and they are the subject of the most colossal commerce of modern times." So equivalent was credit to cash that if credit is "written down on paper" it essentially "become[s] material or corporeal property," according to Macleod.[12] Ellis T. Powell also notes the efficiency of credit, stating that, "There is the minimum wear and tear of the metallic basis, and a coincident tendency to regard it as being only theoretically present," for all financial transactions occur without money ever "leaving the bank."[13]

If, as Checkland asserts, during the whole of the nineteenth century economists vainly sought to discover the rules that governed money and credit, Macleod and Powell are just examples of the many voices engaged in that process in the late Victorian period.[14] As that search intensified, economics took on the mantle of a scientific, mathematical profession. Noting that the rapid, drastic "changes in the value of money" in the 1860s and 1870s made it necessary for increased, current, and continuous "practical study" of money, editor of *The Economist* Walter Bagehot asserted that, "the present time almost *requires*" the "practical study of the money market."[15] In virtual response to Bagehot's call, between 1871 and 1891, there was a rise in journals devoted to economics, and 1,768 articles and essays on monetary concerns were published.[16] Amalgamation and centralization of banking increased in response to the need to address banking crises, inefficient banking practices, and organizational problems.

After reading *Dr. Jekyll and Mr. Hyde*, Andrew Lang asked Robert Louis Stevenson if he knew of the short stories by Poe and Gautier featuring the doppelgänger trope. Stevenson was taken aback. "Yes, I knew William Wilson," Stevenson responds, "but I now hear for the first time (and with chagrin) of the Chevalier Double. Who in hell was he?" Hoping that Poe's tale and Gautier's short story "Le Chevalier Double" had not "cut . . . out" his own, he adds, "My point is the identity with difficulty preserved; I thought it was quite original: a fresh start."[17] Obviously not the first to represent the double, Stevenson, I suggest, was an entrepreneur. That is to say, he pens an astonishing rendition of the Freudian capitalist whose business it is to advertise and distribute hysteria, exchange, fragmentation, and will-fulness as the psychic manifestations of *homo economicus*. Such an interpretation of the famous story of Jekyll and Hyde puts the focus on the seeming cipher Utterson rather than on the sublime schizophrenic protagonist. Indeed, I argue that Utterson's duality instigates the dreamscape of the Jekyll/Hyde plot. Reconstructing the Jekyll/Hyde relationship by taking it literally to the bank, Utterson tracks down his alter ego Jekyll, who has manufactured a means of consuming and incorporating exchange, unlimited fluctuation, production, desire, and panic. Utterson's pursuit engenders, contains, and displaces his own alienation. He ultimately accedes to the capitalist assertion of the individual and his possession of a will: that is, that he is a free agent who possesses himself, something capitalism ostensibly wills to the subject. In a brilliant double twist, Utterson's utterance of the Jekyll/Hyde story under-writes the stalking of his own will and the subliminal incorporation of economic panic into his own body.

Stevenson preempts Freud in suggesting that dreams imitate economic dynamics. In an article entitled "A Chapter on Dreams," published just a year after *Dr. Jekyll and Mr. Hyde* and explicitly citing that tale, Stevenson explains how dreams influenced his writing. Referring to "the little people" or "Brownies" who subliminally influence the writer's storytelling, he gives examples of how the unconscious informs fictional images, plots, and characters during the hypnagogic state. More straightforward and realistic than Freud about the "economics" of dreaming, Stevenson notes that he began to use his dreams when he consciously decided to "turn" them to "account" by writing and selling stories, thus securing "the little people" to help him with the "business" of writing "profitable tales." Thinking his daytime, writerly self controls his storytelling, the Stevenson persona admits that the "Brownies" often manage the writing through the dream work they perform, which is "one-half" the "work" of his authorship.[18]

Explaining that part of *Dr. Jekyll and Mr. Hyde* was written as a result of dream work, Stevenson demystifies the writer. He posits that "For myself — what I call I, my conscious ego, the denizen of the pineal gland unless he has changed his residence since Descartes, the man with the conscience and the variable bank-account . . . — I am sometimes tempted to suppose he is no story-teller at all." In this statement, Stevenson cheekily admits that his writing is as much about his unstable "bank-account" as it is about his ability or desire to write. This admission also implies a sort of identity panic that acknowledges that in the age of science and capital identity is equivalent to one's glands and bank account. Certainly one gathers from this essay that economics were the chief impulse for writing *Dr. Jekyll and Mr. Hyde*: "Then came one of those financial fluctuations to which (with an elegant modesty) I have hitherto referred in the third person," says Stevenson. As a result, the author "went about racking my brains for a plot," finally "dream[ing] the scene at the window, and a scene afterward split in two, in which Hyde, pursued for some crime, took the powder and underwent the change in the presence of his pursuers."[19] Viewing his unconscious as an economic memory bank that accumulates linguistic tropes that eventually compound (reader) interest, Stevenson assumes that identity (the self's credit) is in the bank and the account it gives of the self. As he already understood, modern psychology could not exist without the established language of capitalist economics.

The example Stevenson uses to show how "Brownies" help create his fiction has to do with a hypnagogic economy as well: he explains that the source of one of his stories is a dream in which a young heir kills his father and lives in dread that the father's young, beautiful widow will find out about the murder. Ultimately, the heir learns that she loves him, and thus he inherits the father's large landed property and the beautiful young wife without any accompanying guilt. It is well to remember that the bohemian Stevenson was constantly in debt and usually profligate when he had money, and he frequently looked to his father to bail him out of financial difficulties. As Jenni Calder points out, even at the age of thirty-five, when he wrote *Dr. Jekyll and Mr. Hyde,* Stevenson still could not survive without his father's financial bequests.[20] As is often the case, the well-to-do father loved his son but was stern and demanding nonetheless, expecting him to choose a career worthy of inheriting all the property he willed to Louis. Stevenson the younger felt both defiant and subordinate to his father, loving and resenting him at the same time. According to Malcolm Elwin, Jekyll represents Stevenson's "conscience" that he needed to stop being a "social parasite" by living off his father financially; in contrast, Stevenson's Hyde represents his "self-indulgent impulse" and his resentment towards "the parsimony of his father's allowance."[21] Ironically, *Dr. Jekyll and Mr. Hyde,* which, I argue, manifests Stevenson's subliminal anxieties about paternal wills and inheritances, was the first of Stevenson's writings that established him as a writer who could live by what he made from his writing. Stevenson's dream *work,* then, had paid off with a dream economy, if you will, relieving the author, temporarily, of his anxieties about "financial fluctuation" and his "variable bank-account."

Freud's economic explanation of dreams written in 1900 replaces Stevenson's naïve rendition of the "Brownies" with "entrepreneurs" and "capitalists" but in doing so astonishingly rejects the actual potential economic incentives of dreaming that Stevenson so ingenuously admitted. Freud insisted that displacement, overdetermination, and the relationship between the unconscious and the conscious could be understood in meta-phorical economic terms without having anything to do with fiscal eco-nomics. Writing only a few years after Stevenson's discussion of dream economics, the father of psychoanalysis describes the mechanisms through which dreams manifest the unconscious:

The *motive force* which the dream required had to be provided by a wish; it was the business of the worry to get hold of a wish to act as the motive force of the dream.

The position may be explained by an analogy. A daytime thought may very well play the part of *entrepreneur* for a dream; but the *entrepreneur*, who, as people say, has the idea and the initiative to carry it out, can do nothing without capital; he needs a *capitalist* who can afford the outlay, and the capitalist who provides the psychical outlay for the dream is invariably and indisputably, whatever may be the thoughts of the previous day, *a wish from the unconscious.*

Sometimes the capitalist is himself *the entrepreneur,* and indeed in the case of dreams this is the commoner event: an unconscious wish is stirred up by daytime activity and proceeds to construct a dream. So, too, the other possible variations in the economic situation that I have taken as an analogy have their parallel in dream-processes. The *entrepreneur* may himself make a small contribution to the capital; several *entrepreneurs* may apply to the same capitalist; several capitalists may combine to put up what is necessary for the *entrepreneur.*[22]

Freud's convoluted explanation has convinced the modern age not only that dreams manifest important psychological content but also that the dream's meaning never articulates itself in straightforward terms. Never, for example, does the dream link the psychological problem at issue to an image of its actual source, nor does it imagine that conscious language is capable of explicitly articulating unconscious trauma. Because Freud's system is bankerized – that is, it imagines that the unconscious is incon-vertible and incommensurable – the conscious and unconscious require and never get beyond the need for a middleman. The dynamics of this psychical exchange occurs thus: worry> thought> wish> motive force> dream. In other words, an unconscious trauma or fear attaches to a thought, which generates an unconscious wish (the entrepreneur) that needs a motivating force (the capitalist) to distribute the dream. Hence, through displacement, or a kind of cubism, the dream transfers the psychological trauma onto a seemingly irrelevant image, which then acts as the sign of the trauma and the emotions it produces.

Despite Freud's brilliant plotting of psychic indirection, the fact that he explicitly uses an economic analogy for the production of dreams should not stop one from directly relating psychic trauma to real economic conditions. Stevenson certainly sees the connection. Using the older science of economics to underwrite his new science of the psyche, Freud could not imagine his new science without the established language of capitalist economics, just as nineteenth-century economics turned to the older science of physics for many of its metaphors. The psyche he imagines, the imagination he psychologizes, and the structure of his own imagining are capitalist. Indeed, Freud's construction of the entrepreneur/capitalist who distributes the subject's dreams covers over Freud's establishment of a whole new profession and its consequent economic conditions and trajectories. Undoubtedly his assertion that only a middleman/entrepreneur/ capitalist can elocute and allocate metaphorically the self's original trauma(s) may be a displacement of his own economic requirement that analysands must have a psychiatrist/entrepreneur to translate the subjects' dreams regularly.[23]

It is not that *homo* was not complicated before the Industrial Revolution; it is that the age of *homo economicus* multiplies and economically arranges those complications in almost unlimited ways, as Dickens's *Little Dorrit* portends. Dr. Jekyll's reference to the "polity of multifarious, incongruous and independent denizens" that inhabit and make up his subjectivity illustrates Freud's psychological view of the self (82). As an economic formula, Freud's psychological explanation is analogous to capitalism's Gothic will to unlimited production and thus unlimited desire. The labeling and establishment of new psychic diseases and the suggestion that symptoms are potentially unlimited requires more analyses ergo more psychoanalysts; and the view of the self as an infinitely (unrequited) desiring subjectivity – whose unconscious and psychological traumas are multiple and multiplying in their forms and contents – sustains the psychic cycle of trade. Creating an explicitly named and defined unconscious self with ever increasing needs and problems that require professionals and a professional language to articulate those problems, psychoanalysis banks on panic as it produces a whole economy based on the conviction that the subject is an entity that constantly experiences and represses trauma. As Freud's displaced metaphor of capitalists and entrepreneurs illustrates, it takes an economic language to keep track/account of all the traces of this newly imagined human being. In this Gothic economic construction of the psychic subject at least two conflicting economic expectations are reiterated: the subject must be interpellated as a unified, monolithic individualist but also as an endlessly self-replicating, consumed/consuming multiply selved incorporation.

In essence, Freud's theory of displacement and the dream process illustrates the impending bankerization of the imagination, indicating that the material conditions evoked by the economy act as the transcendental signifier of all other cultural meanings, including the psychological. Representing this Gothic bankerization in a number of ways, *Dr. Jekyll and Mr. Hyde* at the very least shows that the "I" is possibly always already the "not I." The horror of the Victorian Gothic premonition of Lacanian destabilization found in Dr. Jekyll is depicted brilliantly by Stevenson as a simultaneous experience of *déjà vu* and *presque vu* as regards the condition of selfhood under the sign of capitalism. What Stevenson shows is that the modern subject stands in panic and horror at the condition of the self's solipsistic confinement within the construct of selfhood as well as the possibility of the self's utter freedom, the condition of being an invasive/invaded horde and a monolithic, impermeable entity at once.

As *Dr. Jekyll and Mr. Hyde* intuits, only through the process of linguistic signification itself can the economic and psychological make their demands. In Stevenson's Gothic novel the name "Utterson" initiates the narrative, and the character it is attached to appears to be merely a container of the story the reader desires to consume. However, he ends up being, as I argue, the indirect central character whose first utterance, "what was that?" linguistically generates the dreamscape the reader enters (31).[24] In Freudian terms, he is a double self who at times is "eminently human," indicating, it would seem, that the quality of humanness is the feature least to be expected from humankind in Victorian culture. Likewise, he loves the theatre but "had not crossed the doors of one for twenty years" just as he "mortif[ies]" his fancy for "vintages" (29). An entrepreneur who registers the culture's psychic worry that being "eminently human" is a rarity in mechanical, repressed, respectable society, he feels "almost with envy" the "high pressure of spirits involved" in the "misdeeds" of some of his friends (29).

Enfield, Utterson's friend and relative, acts as the capitalist to Utterson's subliminal wish to expand his own desiring economy, reporting to the lawyer the savage behavior of a man economically and socially linked to the respectable Dr. Jekyll. Noting that he does not care to know any further about the connection between Jekyll and Hyde because asking questions is "like starting a stone," Enfield remarks: "You sit quietly on the top of a hill; and away the stone goes, starting others; and presently some bland old bird (the last you would have thought of) is knocked on the head in his own back garden, and the family have to change their name" (33). Though Utterson agrees, he obsesses about the relationship between Hyde and his friend Jekyll and starts the stone rolling. The stone analogy figures into Freud's description of psychoanalysis as a kind of archeological project piecing back together the stones and architecture of the analysand's psyche. The stones of *Dr. Jekyll and Mr. Hyde* lead us back indirectly to Utterson's dream/wish generated by his traumas and distributed through his own capitalist energies to circulate himself as respectable and creditworthy.

In his study of capitalist trauma and the "bankerization" of modern life, Jean-Joseph Goux allows that in the first half of the nineteenth century manufacturing and commercial interests controlled money, whereas in the second half of the century banks replaced industry as the financial center of economic activity. This change occurred because the complexity of transferring huge amounts of capital between large businesses, governments, and other institutions required that such transactions occur on paper as credit rather than through the actual exchange of hefty bundles of cash. Arguing that gold is the fixed center of currency in the same way that reality is the fixed center of the novel and that, previous to bankerization, the two were always convertible, Goux suggests that this stable system ceased as "the (recent) inconvertibility of the monetary sign, and also of property, speculative and stock market values" went in tandem with "the loss of credibility of realist language and the crisis of the foundation of values."[25] As pointed out earlier in this study, for Goux the "inconvertibility" of modern money occurs with the demise of the gold standard (1971 in the United States, 1931 in Britain). At this point, Goux believes, money can no longer be turned into a material equivalent like gold, for it is now a sign that can be exchanged only for other signs, as all signs become cut off from any material reality.[26]

To Goux, the floating currency goes in tandem with the floating signifier, and like money, literature becomes increasingly inconvertible, losing material connection to the real. With money and language cut off from the domain of the real, according to Goux cubism replaces Victorian realistic fiction. The turn away from realistic writing towards symbolism and stream-of-consciousness typifies the transition from Victorian to modernist literature just as cubism moves from partial representation towards complete abstraction.[27] Published on the cusp of bankerization transformations, *Dr. Jekyll and Mr. Hyde* stands in contrast to the sprawling, expansive plotting of multi-decker novels like *Little Dorrit* and *Villette*. Indeed, the muted connection between linguistic signs and the material reality they describe puts readers of *Dr. Jekyll and Mr. Hyde* into a mode of suppressed panic as they struggle to make the signs of this laconic story convert into reality.

The hypotactic, angular, even gaunt snatches that make up the story of Dr. Jekyll might easily be styled as proto-cubist. Sketchy to the point of sharpness, Stevenson's terse tale includes stark moments that are pointedly incommensurable, keenly inconvertible. Likewise, the narrator often provides the bare outlines of a horrifying occurrence, dialogue, or character and then leaves the reader to decipher meaning in the murky aftermath. The narrative structure adds to the obfuscation: characters who want to explain but cannot quite name their condition narrate the Gothic tale.

Beginning with a story within a story, the novella ends with the letters from
two dead men who write at the acme of utter panic. Likewise, because there
is no return by the narrator who began the tale, the ending lacks closure and
a restoration to reality and knowability. For all these reasons, at times the
reader is not sure if the way s/he interprets the seemingly simple, spare
discourse is linked to any authorial intention whatsoever. In fact, the
spareness of the story (its economy, if you will) suggests that the narrative
is itself constrained by the economy of inconvertibility.

That is why it is so disturbing when the trail that leads to knowledge of
Hyde's identity – and thus, of course, of Jekyll's – is one that ends up at the
bank, an odd, even inane location for a Gothic tale and, seemingly, for
searches for the self's provenance. This brings us back to credit. Utterson's
panic about Hyde increases when the Victorian source of legitimacy and
authority – the bank – confirms Hyde's credentials on the two occasions in
the novel in which a state institution interacts with the atavistic doppelgänger. One recalls that the court in *The Woman in White* refuses to recognize
Laura Fairlie's identity because she presents her body rather than paperwork
as proof of who she is; in *Dr. Jekyll and Mr. Hyde*, the bank, on the authority
of Jekyll's unembodied signature, authenticates Hyde's deformed body,
affirming that he is the man he claims to be. Thus, even though it would
be impossible for Hyde to have a birth certificate (he is not born), this man
has the only signs he needs to pass in this culture, the signature of Dr. Jekyll.
The signature only has credit at the bank because Jekyll is a man of means,
meaning, therefore, that Hyde is a kind of entrepreneurial creation of
banking credit. In both cases of stolen identity, or rather, identity lacking
ties to the self, Victorian subjects react with open panic.

The first reference to banking in *Dr. Jekyll and Mr. Hyde* illustrates
identity panic and the concomitant capitalization of personal credit. When
Mr. Enfield tells Utterson about his encounter with a man who collides
with and batters a young girl on the street, the "damned Juggernaut," of
course, turns out to be Mr. Hyde. When the group who gathers round the
girl threatens Hyde with taking away his "credit" and his "name," Hyde
retorts, "If you choose to make capital out of this accident" then "Name
your figure" (31, 32). Enfield explains to Utterson how he and the crowd
settle the matter with the revolting stranger: in lieu of calling the police,
they demand that he pay the girl's family £100. Enfield is shocked when
Hyde breezily enters a nearby building – Dr. Jekyll's residence – and
returns with ten pounds in gold and a check for the remaining amount.
As Enfield comments, "a man does not, in real life, walk into a cellar door
at four in the morning and come out of it with another man's cheque for

close upon a hundred pounds." Hyde brazenly counters, "'I will stay with you till the banks open, and cash the cheque myself'" (32).

On top of Hyde's odd behavior, Enfield hosts Hyde, the doctor, and the girl's father in his private quarters until the next morning when the bank opens for business. Hence this bizarre citizen arrest results in strangely linking the perpetrator, victim, and chief witness of the crime while they remain in self-imposed quarantine at the witness's home for at least a five-hour stint. After breakfasting civilly together – the text also assumes this to be a normal response to the situation – the motley group set off "in a body to the bank" of Coutts & Co (32). The banking house of Coutts, of course, was one of the most reputable in England, whose clients included Charles Dickens as well as many royals, with Queen Victoria a loyal customer. Noting the hierarchical status of different banks, in his article on "Banking" (1856), Edmund Saul Dixon avers that while private banks are "mortal," and "the Bank of England is immortal," "Messrs. Coutts and Co." is all but "apotheosi[zed]."[28] Likewise, Bagehot remarked that the managers of the banks of Hoare's, Child's, Gosling's, and Coutts had "a certain union of pecuniary sagacity and educated refinement which was scarcely to be found in any other part of society."[29]

At the bank Enfield, Hyde, the doctor, and the girl's father wait to make sure that the check Hyde has produced is not a forgery. To Enfield's astonishment, the bank backs the piece of paper as, in fact, a "genuine" check (32). Attempting to explain why he is so disturbed by the whole affair, Enfield remarks that Hyde is "a fellow that nobody could have to do with, a really damnable man; and the person that drew the cheque is the very pink of the proprieties, celebrated too, and (what makes it worse) one of your fellows who do what they call good" (33). Curiously, however, though the group finds Hyde's manners and appearance despicable and they intuit his Gothic propensities, they have no qualms being in close quarters with him – sleeping and eating with him in the same house. They are, however, deeply troubled by his credit with the bank, which provides him with the economic sign of legitimacy – cultural and economic capital.

When in 1887, H. D. Macleod asserted to Parliament that using credit instead of money illustrated that the Victorians had become increasingly civilized, he also implicitly suggested throughout that a most important part of the whole new reliance on credit was the credit or confidence the client had in the banker, banking, and the credit system itself.[30] Enfield's response to Coutts's affirmation of Hyde's identity illustrates the unwritten part of the contract that stipulates that the self only has faith in the Bank of England. If panic means that there is only a belief in the Bank of England, it also indicates that in this Gothic economy a concordant transaction occurs: individuals only come to have credit, identity, and authenticity if the bank believes in them. The capitalist subject gains the bank's imprimatur only by being willing to use the bank and its exchange practices, that is, investing in the idea of exchange itself, exchanging gold for notes and checks and ultimately the money no one sees – credit. To get credit from the bank – to become more civilized – the Victorian subject must invest in being identified and defined by money and the economic system at the same time that the banking system is swiftly becoming based on an ever more tenuous link between credit and identity.

Testifying before a select committee, Bagehot asserted that, "Credit is 'the historical element of political economy'" and that the "opinion people form of one another, which is the basis of banking, necessarily depends upon historical consideration," for it "cannot be changed with the same facility with which you can change any ordinary element in mercantile business."[31] Bagehot thus implies that one's personal credit has more to do with the history of one's relationship with a bank – the paper trail of the accounts one has there – than with autobiographical or biographical accounts that might be inscribed about the self and its meaning. J. W. Gilbart also writes about the cachet one attains by having a bank account, noting that bankers, "for their own interest," are always concerned about the moral reputation of their clients. Thus they will examine a customer's habits to see if he is "speculative, thrifty or prodigal" and will be more likely to lend to a man who owns some property and exhibits "good morals," than to a man with a great deal of property "but of inferior reputation." The word to the wise, then, is that "the establishment of a bank in a place immediately advances the pecuniary value of a good moral character."[32]

Edmund Saul Dixon remarks the same tendency, writing that one of the results of having a banker is that "you have a continual referee to your respectability." In addition, if this "gives credit, and credit is money," keeping a banker also allows one to keep track of the moral credit of other bank clients. As Dixon asserts, most bankers give "information to each other as to the respectability of their customers."[33] When one achieved respectability in the eye of the banker, one apparently had the frightening capacity to check up on one's neighbor's credit, as the accredited banking client became a sorcerer *manqué*. To wit: economist Henry Sidgwick asserted that the primary function of money was not only for the literal and local transfer of a particular commodity but as a medium of exchange in general.[34] It would appear then that the bank's imprimatur gives Hyde the mystified power money has as a "medium of exchange."

Shocked by Hyde's power to make money move, and knowing that the check drawer is his own friend and client Dr. Jekyll, lawyer Utterson asks for more precise details, in particular, if Enfield is positive that Hyde had a key to the check drawer's house and if Enfield quizzed Hyde about "the place with the door" (33). Aware that Jekyll's property includes a seldom-used door in the back that enters into an old laboratory, Utterson probes Enfield to find out how he knows that this entryway and its premises belong to Jekyll. Responding that it certainly seemed unlikely, Enfield explains that "I happen to have noticed his address; he [Jekyll] lives in some square or other" (33). The reader gathers from this Spartan exchange that Utterson knows that the rear door located in a shabby court also provides egress into Jekyll's house, whose front entrance is on a square appropriate to the doctor's gentlemanly wealth and status. By deposing Enfield, Utterson attempts to find out how much his friend knows about Jekyll's identity and if he gives credit to it.

Having heard Enfield's story and disturbed that his doctor friend gives Hyde free entry to his private quarters via the back door, Utterson "haunt(s)" Jekyll's door for days until he sees Hyde (38). Stephen Heath writes that "the organizing image" of Stevenson's tale is "the breaking down of doors," and "learning the secret behind them."[35] Jekyll's description of his transformations into Hyde includes the metaphor that he let the "doors of the prisonhouse" open and that the self is a "fortress" to be blocked from easy access (85, 83). Certainly the psychological connotations of the double doors – the front and rear doors are completely disparate in appearance and so far apart that few can tell that they lead to the same place – illustrate the structure of Jekyll's split psyche. Though the sexual and socio-economic connotations of entrance via the rear door are scandalous or déclassé for Victorians, from another economic perspective, having a back entryway to his property that makes it impossible to tell from the outside that the shabby court actually leads to a thriving, upscale square subverts Jekyll's peers from ostracizing him for extravagant bohemian and criminal behavior. His "coming and going" are, then, concealed (88).

But what is the economy of the obsession with doors and the coming and going, aside from being a means of concealment? In literal terms, we know that the Bank Act of 1844 created an amorphous institution made of two bodies housed within and composing one entity simultaneously considered legally separate. In evidence given to the Banks of Issue Committee, Bagehot, who elsewhere remarked the "peculiar[ity]" of the English banking system, states that, "the accidental combination of the two departments in the same building gives the banking department no aid in meeting a panic."[36] An entity in which the right hand was not to know what the left was doing, the Bank of England was legally required to consider the doors to the two different departments as double doors: they did and they did not have access to each other.

Lord Overstone believed that previous to the 1844 Act the Bank of England was already confused between the bank's issuing and banking duties and that the Act would clarify and permanently separate the two functions. Testifying in 1840 to the Parliament committee on banking, he averred that, "almost all the fallacies which are prevalent on the subject of the circulation or the currency, arise out of a confused view of those two different functions" of the Bank of England as issuer of money and as place of deposit. He also notes the "confusion and derangement" that has occurred "by mingling the management of circulation with banking operations."[37] In another place, Overstone reiterates this point, remarking that, "To mix" banking and issuing is like an "unskillful chemist" who tries to put together "substances which have no affinity, and will not combine, and therefore obtains only a confused and useless mixture, where he looked for a perfect chemical compound."[38]

Jekyll seems to find that perfect (supernatural) chemical compound. In saying that there may be connections between the peculiar doubleness of the Bank of England and the Gothic doppelgängers in *Dr. Jekyll and Mr. Hyde,* I obviously do not argue a one-to-one allegorical relationship. Nevertheless, I do believe there are deep structural similarities revealing that both manifestations are from the same conflicted and increasingly bankerized Victorian culture. If in Victorian culture money is the universal sign or equivalent, then in a real way the double structure of the Bank of England mirrors the doubleness of the commodity, the double or split psyche, and the doubling that occurs in both fictional and economic discourses that describe this doubleness, for when Parliament officially instituted the 1844 Bank Act it legitimized the doubleness of its own identity but also established a new subject identity. As Gordon Bigelow asserts, the 1844 Act created a paradigm shift in that it was part of a new methodology for knowing the world strictly within the modern construction of the economy. Part of that new economic system was to separate the economic from all other areas of human life.[39]

That modern construction is itself dual. As Ann L. Jennings points out, the establishment of economics as a separate field had repercussions for the relations between the state, the private sphere, and the economy.[40] Not only were the public and private spheres separated, there was also a binary between the state and the economy, with the state seen as inhabiting the public sphere and the market the private, as in private versus government business. But this view is reversed when the market was compared to the private domestic sphere: then the economy was viewed as within the public sphere in contrast to the private domestic sphere. Occupying this anomalous position, the economy was the privileged counter in both sets of binaries, having it both ways when it came to the market's responsibilities to the individual and the state.[41] Indeed, the market could prevail in its claims that the state should stay out of private business affairs, while at the same time figuring "Economism" (or "the social prioritizing of market processes as the desiderata of social well-being") as a state function that comes before the family or individual.[42] This interpretation of the amorphous position of the economy in Victorian England goes along with Rondo Cameron's pertinent query: to wit, how did "privately owned profit-making organizations" like the Bank of England obtain sole power to carry out the government's legal, sovereign duty to create, oversee, and maintain the system of currency?[43]

In a way, the Gothic body shared by Jekyll/Hyde is a site where the anomalous and contradictory public and private characteristics of the modern economy compete. Like the larger Victorian economy and the Bank of England, the Jekyll/Hyde economy insists that the public self not know what the private self is doing and vice versa, thus eliding responsibility to both the public and private sectors. For example, in *Dr. Jekyll and Mr. Hyde* a private interpretation of the economy becomes an excuse for Utterson to conceal Jekyll's shenanigans, while a public interpretation allows him to pursue relentlessly the character who has displaced him in Jekyll's will. Further, as doubles in one body unconscious of the other's doings, Jekyll and Hyde constantly make economic and psychic exchanges without ever meeting. This dynamic makes Jekyll's body a clearinghouse, a place where the entrepreneurs' wills are exchanged by their capitalist agents and where the will – responsibility to public and private duties – is contained and ideally elided.[44]

If crisis guarantees or underwrites this new identity, it is also the focal point of panic when economic and psychic crises occur as they are expected to regularly in a capitalist economy. Certainly when exchange, circulation, and transformation take place, Jekyll/Hyde experiences it as the "approaches of the hysteria" (78). Having access to doorways that should be shut to him, Hyde – who should remain hidden – causes bankerization panic in all the characters he meets. A sign of relentless economic sorcery, excess, and inconvertibility, Hyde produces inarticulate anger and panic in others who intuit his Gothic excess and lack. The horrified Utterson, for example, reflects after seeing Hyde for the first and only time, "There *is* something more, if I could find a name for it" (40). Likewise, Lanyon cannot speak what he has seen except in a letter to be opened after his death. In it he writes that when he saw Hyde "change" to Jekyll his "mind submerged in terror" and all he could do was scream "O God!" repeatedly (80). As Jekyll's Freudian displacement, Hyde is so encoded in the psychic condition of the other characters that what he represents about their own bankerization is invisible to them. Signifying the modern condition of (ex)changeability and constant circulation, Hyde represents the bankerization of the self and the equivalency of selves. Cut off from the real, his only purpose is to perform doubleness, circulation, and exchange. Indeed, Hyde would seem to be the embodiment of Jameson's suggestion that under the sign of capitalism the different economic classes dwell as haunted entities in the minds and bodies of their superiors and inferiors.

In the strange, arresting short chapter entitled "Incident at the Window" the motif of the double doorway becomes a window on the bankerized exchange process that Jekyll and Hyde represent. On their weekly walk, Utterson and Enfield greet Jekyll, whom they see looking out an upstairs window of his house. In the midst of their friendly banter with Jekyll, the doctor abruptly disappears from the window. Experiencing *presque vu,* Utterson and Enfield almost observe Jekyll's actual transformation into his Gothic alter ego. But Jekyll, with "an expression" of "abject terror and despair," "instantly thrust[s] down" the window before they can perceive the actual moment of (ex)change. Cut off from their friend, Utterson and Enfield walk away, unable to speak for a while. When they finally do, it is to express in unison the words, "God forgive us" (61). The weird change pictured in Jekyll's window and the obscure exchange of words between Enfield and Utterson afterwards are difficult to decipher completely. But certainly the possibility of seeing the actual exchange process itself in unmediated form generates unmitigated horror in the novel's characters and the reader.

In this nightmarish moment, Utterson and Enfield experience an instant of nauseating *(un)heimlich*: by almost witnessing the mechanics of (ex)change, they know themselves to be subjects who can only read the traces of signs that speak the subject's exchangeability. That almost seen condition of their own exchangeability, the sense of something familiar, leaves them in a condition of panic. When other characters see either one of the doubles, particularly Hyde, they also experience *(un)heimlich,* the mystified after-effect of witnessing the bodily expression of capitalist doubling and exchange. Those who witness the unmediated exchange between and within Hyde and Dr. Jekyll must die, as does Lanyon, the only one to actually see their transformation. Even Lanyon's death is blocked off from the reader's view as though identity panic can only be represented in bankerized, inconvertible form.

The Gothic horror in this novella is not, then, just man's double nature – after all, the first paragraph of the story indicates that Utterson is himself a split personality who has sensual urges that he fiercely suppresses. Duality is a given. What is worse is to see visible what is meant to be invisible in the culture, the act of exchange that turns the commodity, the producer, and the consumer into riven identities always already in the process of being exchanged. Continually exchanging places, bodies, and subconsciousnesses, Jekyll and Hyde are at once a double door, the link and bar to their own and the other's identity. As a result, Jekyll and Hyde can only see their (ex)changes in the "welcom[ing]" reflections of a mirror, the fictional realm of the Imaginary (84). Victorian economists well knew that credit, in financial terms, was a fictional entity, and this novel seems to make an implicit connection between the fictionality of financial credit and the fictionality of personal (character) credit. Referring to commercial enterprise during Charles II's reign, Macleod notes that it was presumed that a bank's business was "to advance Imaginary Money – or Credit – and not Metallic money."[45] Likewise, Gilbart rejoices in the fictionality of finance: referring to what was often called "a system of fictitious Credit," he remarks that even if it is essentially a "fictitious system," its effects are anything but fictitious, for it results in the material conditions a society enjoys. Thus, Gilbart concludes, "If it be a system of bubbles, they are bubbles which, like those of steam, move the mighty engines that promote a nation's greatness and a nation's Wealth."[46] Stevenson's depiction of identity panic consists, in part, of acknowledging the fictionality of personal and financial credit. It also involves knowing that one's condition is equivalent and exchangeable with any other identity and that identity is subject to capitalism's mindless, robotic will to non-containment.

Always on the verge of crisis, capitalism's nightmare and dream, as Marx would suggest, is for unlimited production and consumption and consequent infinite economic exchanges. In keeping with this socio-economic milieu, Jekyll thinks he can control his own economy of desire. "[C]ompound[ing]" an illicit drug, he believes that it will offer him infinite pleasure, experience, and (compound) interest without any repercussions (85). Jekyll is terrified when unlimited exchange interrupts ostensible control of his own identity as Hyde gradually makes exchanges with Jekyll at an ever swifter and more uncontrollable velocity – like the characters meeting and going "at it" in *Little Dorrit*. At this point, Jekyll becomes the victim of his own commodity (the drug he produces) that turns his body and psyche into an exchangeable equivalent in a fluctuating cycle of trade with Hyde. As Jekyll learns, one of the side effects of addiction to endless exchange is an accompanying dependence on the utter lack that produces the will to unlimited production as well as the panic that signals and mediates the transformation between those two conditions.

No less enthralled by the possibility of complete abjectivity than he is by the totalitarianism of unlimited production of desire, Jekyll takes comfort in the fact that he can escape his identity. Referring to Hyde as his "familiar," Jekyll exults,

Think of it – I did not even exist! Let me but escape into my laboratory door, give me but a second or two to mix and swallow the draught that I had always standing ready; and, whatever he had done, Edward Hyde would pass away like the stain of breath upon a mirror; and there in his stead, quietly at home, trimming the midnight lamp in his study, a man who could afford to laugh at suspicion, would be Henry Jekyll. (86)

But quickly Jekyll finds that exchange controls him rather than the other way around: "A moment before I had been safe of all men's respect, wealthy, beloved – the cloth laying for me in the dining-room at home; and now I was the common quarry of mankind, hunted, houseless, a known murderer, thrall to the gallows" (93).

Allen Hoey suggests that Marx's famous C-M-C series essentially illustrates the links between a tenor and vehicle to show the link made by money between two commodities.[47] In this series, the M, the middleman, attaches to itself more power than the commodities, which are supposedly the reason for the use of money. In the same way that the signified is subordinate to the signifier, the items of exchange are subordinate to the means of exchange. In a real way, the M (money/capital) acts as the double doorway between Jekyll and Hyde, who have become exchangeable commodities.[48] As we recall the "cheque" that the bank of Coutts & Co. authorizes for Hyde, it should be understood that the bankerization it represents makes the two identities of Jekyll and Hyde possible for each other and for Victorian society. Coutts accepts Mr. Hyde based upon Jekyll's absent presence – his signature. Giving Hyde the sorcerer's power to move things (to cause movements of capital and commodities between identities), money makes things happen and causes inert commodities to exchange hands, as Marx so dramatically describes. But at the same time, the C-M-C formula makes Jekyll and Hyde subordinate to the exchange process itself, for, ultimately, neither is able to control that process.

The C-M-C process and its resulting identity panic appears in a remarkable admission by Jekyll, who explains what he had to do to obtain his drugs when suddenly he is transformed into Hyde. Strangely, Jekyll keeps referring to Hyde as "he." Then the doctor remarks, "He, I say – I cannot say, I" (94). An extraordinary linguistic chiasmus that mirrors the human doubling occurring in the narrative, this metonymic transcription represents the exchange relationship – the double door – between Hyde and Jekyll. The initial word "He" and the concluding word "I" are simultaneously connected and split by the words "I say – I cannot say." The inconsequential dash subordinates the sign of the subject and his assertion of identity, both binding and canceling the textual relationship between Jekyll and Hyde. Both aggressively asserting and erasing Jekyll's "say[ing]," the dash acknowledges the inconvertibility of signs.[49] When an I cannot say "I," the I is revealed as a fragmented subjectivity. This logical understanding is doubly riven when we recall Lacan's assertion that when one says "I," the entity speaking the "I" is automatically split off from the entity – I – to which I refers. Marx's explanation of money also uncannily describes the identity panic in Stevenson. "If *money* is the bond binding me to *human* life, binding society to me, binding me and nature and man," asks Marx, "is not money the bond of all *bonds*?" Like the Bank of England and Jekyll/ Hyde, money to Marx is at once "the universal *agent of separation*" and "the true *binding agent* – the [universal] *galvano-chemical* power of society."[50]

In this paradigm, continual movement and exchanges produce capital and keep it moving – and Jekyll and Hyde are specific examples of this process as the plot circulates around the circulation of Jekyll/Hyde's will and his check book. In physical terms, Jekyll and Hyde are always on the move, as though the double self within the one body makes it possible for the subject to be in circulation on a double shift as it were, never sleeping, always exchanging personalities and commodities between them. Jekyll's signature also authorizes his will, giving it the "galvano-chemical power" that Marx describes.

The second direct reference to banking in *Dr. Jekyll and Mr. Hyde* reiterates the "galvano-chemical power" of the check. Utterson, who is disturbed by Jekyll's increasingly bizarre behavior, accompanies a detective to Hyde's digs in Soho when it becomes clear that he is the culprit who has brutally murdered Sir Danvers Carew. Investigating the "ransacked" quarters, they find that though "many papers had been burned," they are able to retrieve "the butt end of a green cheque book." The inspector suggests that they proceed to the bank "where several thousand pounds were found to be lying to the murderer's credit" (49). The detective claims that, having the other half of the cane that killed Carew, he now has the evidence to convict the perpetrator. "[A]bove all," however, he has confiscated the partially burned check book, so that all he has to do is wait at Hyde's bank to capture the suspect. As the detective asserts, "You may depend upon it," that "money's life to the man," and thus all he must do to capture the criminal is "wait for him [Hyde] at the bank" when he comes to replenish his wallet (49–50).

If Utterson can be viewed as containing the initiating desire in *Dr. Jekyll and Mr. Hyde*, we might ask not only about the Freudian economy of his dream; we should question also his dream of the economic, that is, the actual financial trajectory of his dream/wish plot. As I conjecture, Utterson decries Jekyll's exchanges with Hyde because the new relationship elides the intimate exchanges between Utterson and Jekyll, ultimately figured by the fact that Jekyll changes his will to name Hyde the beneficiary. As conveyancer of Jekyll's will, Utterson obviously feels a proprietary right to guard the doctor's legacy. But his obsessive pursuit of "Henry Jekyll's favourite," Hyde, suggests that it is almost as if the written will has more authenticity – credit – than Jekyll himself (48). More concerned about Jekyll's "mad will" than anything else, Utterson is strangely detached when he learns that Jekyll may be living a double life (58). Certainly the dour lawyer cares more about the will than that Hyde kills Carew. Indeed, the narrative notes that, "The death of Sir Danvers was, to his way of thinking, more than paid for by the disappearance of Mr Hyde" (56). Thus, when Utterson presses Poole not to say anything about Jekyll's suicide letter, suggesting that, "we may at least save his credit," his concern is as much for Jekyll's bank account as it is for his moral reputation (73).

Utterson finally gets his monomaniacal desire to put the will in the right hands when Jekyll dies. Just before Utterson reads the letters from Lanyon and Jekyll that explain the Gothic horror and end the brief narrative, Utterson's economic dream is fulfilled: "On the desk, among the neat array of papers, a large envelope was uppermost, and bore, in the doctor's hand, the name of Mr. Utterson." Amongst the enclosures are Jekyll's last narrative and his will. To Utterson's surprise "in place of the name of Edward Hyde, the lawyer, with indescribable amazement, read the name of Gabriel John Utterson" (72). Looking at the dead Hyde, he wonders why the man, who "had no cause to like me," had not "destroyed" the will, seeing that he is "displaced" (72). If this novella is about Utterson's own displaced desires and his entrepreneurial efforts to encounter indirectly the capitalist exchanges that allow the subject to believe he possesses a will, credit, and identity, it is at this moment that the lawyer achieves those desires without having any public or private repercussions on his own credit.

His Gothic dream having achieved that goal, the man who uttered the question that began the story concludes by reading and overwriting the letters that end the tale. Concealing the economics of exchange, Utterson immediately focuses on the Gothic narratives by Lanyon and Jekyll that lead the reader away from Utterson's willfulness and lack of (Jekyll's) will. It is his consciousness that allows for the reader to encounter the letter from Lanyon and the "confession" from Jekyll and to conclude with their identity panic, and it is in Utterson's mind that readers confront their own unuttered waking nightmares (97). First and last, in a way, the text centers on the will, a paper document that, like financial credit, is a synecdoche for the subject's personal credit. Utterson's narrative desires to find a subject who wills, and whose integrity, therefore, cannot be breached by the bankerization of the self. The utterances of such a unified self would, like money, hold the power to make things move, to be, in other words, willful.

If, as I suggest, *Dr. Jekyll and Mr. Hyde* may be as much about the displaced Gothic economics of Utterson's desire as it is about the Jekyll/ Hyde duo, one might ask how the tale's ending accomplishes the entre-preneurial trajectory of capitalism. Does it open a double doorway for the reader to encounter the capitalist economics of *unheimlich* or identity panic without paying the price of being responsible for that knowledge in either public or private terms? Does the fear generated by the Gothic tale and its refusal to interrogate the character who initiated it with his interrogatory utterance subliminally require the reader to confront the subject's contain-ment within but responsibility to (ex)change? Given the motif of the double doors, it would seem that the reader might have it both ways, a conclusion that would bankrupt the reading act. Nevertheless, desiring to focus on "the identity with difficulty preserved,"[51] Stevenson describes his own subjectivity as that of a riven man with a "conscience and the variable bank-account." Investing in and interrogating bankerization, the entrepre-neurial Stevenson exhibits an astonishing clarity as he delves into the economics of (his own) dreams and the dreams of economics.

CHAPTER 6

Bankerization panic and the corporate personality *in* Dracula

During the years Bram Stoker worked on *Dracula* (1897), the economy revived itself from the doldrums of the Great Depression. Historians note that between 1893 and 1913 coal and steel production grew, and exports of manufactured goods and raw materials rose, while engineering and ship-building increased. Perhaps the most influential legacy of nineteenth-century industrial capitalism was the laying of the railways, for at the turn of the century 22,000 miles of railway had been put down in Britain.[1] Nevertheless, one Victorian noted of the last decade of the century that they were "long, dragging, dull times."[2] Prices stayed level or fell and unemployment continued. Continuing the extended slump, the banking crisis of 1890 almost sank the Bank of England, which underwrote the House of Barings' bad investments in Argentina. *The Times*, 15 November 1890, reported thus, "Such a week of sensational horrors and heart-rending anxieties as that which is closing to-day can hardly be within the remembrance of the present generation of Englishmen."[3] "No fertile imagination could exaggerate the gravity of the crisis," said economist George G. Goschen, lamenting that the panic "risked the supremacy of English credit."[4] George Bartrick Baker began his article "The Crisis on the Stock Exchange" (1890) with the statement that "Not since the collapse of the City of Glasgow Bank in 1878 has the Stock Exchange been in such a state of nervous apprehension of evil as that which has recently threatened to culminate in a disastrous panic." Describing the debacle, Baker writes that "more than once in the past month we have been on the verge of a financial crisis, perhaps of the first magnitude."[5]

Exports of British capital fell in 1890, and there were crashes of finance companies in 1890–91 and of more banks in early 1892. In 1893 there was a general banking crisis, and, when leading banks felt unable to stop the panic, the British government announced five successive bank holidays to help end the run on banks.[6] In 1894 there were further financial troubles. One pamphleteer complains about the so-called "financial 'genius'" illustrated by bank directors, "who found themselves in control of a large portion of the market." The said directors, according to this writer, "exhibited crass ignorance" regarding economic laws, while also making "the fatal mistake of racing each other, their objective being the payment of the highest possible dividends to their shareholders."[7] As a result, "a severer cycle of depression" occurred and the rates set by the Bank of England were forced to go "abnormally low." With banks undercutting each other's rates of interest, it was no surprise that there was a very reduced dividend at the end of 1894. This same writer worries about the steep decline in profits and remarks that in spite of efforts to hone expenses "to a minimum," nevertheless, at the beginning of 1895, bankers had intense concerns about how to increase their net profits and "restor[e]" dividends "to the old footing."[8]

As L. S. Presnell points out, the near disaster of the Baring Crisis crystallized the British monetary rubric leading towards increased centralization.[9] Thus in the 1890s there was a "revolution in banking" that saw a sharp increase in amalgamations of banks.[10] Indeed, while there were only 44 banking amalgamations between 1844 and 1861 and 138 between 1862 and 1889, the transformation at the end of the century was swift and decisive.[11] In 1886 there were 370 British banks that were partners with around 2,700 local area offices. By 1906, of the 120 joint-stock banks only 20 were left due to mergers and takeovers; of the 250 private banks, only around a dozen remained.[12] For example, Barclay's, one of the "Big Five" amalgamated banks in England, began with 15 linked firms and ended up being a joint-stock company with 180 branches.[13] As F. E. Steele pointed out in 1896, "Barclay's have swallowed a host of banks, metropolitan and provincial," while the Alliance bank and Parr's merged and then took over Consolidated, and Prescott's secured Dimsdale.[14]

Foreign banking fueled a hefty part of bankerization in the 1890s. J. H. Clapham even declares that the deposit of foreign money into British banks was the most significant economic transformation at the end of the century.[15] So crucial was this foreign influx that the inevitable parochialism occurred. An article titled "Lombard Street under Foreign Control" stirred up ethnocentric enmities against the foreign Other when, as Clapham explains, the writer of the article, W. R. Lawson, noted "the prominence of foreign names in the exchange, bill and bullion business." Huth, Haldimand, Meinertzhagen, Rothschild, Hambro, and Goschen were just some of the foreign investors Lawson referred to in his harangue.[16]

In 1897 the famous case of Salomon v. Salomon & Co. Ltd. was heard on appeal before the House of Lords. Owner of a flourishing shoemaking trade, Aron Salomon decided to convert his business from being a one-man operation into a limited liability company under the Companies Act of 1862. To meet the legal requirement of having at least seven shareholders to form the company, Salomon ingeniously retained all but six of the company shares, disbursing the remaining shares to different family members who were otherwise not involved in the business. After he had established his business as a company, the ever-imaginative Mr. Salomon had the company issue debentures to himself as a private individual rather than in his capacity as the manager of the company. When the company was disbanded, a creditor sued the court to decide whether Salomon as an owner of debentures held a privileged position over all other creditors of his company. Furthermore, because Salomon essentially was the only member of his company, the judiciary had to supply an opinion about whether or not the Companies Act allowed for a person being his own preferred creditor. The Court of Appeal decided against Salomon, upholding the view that a company could not be considered as separate from its members. As one of the Lord Justices wrote, "one substantial man and six mere dummies did not make a company."[17]

When Salomon appealed the case to the House of Lords, the august body reversed the court's ruling. Lord Halsbury, for one, declared that it was of singular importance to settle the issue of "whether in truth that *artificial creation of the Legislature* had been validly constituted."[18] The artificial creation referred to was the "corporate personality," a legal fixture in English law from the medieval period. Eighteenth-century scholar William Blackstone explains this anomalous entity in *Commentaries on the Laws of England.* "[A]rtificial persons," he writes, are "bodies politic, bodies corporate" or "corporations" made up of individual persons, and "when [persons] are consolidated and united into a corporation, they and their successors are then considered as one person in law," a unit that "may establish rules and orders for the regulation of the whole."[19] In the Middle Ages the concept of the artificial person or corporate personality was legally used to refer to positions granted official status by the sovereign or the Church, including the positions of city mayor, church dean, and college fellow.[20] The concept of the corporate personality depended upon what is referred to as the fiction theory, which held that the state of necessity created the legal fictional concept of the "personality of a corporate body."[21] In other words, while those who make up a body corporate are real human beings, the personhood of a corporate body is fictional because produced by governmental legislation, thus providing the corporate body with a legal entity. But as Frederick Hallis argues, the main problem with the fiction theory is that members of the corporation are real human beings while the corporation is a separate and fictional entity.[22]

Because "new trading companies were entirely creatures of statute" and there were virtually no laws theorizing commercial entities, the House of Lords used the concept of corporate personality to decide the Salomon case. Thus they ruled that as a company Salomon & Co. Ltd. was a legal artificial personality and therefore distinct and separate from the individuals who made up its membership.[23] Hence, Salomon's creditors had to acknowledge that Salomon's company was authorized to make business agreements with its own members (including Salomon) in the same way that it did with persons not associated with the company.[24] Charles E. F. Rickett and Ross Grantham suggest that this was a momentous decision because it acted as the founding precedent of company law and is thus "treated by judges and academics alike with a reverence bordering on the religious."[25] Revered because the case established that creditors must seek redress from the company and not its individual members, Salomon v. Salomon & Co. Ltd. firmly distinguished between the responsibilities of real and fictional commercial personalities.[26]

Nevertheless, the artificial category of the "corporate personality" had moral and philosophical implications that continue to disturb some legal and economic scholars. Distinguished Victorian jurist Frederic Maitland writes that the corporate personality – which he calls a "miserable being" and a "ghost of a fiction" – required attention because "it has become vastly more important in these last years than it ever was before."[27] Why was Maitland so concerned about the law's effects in the second half of the nineteenth century? Quite simply the answer was that corporations were proliferating across the globe almost exponentially in comparison to the reproductive rates of "natural persons." Thus a greater proportion of legislation was aimed at defining and setting the limits on corporations. In support of his argument, Maitland refers to the American judge who in 1857 declared that, "It is probably true that more corporations were created by the legislature of Illinois at its last session than existed in the whole civilized world at the commencement of the present century."[28] Indeed, between 1863 and 1866 there were 3,500 limited companies added to the number of companies in England.[29] Originally instituted for religious reasons, the corporate personality, it seemed to Maitland, was much more problematic when it referred to the modern commercial company. He feared that corporations, reproducing at a far faster pace than the human population, were a foreign element threatening to have more power than the original corporate personality, the State itself.[30]

While Maitland was troubled about the "subjectification" of the corporation, current economics scholar Paddy Ireland worries that when the company is "reified" by the concept of the corporate personality it further cuts the corporation off from the individual personalities of its shareholders.[31] That is, when the law no longer considers the corporation the sum of its human members but separate from them, then the company becomes an increasingly impersonal entity, or, as L. H. Jenks writes, a company "engaging in economic activity with not so much as a sign of the Capitalist to be seen."[32] Thus, Ireland points out the irony that the company actually increases its impersonality when it becomes a legal personality and that instead of obtaining a kind of moral or essential personhood, this reified personality "in a certain crucial sense, lacks an inherent nature or character."[33] Maitland's contemporary Georg Simmel writes similarly of money, arguing that by virtue of being separated from "all specific contents" and because it "exists only as a quantity," it has the "quality of characterlessness."[34] The contradictions in the fiction theory of corporate personality could not be more telling: the law asserts that the corporation cannot commit treason or other crimes and it cannot act as a trustee or executor, but it does hold proprietary rights. Legally viewed as without a "soul" and, as Maitland summarizes, "incapable of knowing, intending, willing, acting," the corporation is shielded from full liability if it defrauds its members.[35]

Like Maitland, F. E. Steele viewed bankerization as dangerous. Warning that the swift decline in the number of banks caused by amalgamation results in "a banking monopoly," Steele worries that the "conveniences" offered by the banking industry would be reduced and that there could possibly be "a 'corner' in loans." Further, Steele argues that competition within the banking profession is a healthy means of retaining a wide range of banking facilities and services for the customer. Steele was particularly concerned that with banking amalgamation banking practices would become homogeneous and resistant to change. He fears, in other words, that "the reduction to one sombre and uniform *dead* level of a business already sufficiently monotonous" would not be a completely positive transformation.[36] He sees monopolization, then, as a kind of atrophy of banking energy, creativity, and service.

In contrast to the pessimistic views of Maitland and Steele, in his early twentieth-century (1903) discussion of amalgamation, Henry Warren strongly advocated bankerization as a process akin to the establishment of empire. Exulting that as soon as the smaller companies failed "the nearer the reign of the banks approaches," Henry Warren believed that eventually the large banks would form strong connections "because, in business as elsewhere, friendship is centred in the head rather than in the heart." Banks must "draw closer together," argues Warren, for they simply could not survive without centralization. Significantly, Warren suggests that erasing "excessive competition" amongst banks is necessary to forestall client panic, the customers described as those "who in that respect" are the bank's "enemies." Astonishingly, then, Warren sees capitalism as a competition between the customer and business rather than between businesses for the customer's patronage.[37]

I suggest that amalgamations in banking, the concept of the corporate personality, and bankerization might well inform the 1890s English *mise-en-scène* of *Dracula* (1897). Stoker's tale figures two incorporated entities (Dracula and his vampires and Van Helsing and his followers), competing to the death for a complete monopoly on circulation and consumption. In both groups the focus is not on the individual desiring subjectivity but on the meaning and power of the consolidated group. Indeed, Dracula is not only the name of an individual shareholder but also the designation of his corporation, as it were. The term "Dracula" is itself an amalgamation, naming an individual person; an amalgamated corporation of vampires of which he is the brains; a process or procedure of (capitalist) infinite circulation (of the commodity of blood); and the extensive hybrid streams of consciousness (and blood) of a group of accountants (Van Helsing, etc.) who attempt to bankrupt the artificial personality of the incorporated Dracula.[38]

A palimpsest of sorts, *Dracula* maps Victorian psychical derangements onto the Gothic East European vampire myth. Apocalyptic, end-of-the-century, feverish economic consumption in the face of almost monolithic corporate (im)personality underpins this tale that is also relevant to the commercial excesses of the twentieth-century *fin de siècle*. The context for Harker's business visit to Transylvania has everything to do with the fact that London was the world's banker and that its commerce had increasingly to do with banking exchanges of abstract foreign credit while relying less and less on material commercial or industrial ventures such as the building of railways and the production of textiles. Harker comes to Count Dracula to encourage and facilitate his economic exchanges, consumption, and accounting in London. Furthermore, the Count's emigration to England specifically directs the English economy (represented by Harker, Dr. Seward, Renfield, Arthur, and Lucy) to a more obsessive and barely suppressed focus on consumption. Dracula, the foreign investor who attempts corporate/corporal overthrow of competing entities, does exactly what he is supposed to do according to Victorian economic predilections.

Of all the characters in Bram Stoker's novel, the Count is most associated with the "life blood of commerce," money, and banking.[39] As a kind of fictional "corporate personality" who subliminally focuses attention on the bankerization of modern life, Dracula also spearheads what I call bankerization panic – the unrelenting fears about bankerization itself and the concomitant increasing loss of individual personality. Another way to understand this is to suggest that late Victorians experienced a subliminal anxiety about a scenario in which the blood system of every individual body was somehow infused with that of the market that had become distinctly amalgamated and centralized. Ellis Powell provides a particularly shrewd description of this phenomenon, noting that globalization of business sometimes creates "a species of neurasthenia" like that suffered by denizens of the city "in consequence of the incessant pelting of sense-impressions, never for a moment intermitted, upon the personality."[40] As Powell seems to suggest, in the capitalist mode of being it is impossible to escape the feeling of depletion, or of having the sense that one's life is being sucked away by the constant demands of capitalist circulation.

Victorians strongly associated blood circulation with national and international circulation of credit and goods. If Dracula's urge to concentrate England's blood supply into his own incorporated body may be the metaphor of the corporate personality's appropriation of England's economic circulation system, Stoker's famous text is connected with many overdetermined analogies between the economy, circulation of blood, and vampires.[41] Typical representations include, of course, the need of the body politic for money as a "bloodstream whose continuous circulation permeates all the intricacies of the body's organs"[42] as well as the foundational notion that "The life-blood of commerce is credit."[43] H. D. Macleod intones the commonly held metaphorical relationship between the economy and the blood system: the bank's purpose is like that of the human heart, for it "attracts to itself capital, the life blood of commerce," and after amassing "a great reservoir," it drives it through "channels of commerce, vivifying and nourishing it, and spreading vigour and health through the whole commercial body."[44] Asserting that the Bank of England is "the centre of the nervous system of commerce," George H. Pownall is much in agreement with his contemporary Robert Ewen, who states in the 1890s that, "Ready money is the life-blood of trade" and capital needed to be "got more widely distributed."[45] Viewing bankers as "the prime movers in trade circles," Ewen contended that they must "send out the money and keep it circulating through all the arteries of trade and commerce" as "fast as it comes in."[46] The intense economist also worries that there was probably too much "*dead* stock of capital" in the Bank of England because too much money was "lying . . . idle" in many of the larger banking houses.[47]

Of course the way Victorians saw the link between Jewish bankers and usury added to the vampiric associations. Marx subliminally affirmed the connection when he threw down the following gauntlet: "Capital is dead labour," that "vampire-like, only lives by sucking living labour, and lives the more, the more labour it sucks."[48] As seen in the chapter on *Little Dorrit*, Edmund Saul Dixon's essay on banking implicitly likens the "immortal" Bank of England to a vampire when it notes that the revered bank "assimilates into its own substance two-thirds of the blood which flows no longer in the veins of departed banks."[49] So enmeshed in the rhetoric is the relation between vampirism and money that in 1887, George C. S. Churchill entitles an essay about the debate between monometallism and bimetallism "Vampire Gold," and he never needs to refer to "vampire" again to make his position clear.[50] Similarly, Marxist economist Mikhail Tugan-Baranovsky writes in 1901 that "Panic is the death of credit," but that "credit has the ability to return to life," for "Credit dies, to be resurrected" in the regular cycle of credit.[51]

In the world of Victorian banking, as Dracula learns, not to circulate is to be (Un)dead. The narrative immediately engenders the vampire's commercial trip to England to put his property – his caskets and his hoard of old gold coins from various nations – in motion because to stay in the mercantile Transylvanian economy ensures his idleness and death, hoarding being anathema to Victorian economists immured in an economy based on abstract credit. The most voracious of Anglophiles (pun intended), Dracula consumes books on English practices and quickly finds that hoarding gold will only make him forever "*dead*" and "lying idle" in dusty vaults.[52] Thus, the Count demands to hear all the financial "means of making consignments and the forms to be gone through" and the information Jonathan has collated regarding Dracula's recently purchased homes in England.[53] Harker compliments Dracula's commercial savvy, saying, "For a man who was never in the country, and who did not evidently do much in the way of business, [Dracula's] knowledge and acumen were wonderful" (37). Recalling that, "There was a certain method in the Count's inquiries," Harker remembers that Dracula asked questions about "legal matters and on the doing of certain kinds of business" (36). Dracula encapsulates, then, Fred Botting's description of late capitalism, with "the combination of rapid technological advances and performative economic imperatives" increasing "circulation and expenditure so that excess has become the norm."[54]

Becoming sophisticated about the complex signs of capital, the Count seems well able to use many different forms of money. Additionally, in contrast to the descriptions of other characters in the novel, the narrative depicts the Count in banks, shows that he knows in detail what kinds of money forms he carries, and explicitly exhibits his detailed knowledge of his real estate portfolio, along with the precise locations at "197, Chicksand Street, Mile End New Town," and "Jamaica Lane, Bermondsey" and "No. 347, Piccadilly" (229, 239). Furthermore, the reader sees his "invoice[s]" and watches him make financial exchanges "in notes 'over the counter,'" and we know his real estate agents by name, "Mitchell, Sons and Candy" (200, 239). It is conjectured that never before or since has a terrifying supernatural archetypal villain displayed such almost comically mundane knowledge about the "characterless" entity of money.

If we see little of the financial doings of the English and American characters, it is certainly not because they are not interested in Dracula's finances and property. Harker worries that Dracula will invade "the City itself" (229), the London financial center that Lucy Snowe idolizes. A careful reading of the text – that is filled with an array of the most terrestrial of business discourses, including wills, bills of sale, receipts of service, and legal descriptions of parcels of land, and references to mortmain – supports the argument that Van Helsing becomes as obsessed with tracking Dracula's paper trail as he is with avenging Dracula's bloody deeds. Certainly his pursuit of Dracula, like Utterson's of Hyde, conceals the inroads he makes on another's economic and personal property. For one thing, in attempting to bring about Dracula's downfall, the Dutchman worries about the many houses Dracula has purchased. In particular, he notes that, "he will have deeds of purchase," "cheques," "paper," and other "belongings" that need to be tracked down (255). When searching Dracula's Piccadilly house, Van Helsing and his followers find its "title deeds" in "a great bundle" as well as "deeds of the purchase of the houses at Mile End and Bermondsey." There they also locate the keys to his other houses (262).

The text also associates Dracula's very body with money. When Van Helsing and crew pursue Dracula to one of his estates, Harker lunges at the Count with his Kukri knife, puncturing not the vampire's skin but his outer garment, instead. Bizarrely, the Count gushes money: "the point [of the knife] just cut the cloth of his coat, making a wide gap whence a bundle of bank-notes and a stream of gold fell out" (266). Immediately after this, the narrator describes how in the midst of fleeing his pursuers, the Count fumbles to retain his cash: "The next instant, with a sinuous dive he swept under Harker's arm, ere his blow could fall, and, grasping a handful of the money from the floor, dashed across the room, threw himself at the window." Subdued by the need for cash itself, Dracula looks like a bumbling Keystone Cop rather than a supernatural genius, and this fiscal humiliation begins his unraveling. When the Count "tumble[s] into the flagged area below" two noises stand out: "the sound of the shivering glass" and the "'ting' of the gold, as some [of Dracula's much scrambled for] sovereigns fell on the flagging" (267). By this point, it is as though the "ting" of money and Dracula's apparel have become the synecdoche for the fictional personality named the Count. In this ludicrous sequence, after Dracula runs from the scene with the moneys he is able to retrieve, Van Helsing pockets the rest of the cash, titles, and deeds, because, he says, it will stop Dracula from having the resources he needs to continue his horrific plans. The novel never mentions these financial assets again, and one has to wonder if Van Helsing has appropriated them as a finder's fee for having, in multiple ways, bankrupted the Count. At the very least, Van Helsing proves to be as savvy and persistent a consumer as Dracula.

Subliminally illustrating the idea that "the life-blood of the nation is money" that circulates eternally, Stoker's all-engrossing novel demands that readers, along with every character in *Dracula* (1897), acknowledge that in order for the fictional personality of Dracula to exist they must bank on his business – his consumption and production of blood, the commodity that endlessly circulates – and keep and reread compulsive accounts of the frenzied circulation and panic he produces amongst the English *homo economicus*. Studded with characters obsessively recording the fevers, nightmares, and illnesses that are circulated by the Count's business, *Dracula* is always in a state of suppressed or palpable hysteria. Indeed, Freud's assertion that the most inadvertent of words might bear profound subliminal psychic trauma is apparent in this text: the terrifying "Count" named Dracula whose consumption is overdetermined may be a synecdoche for the consumption and (ac)counting that dominate the lives of the English characters. Harker's comic obsession with consuming and keeping track of Transylvanian cuisine and customs, Lucy's coy pleasure in counting her suitors, and Mr. and Mrs. Harker's thinly disguised efforts to enter a higher station through their superb accounting skills end up being projected onto the foreign consumer Dracula.

Such consuming practices fulfill Henry Mayhew's nightmare about monomaniacal Victorian consumption. As Mayhew almost hysterically states, "Everything, is sacrificed" in the "struggle to live ... *merely*" as the "Mind, heart, soul," become completely "absorbed in the belly." As Mayhew worries, it seems that "our social state had a tendency to make the highest animal sink into the lowest" and "rudest" level of animal life, "a locomotive stomach."[55] The insane, Renfield, and the normal, Van Helsing's company of vampire combatants, keep excruciatingly detailed diaries of their frenzied dread of and addiction to consumption, thus quadrupling the psychic distortion so illustrative of Lucy Snowe's obsessive diary accounts of panic. *Dracula*, I suggest, then, would not be the terrifying text that it is if it did not include subliminal representations of endless economic circulation as well as actual instances of financial accounting and banking transactions occurring in heightened states of panic. Analogous to the panicked blood transfusions that temporarily revitalize the increasingly fictional personalities of their recipients, Lucy and Mina, these transactions generate a subliminal *frisson* that only the economic subject can experience.

If the money market is "all-engrossing" and unlimited, as Marx suggests, when Jonathan Harker makes the statement that he will let nothing interfere with business there is a gap in the text. What he will not acknowledge is that the panic that overtakes him completely is a result of his business with a corporate personality who threatens to merge with and then consume him. The subliminal traces of bankerization panic are provocative as banking panic becomes the modern subject's infinite subliminal, hysterical response to the monolithic success of bankerization. Through business transactions with Dracula, Harker learns to circulate circulation, to participate in "all-engrossing" consumption, and to fixate on his own panicked psychic and bodily responses to that eternal cycle of consumption and circulation. As the bankerization of Dracula occurs and the Count assumes the impersonality, subjectification, and reification of the corporate personality, Harker and the other shareholders in his corporate band (I will be coy enough to note that there are six, as legally required to have a company: Jonathan, Mina, Van Helsing, Arthur, Dr. Seward, and Quincey Morris) become increasingly intent upon keeping a record of their psycho-economic panic.

In a novel in which the Gothic is amalgamated with the economic, keeping accounts of the haunted psychic life is a subliminal reiteration of keeping financial accounts. Essentially, the structure of the novel itself is a strict accounting, and its reliance on shorthand is similar to the accounting format that Stoker recommended for clerks of petty sessions, as will be examined presently. In any case, the novel encourages keeping an (ac)count of a Count who is obsessive about keeping a count of his property (including his fifty coffins) in order to protect it from economic interlopers. As Van Helsing tells Seward, "Take then good note of it. Nothing is too small. I counsel you, put down in record even your doubts and surmises.

Hereafter it may be of interest to you to see how true your guess" (112). Obediently doing accounts, Seward is involved constantly with "posting up my books" (129). Dracula's simulacrum, Renfield, also keeps strict numerical accounts of his property. "[A]lways jotting down something," Renfield "keeps a little notebook in which" complete pages "are filled with masses of figures, generally single numbers added up in batches, and then the totals added in batches again, as though he were 'focussing' some account, as the auditors put it" (69). The most orally consumptive, anal retentive, hysterically accounting/accountable human in the novel, Renfield, is, in other words, a model and touchstone for 1890s "vitiated" economic man.

In fact, by the end of the century, bankerization accompanied an increasing psychologization of *homo economicus*. The recognition that "In economy, as in all other social phenomena, psychological facts play an important part" was in keeping with the growing need of the professions to keep painstaking accounts of every aspect of society, including mental and economic transactions.[56] It will be remembered that John Mills declared that just as the economy goes through cycles, so too does the businessman's psyche. According to Mills, progressing from youthful buoyancy and sanguinity about the economy, the businessman's mind reaches a peak with the exultation of hopes fulfilled. Then with the stagnation of capital, it moves towards the decline and death of fiscal optimism and relies on the younger generation of businessmen to begin the cycle anew.[57] In an eccentric rendition of this psychological approach, at mid-century N. C. Frederickson argues that "incessant waves" move the "sea of prices and values" and that these are created by the human mind, which is itself free-floating and wave-like. Explaining that the dynamic motions of the economy "depend largely on the mental waves in the human world," Frederickson describes the way men "move together" and "follow in the same waves of mood," often "running one after the other" like sheep.[58]

In *Economic Crises* (1900), Edward Jones continues the focus on the psychology of *homo economicus*, but, like Mills and Frederickson, illustrates the amalgamation (and increasingly impersonal corporate personality) of that previously individualized entity. Arguing that the market system forms men's minds to become focused monomaniacally on the economy, Jones suggests that "crises rest ultimately ... upon a self-interest so unduly developed as to shut out a proper regard for the social side of economic life." Jones notes that a group psyche grows out of capitalist societies, which are by definition maniacally concentrated on the economy. According to Jones, drastic population increases in major cities produce psychological miasmas that affect the economic decisions people make. Such concentrated levels of habitation force "intimate association in a sense in which no previous system ever did" and thus tend "to vitiate the economic reasoning of those who are subject to market influences." Fearing that the masses of individuals in the city become like one body making irrational economic decisions, Jones suggests, with a degree of panic, that the lifestyle choices and socio-political opinions of city dwellers become as "epidemic and contagious" as any disease. Jones also warns that this "mental contagion" cannot help but produce "feverish and fatuous social struggles for wealth."[59]

These late Victorian examples of economic group psychology may partially help to understand the Van Helsing crew and its hysterical concentration on Dracula's property and his bankerization. Ellis T. Powell's bizarre *The Evolution of The Money Market 1385–1915* includes a history of the legal concept of the "characterless" corporate personality that is, in many ways, also an eerie analogue to the amalgamated, infinite energy that Count Dracula represents to the Van Helsing company – and which they compete with when forming their own centralized group. Using the Bank of England as the template, Powell refers to the nineteenth-century *fin de siécle* financial system as becoming an "organised, coherent and centralised financial force" as it "grows . . . towards increasing complexity of structure and enhanced capacity of self-protection, self-adaptation, and self-repair." In melodramatic flourishes, Powell lauds the corporate personality, almost as though it is a supernatural, reified entity. As Powell suggests, "[t]he yearning for unbroken continuity, as a guarantee of stability" engenders these "corporations which never [die]." In addition, this Mengelean "deathless corporate organism" is "capable of accumulating and transmitting experience by means of a corporate identity" that is "the same from age to age" and that gains experience "stretching across the centuries."[60]

According to this interpretation of the anomalous corporate personality, the knowledge and experience the corporate personality obtains is in some way materially incorporated into the corporation and passed on genetically, thus further strengthening and enlarging it. Merging Gothic supernatural power with evolutionary theory, Powell argues that this "financial organism" holds power over less exuberant entities. With this intensification of power, knowledge, and energy, the Bank of England, according to Powell, is a living, conglomerate entity, a "deathless," "corporate personality" that becomes "a conscious," permanent "self." Like a science fiction monster, this organism is "ceaseless[ly]" aware not only of the economic world but, eerily, of its own awareness.[61] That this corporate personality is more potent than individuals is due to the fact that the banking conglomeration has evolved to having a "common brain" that protects its "far-flung financial interests."[62] The bank directors constitute the "brain" of this overdetermined "organism" while the workers compose the "nervous system."[63]

Powell sees the body politic as best represented by the banking industry instead of the State, and thus he has no trouble appropriating the long-established personification of the State as representative of the body politic. Banks, he assumes, are more proficient, because the bank learns increasingly how to defend itself against failure through unified and coordinated transactions. In his schema, the Bank of England's "persistent and ceaseless" awareness causes increased coordination, coherence, and continuity. Because banks are so much more intensely adapted to the economy, Powell believes that "the radical question is not what a given individual thinks his needs to be, but what an organised and competent authority, looking at the social rather than the individual aspect, assesses them at." In his judgment, because the bank has the most accurate knowledge of the client's monetary accumulations, it can best assay how to use the client's money to the best advantage. Powell glibly asserts that this centralized financial "organism," is better situated than its "biological analogue," individual human beings, because the bank "can ruthlessly destroy vestigial structures which may threaten its welfare." Those "vestigial structures" are financial institutions that cannot adapt to economic change.[64]

Powell's overdetermined view of the English banking system's corporate personality causes him to assume absolute morality in its leaders: he believes, in other words, that the men who compose the top echelons of the corporate personality feel a kind of *noblesse oblige* towards society far beyond what individuals can express, and that this makes them capable "in their fiduciary capacity, of a toil, a sacrifice, a daring, otherwise beyond achievement, and even beyond contemplation." These new Supermen, or "artist[s] in credit," replace physical aggression with the more subtle power of the psyche so that their individual personalities together, drawing from the masses of workers they employ, merge to create an entity that can perform previously unheard of economic feats.[65] It is not that Victorians had not thought of this before. James William Gilbart devotes a whole chapter to "Moral and Religious Duties" of public companies in his *A Practical Treatise on Banking* (1860). Here he notes that the relation between public companies and "Deity" is a "relation of obligation."[66] The terrifying quality of Powell's rendition of this corporate hagiography is that it is a corporate personality, thus a fictional person legally conceived of as proprietary, without a "soul," and without intent, while shielded from full liability if it defrauds its members.[67] Further, at the same time that Powell imagines the sacred benevolence of this amalgamated organism, he also optimistically contends that, "Towards a world control, therefore, the ambitions of finance already turn, sighing for fresh worlds to conquer."[68]

Let us remember that we are talking about bankers here, not vampires or vampire hunters. Nevertheless, I would argue that the breathtakingly optimistic rhetoric Powell displays regarding the corporate personality's benevolence participates in the same Gothic fear and yearning for amalgamation, incorporation, circulation, and panic that are key to the novel *Dracula*. A novel whose horror, in part, is the result of the mono-maniacal consuming practices of its eponymous protagonist, *Dracula* incorporates the reader into a mode of subliminal panic about and yearn-ing for amalgamation and centralization, paralleling those same processes occurring in the economy at the end of the nineteenth century. From the beginning of the novel, the financial is the actual ground of all meaning, for as Harker remarks, despite the frightening places he must travel to in order to do his job, "there was business to be done, and I could allow nothing to interfere with it" (13). This attitude accommodates the paradigm shift Gordon Bigelow refers to as occurring in nineteenth-century England – a transition towards the individual being constituted within an "all-engrossing" economy.[69] Within this episteme even a larger-than-life figure like Count Dracula must be seen to count and account for his drachmas, as it were.

Likewise, the glorified fight to the death between emergent and residual banking systems Powell remarks on is similar to the world-shaking struggle between the best of humans, the English, and Dracula's amalgamated corporate personality constituted by his vampire underlings. As Dracula's increasing power over England's metaphorical and literal blood supply causes increased panic amongst Van Helsing's tight-knit followers, they recognize that they must void his access to banking, money, and landed property before they can deter his access to their English bloodlines. By merging their forces, Van Helsing and company form a kind of corporate personality that acts in fiduciary power for all of England against Dracula's company (of vampires). Also like Powell's narrative about the self-sacrificing English banking brain trust that naturally considers the good of its clients, Van Helsing appeals to the increasingly centralized, coordinated brain trust of his small band of patriots, saying, "it is a terrible task that we undertake, and there may be consequence [*sic*] to make the brave shudder. For if we fail in this our fight he must surely win; and then where end we? ... to fail here, is not mere life or death. It is that we become as him; that we henceforward become foul things of the night like him" (209). In a purple patch, he admonishes them: "I have hope that our man-brains that have been of man so long and that have not lost the grace of God, will come higher than his child-brain that lie [*sic*] in his tomb for centuries, that grow [*sic*] not yet to our stature, and that do only work [*sic*] selfish and therefore small" (294).

Certainly the rhetoric in the Gothic horror story *Dracula* shares a code with Powell's economic text. Van Helsing's rhetoric about man-brains and child-brains, like Powell's about the brain of the corporate personality, combines the Gothic and the evolutionary to describe an amalgamated, increasingly powerful entity. Compare, for instance, Powell's description of the "deathless" eternal corporate personality of the modern banking system summarized above with Van Helsing's description of Dracula:

All through there are signs of his advance; not only of his power, but of his knowledge of it ... in him the brain powers survived the physical death; though it would seem that memory was not all complete. In some faculties of mind he has been, and is, only a child; but he is growing, and some things that were childish at the first are now of man's stature. He is experimenting, and doing it well; and if it had not been that we have crossed his path he would be yet – he may be yet if we fail – the father or furtherer of a new order of beings, whose road must lead through Death, not Life. (263)

Here, just as the banking system in Powell's rendition increases in its ability to repair and adapt itself to changes in economic patterns, so, too, does Dracula become more astute in his adaptation to England and his "self-repair" through accessing more sources to supply his own blood bank. In both Powell's narrative of banking and Stoker's *Dracula*, awesome sub-liminal bankerization produces a colossal corporate personality that has exponentially magnified powers.

Furthermore, like the centralized bank Powell imagines, over the centuries Dracula has expanded and concentrated his power. As Van Helsing explains, "This vampire which is amongst us is of himself so strong in person as twenty men; he is of cunning more than mortal, for his cunning be the growth of ages" (209). Van Helsing also reminds Mina that Dracula's emigration from Transylvania ("The very place, where he have [*sic*] been alive, Un-dead for all these centuries") to England represents the "work of centuries." Like the economic engine Macleod describes, Dracula is always going "at it"; with "persistence and endurance," says Van Helsing, their nemesis comes "again, and again, and again" to find "the place of all the world most of promise for him. Then he deliberately sets himself down to prepare for the task" (278, 279). Similarly, Harker worries that Dracula "carefully thought out" everything "systematically and with precision.

He seemed to have been prepared for every obstacle which might be placed by accident in the way of his intentions being carried out" (200). Like the "deathless" corporate personality of the bank whose will is a "living organism," Dracula, the Un-dead, has a growing, progressing "brain" whose powers are masterful for "all the forces of nature that are occult and deep and strong must have worked together in some wondrous way" to create him (264, 278).

How does the corporate personality of Dracula, the epitome of the monolithic banking entity Powell describes, meet his match? We might return to Clapham's statement that at the end of the century, the most significant aspect of financial London was the rising amount of money deposited by foreigners.[70] Needless to say, Dracula is a fictional rendition of one of those foreigners.[71] An invading foreign element who threatens the aristocratic bloodlines of England, Dracula is elementally disturbing as a fiscal threat – it is particularly horrifying to Harker and friends that they cannot track down all of Dracula's bank accounts and financial transactions. While his bloodline and identity are at once exhausted and artificially replenished, Dracula freely circulates at the same time that he is quite literally contained. A body fed upon miscegenation, as it were, Dracula is an amalgamation of different bloods, from the "whirlpool" of Eastern European blood to the bloodlines of all the English characters he sucks (33). One of the dangers of Mina and Lucy becoming vampires is that their ostensibly pure English blood will become just as mongrelized as the blood that streams through Dracula's veins. Thus the Englishmen must restrict Dracula's bankerization through their own consolidation of power to avoid English bankruptcy.[72]

Covering over the psychic distress it initiates, capitalism engenders in late nineteenth-century England a group mentality that eases its hysterical desire by tracking the unlimited consumption of the foreign Other and thus consolidating its own English (in)corporation with an amalgamated record of the transactions that authenticate its corporate personality and justify the destruction of competitors. And consolidate and centralize it does. Dracula's hold on Lucy Westenra in blood and body is nothing compared to Arthur's ability, with the help of his incorporated friends, of obtaining and consolidating property rights. As Mrs. Westenra's solicitor explains, "with the exception of a certain entailed property of Lucy's father's which now, in default of direct issue, went back to a distant branch of the family, the whole estate, real and personal, was left absolutely to Arthur Holmwood." If she had left her property to her daughter rather than disinheriting her, the property would have been free floating, "'For by her [Mrs. Westenra] predeceasing her daughter [Lucy] the latter would have come into possession of the property, and, even had she only survived her mother by five minutes, her property would, in case there were no will – and a will was a practical impossibility in such a case – have been treated at her decease as under intestacy'" (151). Arthur's consolidation of fiscal and landed property from his father and from Lucy ensures that English nobility and England will remain the supreme corporate personality – they will have their will and their way.

It is important to recognize that the Van Helsing group's documentation of Dracula's bankruptcy both conceals and authorizes Arthur's consolidation of his own estate with Lucy's inheritance. The group's accounting is full of compound interest, if you will, a point I focus on in ending this chapter. If legal and financial documents were Stoker's forte, he viewed that work as making his literary writing better, saying of his five years as clerk, that he agreed with Bacon that, "Writing maketh an exact man."[73] His work as the chief financial officer for the famous Victorian actor Henry Irving underwrites the subliminal banking rhetoric in *Dracula*. In this capacity, the Irish writer and clerk made sure that he was the one and only authority to whom all fiscal information was referred. As Stoker asserts, "The only possible safeguard that I know of is strict reticence at headquarters, and the formulation of such a system of accounts as makes it impossible for lesser officials to know any more than their own branch of work entails." Thus as the manager of Irving's accounts, Stoker ensured that "officials either received money for handing in to me or paid out money given to them for the purpose. None of them did both."[74] The masterful brain overseeing Irving's messy, wasteful economic practices, Stoker attempted to centralize and order the actor's accounts. Dracula takes a page from Stoker's business practices. When asking Harker questions "on legal matters and on the doing of certain kinds of business," the Count guarantees that he is the master of financial affairs by having different barristers handle each of his real estate transactions so that no one barrister will have complete knowledge of his business dealings (36).

As a prodigious clerical mind, Mina undermines Dracula by amalgamating the records on Dracula's doings. Stoker knew of what he spoke when he described Mina's collation of documents. A writer of Gothic tales and a clerical treatise, Stoker penned both *Dracula* and *The Duties of Clerks of Petty Sessions in Ireland*. The juxtaposition of the sensational Gothic thriller with the mind-numbing, technical accounting guide caused Anthony Boucher to ask, "How did the most successful horror novel in the English (and possibly in any) language come to be written by a man whose first published book was entitled *The Duties of Clerks of Petty Sessions*

in Ireland?"[75] I suggest that in both texts Stoker participates in the
centralizing practices occurring in Victorian financial and accounting
systems. In regards to his first book, as a petty clerk in Ireland's judicial
system, Stoker desired to correct the inefficiency resulting from local
control of guidelines for petty clerks. Discussing the fact that he has
centralized all the papers referring to the accounting process for such clerks,
Stoker writes that his book is a "collation of the enormous mass" of multiple
materials, including, "Statutes, General Orders, Circulars, Law Opinions,
Files of Papers, Registry Books, Returns, &c." that had been accumulating
since 1851. Wanting "to ensure, as far as possible, the most rigid accuracy in
the statements set forth," Stoker admits that his compilation includes many
"amalgamations" of the said materials as well as changes in "the original
wording." Merging advice gained from his own experience as auditor with
suggestions from the many petty clerks who wrote to him with their
suggestions for improvement of the system, Stoker wanted to create "a
certain uniformity of method" to auditing.[76]

This uniformity serves to create an organized narrative for each case that
came before the court. For example, Stoker suggests that when there are
many witnesses "the file of Information should be arranged and pinned
together in such manner as may best serve to give a connected account of
the transaction, and form a regular chain of evidence." Nevertheless, of
course, this uniformity was achieved at the expense of retaining unedited,
verbatim reports from witnesses. To counter this quibble, Stoker explains
that, "Where I have changed the original wording or effected amalgamations
I have referred to the authorities." In addition, astonishingly, the former
petty clerk asserts that one of the benefits of his amalgamations is that the
primary materials "need never be referred to again" as the clerk's amalgamated records form a narrative as admirably coherent as a novel's plot.[77]

It is now a literary given to suggest the significance of the fact that
Dracula is an amalgamation and centralization of individual accounts. But
it is important to connect Stoker's clerking guide to this observation.
Jonathan's account initiates the novel by saying, "Let me begin with facts –
bare, meagre facts, verified by books and figures, and of which there can be
no doubt" (35). Asserting the authority of his narrative, Harker explicitly
nods in the direction of verbatim reportage, but in reality, and implied in
his statement, his is a cut-and-paste narrative that ostensibly can be "verified"
by consulting the original "books and figures" it summarizes. An advocate
of acute amalgamation rather than verbatim accuracy when it came to
clerking, Stoker, as accountant and editor, suggests that piecing together
disparate facts by different authors creates an orderly, linear, chronological

outline through which a realistic narrative understanding of the court case can be ascertained. *Dracula* is the exact prototype for Stoker's ideal clerical record, for the premise of the narrative is that the story only exists because the characters are excellent not only at keeping records but at amalgamating those records to form a narrative.[78]

The final paragraphs of the novel reiterate the nation-State's reliance upon bankerization, centralization, and amalgamation. As the triumphant corporation of Mina, Jonathan, Dr. Seward, and Van Helsing admit, "We were struck with the fact, that in all the mass of material of which the record is composed, there is hardly one authentic document; nothing but a mass of type-writing ... We could hardly ask anyone, even did we wish to, to accept these as proofs of so wild a story" (326–27). So profuse with business documents, banking transactions, and clerical accountings, *Dracula* seems a text with no gaps. The novel's motto might be, "Take then good note of it. Nothing is too small" (112). Mina's faultless clerical and financial digest is a touchstone because it takes note of the smallest fragments of information and collates them with other bits to present a seemingly infallible, factual – economic – account.

Even the tiny gap or puncture wound in a neck is not too small. But that infinitesimal bloody gap that Dracula incises in the body – the tiny punctures to the neck that allow for bloodletting and circulation – engenders the novel's bankerization panic and the realization that the economic account always already immerses itself in and elides emotional and economic bankruptcy. Mina's amalgamation of documents is reminiscent of Adam Smith's directions for dealing with gaps in the economic record. It will be remembered that, asserting that the economist "should never leave any chasm or Gap in the thread of the narration," Smith commented that one way to fill the gap between cause and effect was by using literary tropes "*which often had nothing in the bringing about the series of the events.*"[79] A prodigious literary trope, Dracula, as a reified gap and a producer of gaps, perhaps subliminally counts the costs of the culture's investment in consumption. As trope Dracula highlights the nauseating multiplication of the artificial corporate personality and the "hegemony," Ellis Powell's word choice, that economically obsessed "personality" has over its shareholders and other "natural persons." Mina's collation of records just allows the English brand of the corporate personality to engage "in economic activity with not so much as a sign of the Capitalist to be seen."[80] Without a "soul," this English artificial corporation – of Arthur *et al.* – is legally, as Maitland surmises, "incapable of knowing, intending, willing, acting," at the same time being shielded from full liability if it defrauds its public.[81]

Notes

1 BANKING ON PANIC: THE HISTORICAL RECORD AND A THEORETICAL FRAME

1 Charles Dickens, *Little Dorrit* (Oxford: Clarendon Press, 1979): 384. Used by permission of Oxford University Press.

2 Walter Bagehot, "The Money Market No. III: What A Panic Is And How It Might Be Mitigated," in *The Collected Works of Walter Bagehot*, ed. Norman St. John-Stevas (London: The Economist, 1978): IX: 435. Reproduced by permission of Oxford University Press.

3 *Ibid.*, IX: 435–39; 435; Judith Halberstam, *Skin Shows: Gothic Horror and the Technology of Monsters* (Durham: Duke University Press, 1995): 102.

4 See, for example, Kurt Heinzelman, *The Economics of the Imagination* (Amherst: University of Massachusetts Press, 1980); Jean-Joseph Goux, "Banking on Signs," *Diacritics*, 18 (Summer 1988): 15–25 and "Cash, Check, or Charge?" in *The New Economic Criticism: Studies at the Intersection of Literature and Economics,* ed. Martha Woodmansee and Mark Osteen (London: Routledge, 1999): 114–27; Marc Shell, *The Economy of Literature* (Baltimore: Johns Hopkins University Press, 1978); Patrick Brantlinger, *Fictions of State: Culture and Credit in Britain, 1694–1994* (Ithaca: Cornell University Press, 1996).

5 I am indebted to both Cambridge readers of this typescript for their enormously helpful comments; the first reader's insights served to enrich this section of my discussion.

6 Linda J. Nicholson, *Gender and History: The Limits of Social Theory in the Age of the Family* (New York: Columbia University Press, 1986).

7 Mary Poovey, *Making a Social Body: British Cultural Formation 1830–1864* (Chicago: University of Chicago Press, 1995).

8 Raymond Williams, *Marxism and Literature* (Oxford: Oxford University Press, 1977); Ellis T. Powell, *The Evolution of The Money Market 1385–1915* (1915; New York: Augustus M. Kelley, 1966): 296–97.

9 Fredric Jameson, *The Political Unconscious: Narrative as a Socially Symbolic Act* (Ithaca: Cornell University Press, 1981): 40; Fredric Jameson, "Marx's Purloined Letter," in *Ghostly Demarcations: A Symposium on Jacques Derrida's "Specters of Marx"* (London: Verso, 1999): 26–67; 49.

10 Mr. Lalor quoting Gibbon Wakefield; cited in Bagehot, "Money and Morals – I," in *The Collected Works of Walter Bagehot,* IX: 276–83; 279.

11 As early as 1892, one Victorian economist argues that there is no "definite body of truths" central to the study of economics while he "insist[s] on the relativity of Economic Doctrine" and argues that there are narrow limits of place and time within which generalizations about real economic situations can be viewed as accurate (Professor W. Cunningham, "The Relativity of Economic Doctrine," *The Economic Journal,* ed. F. Y. Edgeworth [1892; London: Wm. Dawson & Sons, 1966] II: 1–16; 1, 3, 5, 9).

12 Amy Koritz and Douglas Koritz, "Symbolic Economics: Adventures in the Metaphorical Marketplace," in *The New Economic Criticism,* 408–19; 409; Martin Hollis and Edward J. Nell, *Rational Economic Man: A Philosophical Critique of Neo-Classical Economics* (Cambridge: Cambridge University Press, 1975): 85.

13 Hollis and Nell, *Rational Economic Man,* 112; see also Keith Tribe, *Land, Labour and Economic Discourse* (London: Routledge & Kegan Paul, 1978): 146–48.

14 Cited in Heinzelman, *Economics of the Imagination,* 97.

15 See Donald N. McCloskey, "Storytelling in Economics," in *Narrative in Culture: the Uses of Storytelling in the Sciences, Philosophy, and Literature,* ed. Christopher Nash (London: Routledge, 1990): 5–22; 7. Warren J. Samuels, "Introduction," in *Economics as Discourse: An Analysis of the Language of Economists,* ed. Warren J. Samuels (Boston: Kluwer Academic Publishers, 1990): 1–14; 4–5, 7. In *Manias, Panics and Crashes: A History of Financial Crises* (New York: Basic Books, 1978), Charles P. Kindleberger's whole premise is that economics, the market, investors, etc., are as irrational as they are rational.

16 Tribe, *Land, Labour and Economic Discourse,* 145, 5, 127.

17 Samuels, "Introduction," in *Economics as Discourse,* 7.

18 In "The Significance of Significance: Rhetorical Aspects of Statistical Hypothesis Testing in Economics," in *The Consequences of Economic Rhetoric,* ed. Arjo Klamer, Donald N. McCloskey, Robert M. Solow (Cambridge: Cambridge University Press, 1988): 163–83; 163, Frank T. Denton remarks that when one accepts a statistical model, she must accept the narrative implied by the data "as if they were a sample from an unseen (and unseeable) parent population or the product of an invisible generating mechanism." See also Cristina Bicchieri's "Should a Scientist Abstain from Metaphor?" in *Consequences of Economic Rhetoric,* 100–14; 107.

19 McCloskey, "Storytelling," 9; McCloskey suggests that economics is just as subject to reader-response critique as fiction because it involves authorial intentions and includes aporias requiring the reader to be part author ("Storytelling," 19, 20).

20 Adam Smith, cited in Mary Poovey, *A History of the Modern Fact: Problems of Knowledge in the Sciences of Wealth and Society* (Chicago: University of Chicago Press, 1998): 245, emphasis added.

21 A. W. Coats, "Economic Rhetoric: the Social and Historical Context," in *Consequences of Economic Rhetoric,* 64–84.

22 See *New Economic Criticism, Diacritics,* 18 (Summer 1988), and Poovey's *Modern Fact* for a good overview and example of the New Economic Criticism. Culture can be understood through New Economic Criticism, according to Koritz and Koritz in *New Economic Criticism,* 408, as "deployment of economic language to describe the circulation of cultural practices, tastes, and styles, which is supposed to refer the cultural to the economic in order to assert the impossibility of extricating the one from the other."

23 John Vernon, *Money and Fiction: Literary Realism in the Nineteenth and Early Twentieth Centuries* (Ithaca: Cornell University Press, 1984): 96; Christina Crosby, "Financial," in *A Companion to Victorian Literature & Culture,* ed. Herbert F. Tucker (Oxford: Blackwell, 1999): 225–43; 226.

24 Warren Montag, "Spirits Armed and Unarmed: Derrida's *Specters of Marx,*" in *Ghostly Demarcations,* 68–82; 79.

25 Cited in Maggie Kilgour, *The Rise of the Gothic Novel* (London: Routledge, 1995): 222.

26 Rastko Močnik, "After the Fall: Through the Fogs of the 18th Brumaire of the Eastern Springs," in *Ghostly Demarcations,* 110–33; 111.

27 Rondo Cameron, *Banking in the Early Stages of Industrialization: A Study of Comparative Economic History* (New York: Oxford University Press, 1967): 41; Goux, "Cash, Check, or Charge?," 122; on bankerization, see also Brantlinger, *Fictions of State,* Georg Simmel, *The Philosophy of Money* (1900; London: Routledge & Kegan Paul, 1978), and Walter Benn Michaels, *The Gold Standard and the Logic of Naturalism: American Literature at the Turn of the Century* (Berkeley: University of California Press, 1987).

28 Karl Marx, *Capital: A Critique of Political Economy* (Moscow: Foreign Languages Publishing House, 1959): III: 593.

29 *Ibid.,* III: 394.

30 Gordon Bigelow, "Market Indicators: Banking and Domesticity in Dickens's *Bleak House,*" *ELH,* 67 (2000): 589–615; 593.

31 Goux, "Banking on Signs," 20; Philippe Forest, "Jean-Joseph Goux – Money Signs," *Art Press,* 261 (2000): 20–25; Brantlinger, *Fictions of State.*

32 Letter to G. C. Lewis, 24 November 1857, in *The Correspondence of Lord Overstone,* ed. D. P. O'Brien (Cambridge: Cambridge University Press, 1971): II: 823.

33 Bertram W. Currie, 8 July 1887, in *British Parliamentary Papers: Second and Final Reports From the Royal Commission on the Recent Changes in the Relative Values of Precious Metals with Minutes of Evidence, Appendices and Index 1888* (Shannon, Ireland: Irish University Press, 1969): V: 47.

34 Bagehot, "The Money Market No. 1: What the Money Market Is, and Why It Is So Changeable," in *The Collected Works of Walter Bagehot,* IX: 421–26; 421.

35 Dickens, *Little Dorrit,* 384.

36 Heilbronner, "Economics as Ideology," in *Economics as Discourse,* 101–16; 107.

37 H. D. Macleod, evidence of 18 July 1887, in *British Parliamentary Papers: Second and Final Reports 1888,* V: 73.

38 George H. Pownall, "Bank Reserves," *The Economic Journal*, 9.35 (1899; London: Wm. Dawson & Sons, 1966): 394–410; 401. In this same article, Pownall notes that the clearinghouse, what Pownall calls "a masterpiece of mechanism," was where banks met to remit the checks they had received from each other's customers and exchange the cash owed on those transactions (402).

39 Bagehot, "The General Aspect of the Banking Question, No. 1," in *The Collected Works of Walter Bagehot*, IX: 318–25; 319.

40 Henry Sidgwick, *The Principles of Political Economy* (London: Macmillan, 1883): 231, 240, 241. Economics and the supernatural confront one another in Sidgwick's "A Census of Hallucinations," *The New Review*, 4 (January 1891): 52–59; 52, where Sidgwick appealed to readers for help in the research he and American philosopher and scientist William James were conducting to scientifically trace the causes of apparitions of persons dying at the very same moment that they are seen in an apparition (52, 53).

41 L. S. Presnell, "Public Monies and the Development of English Banking," *Economic History Review*, n. s. 5.3 (1953): 378–97; 380.

42 John Mills, "On Credit Cycles and the Origin of Commercial Panics, in *Transactions of the Manchester Statistical Society* (1868), in *Business Cycle Theory: Selected Texts 1860–1939*, ed. Harald Hagemann (London: Pickering & Chatto, 2002): I: 57–88; 65; Karl Marx, *Capital: A Critique of Political Economy* (Chicago: Charles H. Kerr, 1909): III: 696.

43 Poovey, *Modern Fact*, 27.

44 Thomas DiPiero, "Buying into Fiction," *Diacritics*, 18 (Summer 1988): 2–14; 7.

45 Goux, "Cash, Check, or Charge?," 115; Forest, "Jean-Joseph Goux," 20–25.

46 Bigelow, "Market Indicators," 593.

47 Alvin H. Hansen, *Business Cycles and National Income* (New York: W. W. Norton, 1951): 4.

48 The most comprehensive definition of this term, I find, is that of Stephen Resnick and Richard Wolff, who argue in "Marxian Theory and the Rhetorics of Economics," in *The Consequences of Economic Rhetoric*, 47–63; 53, 57, that the term "overdetermination" assumes that an event "is caused by innumerable influences emanating from all the other events in the social totality." In other words, "There is no essence in society from which the behaviors of all other social aspects can be derived as necessary effects. Rather, each aspect of society is understood to exist, to be constituted, as the site of the combined influences emanating from all the others."

49 Jameson, *Political Unconscious*, 40.

50 *Ibid.*, 66, 125.

51 Vernon, *Money and Fiction*, 17.

52 Jerrold E. Hogle, "Introduction: the Gothic in Western Culture," in *The Cambridge Companion to Gothic Fiction*, ed. Jerrold Hogle (Cambridge: Cambridge University Press, 2002): 1–20; 2.

53 Cited in Kilgour, *Rise of the Gothic Novel*, 220; David Punter, *Gothic Pathologies: The Text, the Body, and the Law* (Houndsmills, Basingstoke: Macmillan, 1998): 9, 14.

54 Julian Wolfreys, *Victorian Hauntings: Spectrality, Gothic, the Uncanny and Literature* (New York: Palgrave, 2002): 8.

55 Paula R. Backscheider, *Spectacular Politics: Theatrical Power and Mass Culture in Early Modern England* (Baltimore: Johns Hopkins University Press, 1993): 150.

56 Hogle, "Introduction," 3; Annette Kuhn; cited in Kelly Hurley, "British Gothic Fiction, 1885–1930," in *The Cambridge Companion to Gothic Fiction,* 189–207; 194; and see also Fred Botting, "Aftergothic: Consumption, Machines, and Black Holes," in *The Cambridge Companion to Gothic Fiction,* 277–300; 280.

57 David Punter, *The Literature of Terror: A History of Gothic Fictions from 1765 to the Present Day* (London: Longman, 1980): 1–2; see also, Kelly Hurley, "British Gothic Fiction, 1885–1930," 193.

58 Wolfreys, *Victorian Hauntings,* 9, 25, 13.

59 *Ibid.,* 9.

60 Punter, *Gothic Pathologies* 1; James R. Kincaid, "Designing Gourmet Children or, KIDS FOR DINNER!," in *Victorian Gothic: Literary and Cultural Manifestations in the Nineteenth Century,* ed. Ruth Robbins and Julian Wolfreys (Basingstoke: Palgrave, 2000): 1–11; 3.

61 Wolfreys, *Victorian Hauntings,* 13.

62 Hogle, "Introduction," 1.

63 Joseph A. Schumpeter, *Essays: On Entrepreneurs, Innovations, Business Cycles, and the Evolution of Capitalism,* ed. Richard V. Clemence (1951; New Brunswick: Transaction, 1989): 11; R. H. Mottram, *Miniature Banking Histories* (London: Chatto and Windus, 1930): 198; D. N. McCloskey, "The Industrial Revolution 1780–1860: a Survey," in *The Economic History of Britain since 1700,* ed. Roderick Floud and Donald McCloskey (Cambridge: Cambridge University Press, 1981): 1: 103–27; 104; S. G. Checkland, *The Rise of Industrial Society in England, 1815–1885* (London: Longman, 1964): 190; Kindleberger, *Manias, Panics and Crashes,* 27.

64 Albert Gallatin; cited in Hansen, *Business Cycles,* 217; and D. Morier Evans, *The History of the Commercial Crisis, 1857–58* (1859; New York: Augustus M. Kelley, 1969): 1.

65 Hansen, *Business Cycles,* 6, 4; Arthur F. Burns and Wesley C. Mitchell, *Measuring Business Cycles* (New York: National Bureau of Economic Research, 1946); cited in Hansen, *Business Cycles,* 7.

66 François Crouzet, *The Victorian Economy* (New York: Columbia University Press, 1982): 63; N. C. Fredericksen, "Periodicity of Crises, Liquidations and Expanding Periods," *The Bankers' Magazine,* 53 (January 1892): 189–98; 189.

67 John Benjamin Smith, "An Inquiry into the Causes of Money Panics, and of the Frequent Fluctuations in the Rate of Discount" (London: Simpkin, Marshall, 1866): 15.

68 Rondo Cameron, *Banking in the Early Stages of Industrialization,* 18; Peter Mathias, *The First Industrial Nation: An Economic History of Britain 1700–1914* (New York: Charles Scribner's Sons, 1969): 236; McCloskey, "The Industrial Revolution," 103–42; 103.

69 Powell, *Evolution of the Money Market,* 287; Checkland, *Rise of Industrial Society,* 36.

70 John Clapham, *An Economic History of Modern Britain: Machines and National Rivalries (1887–1914)* (Cambridge: Cambridge University Press, 1968): III: 292.

71 Malcolm Dillon, *The History and Development of Banking in Ireland From the Earliest Times to the Present Day* (London: Effingham Wilson & Co., 1889): III–12.

72 Eric Partridge's *A Dictionary of Slang and Unconventional English,* ed. Paul Beale (1961; London: Butler & Tanner, 2002): 480 notes that this slang came into practice around 1880. Of course, Christina Rossetti's "Goblin Market" perfectly fuses the supernatural and economic meanings of the term "goblin." In addition, the association of "goblin" with money is reminiscent of the supernatural depiction of Bertha in *Jane Eyre*: Brontë describes her as like a vampire, and her laughter is strangely referred to as the "goblin ha ha"; similarly, in *Wuthering Heights,* Heathcliff is referred to as a "goblin." In both cases, the text covers over the economic crisis experienced by the characters with descriptions of their abjectness as located in the supernatural.

73 Ian P. H. Duffy, *Bankruptcy and Insolvency in London During the Industrial Revolution* (New York: Garland, 1985): 168, 372, 374; Barbara Weiss, *The Hell of the English: Bankruptcy and the Victorian Novel* (Lewisburg, PA: Bucknell University Press, 1986): 179, 180.

74 *The Annual Register, or a View of the History and Politics of the Year 1852* (London: Woodfall and Kinder, 1853): 456; *The Annual Register, or a View of the History and Politics of the Year 1853* (London: Woodfall and Kinder, 1855): 408; *The Annual Register, or a View of the History and Politics of the Year 1857* (London: Woodfall and Kinder, 1858): 523; Weiss, *The Hell of the English,* 179–80; as Weiss points out in *The Hell of the English,* 177, bankruptcy statistics are not fully accurate for a number of reasons, including changes in the law and the knowledge that official statistics do not cover all the cases of bankruptcy that occurred.

75 "Financial and Commercial Embarrassments," *The Bankers' Magazine,* 45 (1885): 216–217.

76 See note 8 of this chapter.

77 Alvin H. Hansen, cited in Wesley C. Mitchell, *Business Cycles: The Problem and Its Setting* (New York: National Bureau of Economic Research, 1927): 31; Mitchell, *Business Cycles,* 61.

78 McCloskey, "Storytelling," 7; Jürg Niehans, "Juglar's Credit Cycles," in *History of Political Economy* 24.3 (1992): 545–69; 545.

79 Checkland, *Rise of Industrial Society,* 426; see the range of commentary illustrating this point in the following: A. Anderson, *The Recent Commercial Distress; or, The Panic Analysed: Showing the Cause and Cure* (London: Effingham Wilson, 1847), BL 8245.d.6; Sigma, "Money: How the Banks Make it Scarce and Dear! The Remedy! The Banks and Their Stability!" (Melbourne, R. M. Abbott, 1871), BL 8228.d.64. (3.); Hamer Stansfeld, *The Currency Act of 1844, The Cause of the Panic of October 1847, and the Generator*

of Monetary Panics Periodically (London: Effingham Wilson, Royal Exchange, 1854); Henry Sidgwick, *Principles of Political Economy* (London: Macmillan, 1901); James Robinson, *The National Distress, and its Remedy* (London: Simpkin, Marshall, & Co., 1843) BL 1391.g.33. (8.).

80 Crouzet, *The Victorian Economy*, 321; Coats, "Economic Rhetoric," 71–72.

81 Lord Overstone (Samuel Jones Loyd), *Reflections Suggested by a Perusal of Mr. J. Horsley Palmer's Pamphlet on the Causes and Consequences of the Pressure on the Money Market* (London: Pelham Richardson, 1837): 44, UL: E.837; Samuel Mountifort Longfield at about the same time made the literal circular argument, writing his trade cycle description in a circle on the page as follows: "Sudden Cessation – Paralysis – Distrust – Panic – Bankruptcies – Caution – Confidence – Liveliness – Over-Trading – Great apparent Prosperity." (Samuel Mountifort Longfield, "Banking and Currency," Part II *Dublin University Magazine*, 86 (February 1840): 218–33; 223. A cartoon featured in *The Washington Post* has a business reporter stating "Today the stock market sputtered ... dropped ominously ... plunged to new lows ... then suddenly showed signs of life ... rebounded ... recovered miraculously ... then dipped ... and ended the day unchanged from yesterday" in a modern telescoped version of Overstone's description of the cycle of trade (Schwadron, untitled cartoon, *The Washington Post National Weekly Edition*, 8–14 January 2001: 35).

82 Samuel Jones Loyd, *Remarks on the Management of the Circulation; and on the Condition and Conduct of the Bank of England and of The Country Issuers, During the year 1839* (London: Pelham Richardson, 1840): 28, 4, 5, 13, 14, 18, HM 280948.

83 Checkland, *Rise of Industrial Society*, 426.

84 Cited in Margaret Schabas, *A World Ruled by Number: William Stanley Jevons and the Rise of Mathematical Economics* (Princeton: Princeton University Press, 1990): 78.

85 William Stanley Jevons, "The Periodicity of Commercial Crises and its Physical Explanation" (1884), in *Readings in Business Cycles and National Income*, ed. Alvin H. Hansen and Richard V. Clemence (New York: W. W. Norton, 1953): 83–95.

86 Checkland, *Rise of Industrial Society*, 426.

87 John Stuart Mill, "Of the Tendency of Profits to a Minimum," in *Principles of Political Economy*, in *Readings in Business Cycles and National Income*, 74; Kyun Kim, *Equilibrium Business Cycle Theory in Historical Perspective* (Cambridge: Cambridge University Press, 1988): 21; Niehans, "Juglar's Credit Cycles," 563–64.

88 Evans, *History of the Commercial Crisis*, 11; Edward D. Jones, *Economic Crises* (New York: Macmillan, 1900): 207.

89 Mills, "On Credit Cycles," I: 57–88; 63; see also Hansen, *Business Cycles*, 267.

90 Hansen, *Business Cycles*, 220.

91 Mills, "On Credit Cycles," I: 63; see also T. S. Ashton, *Economic and Social Investigations in Manchester, 1833–1933* (London: P. S. King & Son, 1934): 78.

92 Hansen, *Business Cycles*, 218; Niehans, "Juglar's Credit Cycles," 550–51.

93 Cited in Niehans, "Juglar's Credit Cycles," 549.

94 Robert Mushet, cited in Lawrence H. White, *Free Banking in Britain: Theory, Experience, and Debate, 1800–1845* (Cambridge: Cambridge University Press, 1984): 104.

95 Felix Schuster, "The Bank of England and the State," a Lecture Delivered on 14 November 1905 (Manchester: Manchester University Press, 1906): 17; Powell, *Evolution of the Money Market*, 258.

96 Smith, "An Inquiry into the Causes of Money Panics," 7.

97 Bagehot, "Evidence Given Before the Banks of Issue Committee 22 July 1875," in *The Collected Works of Walter Bagehot*, XI: 105–55; 109, 125.

98 In 1946 the Bank of England Act legally formalized the Bank's responsibility as a central bank by nationalizing the corporation (W. T. Newlyn and R. P. Bootle, *Theory of Money* [Oxford: Clarendon Press, 1978]: 9).

99 The banking school theorists like Thomas Tooke believed that, as Lloyd Alvin Helms in *The Contributions of Lord Overstone to the Theory of Currency and Banking* (Urbana, Illinois: University of Illinois Press, 1939): 122 explains, "the circulation had no effect as an original operative cause of change in price" and thus suggested that there was no need to ensure limitations on the bank's issuance of money during times of crisis.

100 See *ibid.*, 116.

101 Michael D. Bordo, *The Gold Standard and Related Regimes: Collected Essays* (Cambridge: Cambridge University Press, 1999): 63.

102 Cited in John Clapham, *The Bank of England: a History* (Cambridge: Cambridge University Press, 1945): II: 287.

103 Jacob Viner, *Studies in the Theory of International Trade* (New York: Harper & Brothers Publishers, 1937): 218–19.

104 Cited in John P. Gassiot, *Monetary Panics and Their Remedy, with Opinions of the Highest Authorities on the Bank Charter Act* (London: Effingham Wilson, 1867): 48.

105 Charles Neville Ward-Perkins, "The Commercial Crisis of 1847," in *Oxford Economic Papers* (January 1950): 75–94, in *Readings in Business Cycles and National Income*, 1–21; 17.

106 Cited in O'Brien, *Correspondence*, II: 812.

107 Mathias, *First Industrial Nation*, 38; Crouzet, *The Victorian Economy*, 321.

108 Pownall, "Bank Reserves," *The Economic Journal*, ed. F. Y. Edgeworth and Henry Higgs, 9 (London: Macmillan, 1899): 394–410; 400; Crouzet, *The Victorian Economy*, 321.

109 Robert Ewen, "Banking Revolution," *The Westminster Review*, 150 (December 1898): 641–46; 641; see also Crouzet, *The Victorian Economy*, 331, and R. S. Sayers, "Revisions in Economic History: XIII. The Development of Central Banking after Bagehot," *Economic History Review*, n. s. 4.1 (1951): 109–16; 113.

110 Sayers, "Revisions in Economic History," 113.

111 Powell, *Evolution of The Money Market*, 247, 201.

112 Pownall, "Bank Reserves," 403.

113 Sayers, "Revisions in Economic History," 116; Cameron, *Banking in Early Stages*, 304, cited in Michael Collins, "Long-Term Growth of the English Banking Sector and Money Stock, 1844–80," *Economic History Review*, n. s. 36.3 (August 1983): 374–94; 381. This attitude was accompanied by a conceptual inability to consider using fiscal strategies to help the economy. As Frank Whitson Fetter explains, unlike the modern period, in the nineteenth century there was "no belief that by fiscal policy the economy could be stimulated" (*The Economist in Parliament* [Durham, NC: Duke University Press, 1980]: 111).

114 See Pownall, "Bank Reserves," 407; Sayers, "Revisions in Economic History," 113; T. R. R. Davison, *Bankruptcy Reform: Prefatory Remarks, and Two Letters Reprinted from "The Economist"* (London: Effingham Wilson, Royal Exchange, 1879): 9, BL 8229.cc.12. (12.); and Douglas K. Adie, "English Bank Deposits before 1844," *Economic History Review*, n. s. 23.2 (August 1970): 285–97; 289.

115 Cited in Clapham, *The Bank of England*, II: 361; 362.

116 *The Bankers' Magazine* 45 (1885): 547–48.

2 GOTHIC ECONOMIES IN BAGEHOT, MARX, AND LORD OVERSTONE

1 T. E. Gregory, *Select Statutes, Documents & Reports Relating to British Banking 1832–1928* (1929; New York: Augustus M. Kelley, 1964): I: x; Philippe Forest, "Jean-Joseph Goux – Money Signs," *Art Press*, 261 (2000): 20–25.

2 Charles P. Kindleberger, *Manias, Panics and Crashes: A History of Financial Crises* (New York: Basic Books, 1978): 27.

3 Hamer Stansfield, *The Currency Act of 1844, The Cause of the Panic of October 1847, and the Generator of Monetary Panics Periodically* (London: Effingham Wilson, Royal Exchange, 1854): 19; Sigma, "Money: How the Banks Make it Scarce and Dear! The Remedy! The Banks and Their Stability!" (Melbourne, R. M. Abbott, 1871): 13, BL 8228.d.64. (3.).

4 R. Legg, *How to Prevent Monetary Panics by Reform in Banking* (London: Effingham Wilson, n. d.): 9, UL [G. L.] E.871.

5 J. H. Macdonald, *The Errors and Evils of the Bank Charter Act of 1844* (London: Richardson Brothers, 1855): 4, 3, 11, 19, UL [G. L.] E.855.

6 Samuel Mountifort Longfield, "Banking and Currency." Part II, *Dublin University Magazine*, 86 (February 1840): 218–33; 222; see also Lawrence H. White, *Free Banking in Britain: Theory, Experience, and Debate, 1800–1845* (Cambridge: Cambridge University Press, 1984): 108–09; James Taylor, *Money Should Be The Servant of the People Not Their Master: A Letter to William Leatham, Esq.* (London: Pelham Richardson, 1842): 11, UL E. 842.

7 R. H. Mottram, *Miniature Banking Histories* (London: Chatto and Windus, 1930): 198, 202.

8 Amasa Walker, "Lord Overstone on Metallic and Paper Currency," *Merchants' Magazine* (February 1859): 2, UL [Gold] [G. L.] E.859.

9 Macdonald, *The Errors and Evils of the Bank Charter Act*, 6, 14, 9, 24–25.

10 Francis Playford, *Practical Hints for Investing Money: With an Explanation of the Mode of Transacting Business on The Stock Exchange* (London: Smith, Elder, 1855): 79–80, UL [G. L.] E.864; *The Railway Investment Guide: How to Make Money by Railway Shares; Being a Series of Hints and Advice to Parties Speculating in the Shares of British, Colonial, and Foreign Railways* (London: G. Mann, n. d.): 2, UL I1.845. (3); J. R. McCulloch letter to Lord Overstone 20 November 1857, in *The Correspondence of Lord Overstone*, ed. D. P. O'Brien (Cambridge: Cambridge University Press, 1971): II: 812.

11 E. T. Freedley, *Opportunities for Industry and the Safe Investment of Capital; or, A Thousand Chances To Make Money* (Philadelphia: J. B. Lippincott, 1859): 9–10, UL [Gold] [G. L.] 1859.

12 Overstone, letters 5 November 1863 to G. W. Norman and 24 October 1863 to G. W. Norman, in *Correspondence*, III: 1018, 1017.

13 *The Times*, 9 May 1866, cited in John Clapham, *The Bank of England: A History* (Cambridge: Cambridge University Press, 1945): II: 263.

14 Cited in Gregory, *Select Statutes*, II: 136.

15 "The Panic of 1866," *The Bankers' Magazine* (London: Waterlow & Sons, 1886): XLVI: 1013–17; 1014; *The Times*, 15 November 1890, cited in Gregory, *Select Statutes*, II: 188–89.

16 See chapter 1, note 2; Bagehot, "A General View of Lombard Street," in *The Collected Works of Walter Bagehot*, ed. Norman St. John-Stevas (London: The Economist, 1978): IX: 69–84; 73.

17 My thanks to Timothy Alborn for suggesting the Wilson/Bagehot letters to me.

18 *The Love-Letters of Walter Bagehot and Eliza Wilson, Written from 10 November, 1857 to 23 April, 1858*, ed. Mrs. Russell Barrington (London: Faber and Faber, 1933): 18.

19 *Ibid.*, 23, 26, 47.

20 *Ibid.*, 57, 65, 150, 31.

21 *Ibid.*, 46–47.

22 *Ibid.*, 80, 33, 185.

23 *Ibid.*, 102, 57,

24 *Ibid.*, 188, 102.

25 Walt W. Rostow, "Bagehot and the Trade Cycle," in *The Economist 1843–1943: A Centenary Volume* (Oxford: Oxford University Press, 1943): 156.

26 *The Love-Letters of Walter Bagehot and Eliza Wilson*, 53.

27 *Ibid.*, 196, 197, 116.

28 *Ibid.*, 108, 153, 191.

29 *Ibid.*, 200, 157, 164.

30 *Ibid.*, 152, 119, 120, 122, 203.

31 *Ibid.*, 136–37, 189, 55. Dickens's *Our Mutual Friend* also figures the happy couple Bella and Harmon realizing their erotic climax at the bank.

32 Michael Sprinker, "Introduction," in *Ghostly Demarcations: A Symposium on Jacques Derrida's "Specters of Marx"* (London: Verso, 1999): 1–4; 3.

33 Jacques Derrida, *Specters of Marx: the State of the Debt, the Work of Mourning, and the New International* (New York: Routledge, 1994): 113, 142–45.

34 *Ibid.*, 37, 45.

35 Fredric Jameson, "Marx's Purloined Letter," in *Ghostly Demarcations*, 26–67; 49.

36 Georg Lukács, *History and Class Consciousness: Studies in Marxist Dialectics* (1968; Cambridge, MA: MIT Press, 1971): 83.

37 Kurt Heinzelman, *The Economics of the Imagination* (Amherst: University of Massachusetts Press, 1980): 180.

38 Marx and Engels; cited in *ibid.*, 180.

39 Walter Benn Michaels, *The Gold Standard and the Logic of Naturalism: American Literature at the Turn of the Century* (Berkeley: University of California Press, 1987): 178.

40 Regarding chiasm in Marx, see Rastko Močnik, "After the Fall: Through the Fogs of the 18th Brumaire of the Eastern Springs," in *Ghostly Demarcations*, 110–33; 112.

41 Lukács, *History and Class Consciousness*, 181.

42 Karl Marx and Friedrich Engels, *The Communist Manifesto* (1848; Peterborough, Ont., Canada: Broadview, 2004): 67; Marx, *Capital* (Chicago: Charles H. Kerr, 1909): III: 966.

43 Marx, *Capital* (Chicago: Charles H. Kerr, 1926): I: 257.

44 Marx, *Capital* (1909): III: 948.

45 Marx, *Capital* (1926): I: 81.

46 *Ibid.*, I: 83.

47 *Ibid.*, I: 81–82.

48 Derrida, *Specters*, 151; Jameson, "Marx's Purloined Letter," 56.

49 Marx, *Capital* (1909): III: 948.

50 Marx and Engels; cited in Heinzelman, *Economics of the Imagination*, 178.

51 Heinzelman, *Economics of the Imagination*, 181.

52 Marx, *Capital* (1909): III: 460.

53 Marx, *Capital* (1926): I: 170–71.

54 Marx, *Capital* (1909): III: 298.

55 Marx, *Capital* (1926), I: 154–55; cited in Heinzelman, *Economics of the Imagination*, 177.

56 Cited in Heinzelman, *Economics of the Imagination*, 96.

57 Marx, *Capital* (1926): I: 172.

58 *The Communist Manifesto, Principles of Communism and the Communist Manifesto After 100 Years* (New York: Monthly Review, 1964): 1–62.

59 Marx, *Capital* (1909): III: 292.

60 Simon Clarke, *Marx's Theory of Crisis* (London: St. Martin's Press, 1994): 175, 280.

61 Cited in Mark Osteen, "The Treasure-House of Language: Managing Symbolic Economies in Joyce's *Portrait*," *Studies in the Novel*, 27 (Summer 1995): 154–68; 162.

62 Marx, *Capital* (1909): III: 568.

63 Henryk Grossman, *The Law of Accumulation and Breakdown of the Capitalist System: Being Also a Theory of Crises* (London: Pluto Press, 1990): 181.

64 Marx, *Capital* (1909): III: 660, 653.

65 *Ibid.*, III: 658, 662–63.

66 *Ibid.*, III: 495–96, 499–500. Overstone's calm attitude towards banking panic was surely influenced by his own monetary situation. In "Summary of My Personal Property for the Guidance of My Executors, March 1881" Overstone's list of his property includes "320,000 in new 3 per cents; 300,000 in consols; and railway securities Lancaster and York and Debenton [?] stock 70,000; North Eastern 60,000; North Western, 40,000; Great Northern, 30,000; South Western, 40,000; Great Western, 20,000; Midlands, 30,000; Great Northern other stocks, 40,000 and 26,337" (UL MS 804/2171/4).

67 Marx, *Capital* (New York: Vintage, 1981): III: 689, 563.

68 *The Times*, cited in *Correspondence*, I: 45.

69 Overstone, letter to Henry Brookes; cited in *Correspondence*, I: 64; Overstone, *Reflections Suggested by a Perusal of Mr. J. Horsley Palmer's Pamphlet on the Causes and Consequences of the Pressure on the Money Market* (London: Pelham Richardson, 1837): 44, UL E.837.

70 Overstone, *Remarks on the Management of the Circulation; and on the Condition and Conduct of the Bank of England and of the Country Issuers, During the Year 1839* (London: Pelham Richardson, 1840): 104, HM 280948.

71 Overstone, *Correspondence Between The Right Hon. Lord Overstone and Henry Brookes, Esq.*, rpt from the special supplements of the *Money Market Review* (London: Effingham Wilson, Royal Exchange, 1862): 8–9, UL [Gold] [G.L.] E. 862.

72 *Ibid.*, 15, 21, 22.

73 *Ibid.*, 23, 33.

74 *Ibid.*, 34–35.

75 Walter Besant, "Literature as a Career," in *Essays and Historiettes* (London: Chatto & Windus, 1903): 308–36; 315.

76 Friedrich Nietzsche, *The Will to Power*, in *The Complete Works of Friedrich Nietzsche*, ed. Oscar Levy (New York: Russell & Russell, 1964): 15 (anecdotes 814, 887, 888, 889, on pp. 321–25).

77 Charlotte Brontë (CB), letter to Ellen Nussey, 23 January 1846, in *The Letters of Charlotte Brontë*, ed. Margaret Smith (Oxford: Clarendon Press, 1995): I: 444.

78 CB, letter to Ellen Nussey, 14 April [1846], in *ibid.*, I: 463.

79 CB, letter to Ellen Nussey [13 December 1846], in *ibid.*, I: 507.

80 In *The Letters of Robert Louis Stevenson July 1884–August 1887*, ed. Bradford A. Booth and Ernest Mehew (New Haven: Yale University Press, 1995): V: 171.

81 Bram Stoker, *Personal Reminiscences of Henry Irving* (New York: Macmillan, 1906): II: 312.

82 Barbara Belford, *Bram Stoker: A Biography of the Author of Dracula* (New York: Alfred A. Knopf, 1996): 269n, 77.

83 Charles Dickens and W. H. Wills, "A Review of a Popular Publication," *Household Words*, 1 (27 July 1850): 426–31; 426.

84 Charles Dickens and W. H. Wills, "The Old Lady in Threadneedle Street," *Household Words*, 1 (6 July 1850): 337–42; 339.

85 Cited in Jean-Joseph Goux, *The Coiners of Language* (Norman: University of Oklahoma Press, 1994): 94.
86 *Ibid.*
87 Mark Osteen, "The Treasure-House of Language: Managing Symbolic Economies in Joyce's *Portrait*," *Studies in the Novel*, 27 (Summer 1995): 154–68; 162.
88 *Ibid.*

3 THE GHOST AND THE ACCOUNTANT: INVESTING IN PANIC IN
VILLETTE

1 Arthur D. Gayer, W. W. Rostow, and Anna Jacobson Schwartz, *The Growth and Fluctuation of the British Economy 1790–1850, An Historical, Statistical, and Theoretical Study of Britain's Economic Development* (1953; New York: Barnes & Noble, 1975): I: 304–06; S. G. Checkland, *The Rise of Industrial Society in England, 1815–1885* (London: Longman, 1964): 17.
2 Gayer, Rostow, Schwartz, *Growth and Fluctuation*, 304–06; Charles Neville Ward-Perkins, "The Commercial Crisis of 1847," in *Oxford Economic Papers*, 75–94, in *Readings in Business Cycles and National Income*, ed. Alvin H. Hansen and Richard V. Clemence (New York: W. W. Norton, 1953): 1–20; 3; John P. Gassiot, *Monetary Panics and Their Remedy, With Opinions of the Highest Authorities on the Bank Charter Act* (London: Effingham Wilson, 1867): 17.
3 Gassiot, *Monetary Panics and Their Remedy*, 5, 17; Ward-Perkins, "The Commercial Crisis of 1847," 12. "Report from the Secret Committee of the House of Lords on the Commercial Distress" (28 July 1848); cited in T. E. Gregory, *Select Statutes, Documents & Reports Relating to British Banking 1832–1928* (1929; New York: Augustus M. Kelley, 1964): II: 39, 40.
4 D. P. O'Brien, "Monetary Base Control and the Bank Charter Act of 1844," *History of Political Economy*, 29.4 (1998): 593–633; 626; Checkland, *Rise of Industrial Society in England*, 36, 37; Gayer, Rostow, Schwartz, *Growth and Fluctuation*, 305.
5 Cited in John Clapham, *The Bank of England: A History* (Cambridge: Cambridge University Press, 1945): II: 205.
6 Ward-Perkins, "The Commercial Crisis of 1847," 5; Alexander Matheson, letter to Donal Matheson, Jardine–Matheson MSS; cited in *ibid.*, II: 207.
7 Clapham, *Bank of England*, II: 207.
8 A. Andréadès, *History of the Bank of England 1640 to 1903* (1909; New York: Augustus M. Kelley, 1966): 336–37.
9 Cited in Gregory, *Select Statutes*, II: 34; "Report From the Secret Committee of the House of Lords"; cited in Gregory, *Select Statutes*, II: 39, 40.
10 C. P. Hill, *British Economic and Social History 1700–1939* (London: Edward Arnold, 1961): 170.
11 *Ibid.*, 169, 170; Checkland, *Rise of Industrial Society*, 38.

12 William John Lawson, *The History of Banking* (Boston: Gould and Lincoln, 1852): 249.

13 Alison Milbank, "The Victorian Gothic in English Novels and Stories, 1830–1880," in *The Cambridge Companion to Gothic Fiction*, ed. Jerrold E. Hogle (Cambridge: Cambridge University Press, 2002): 145–66; 155.

14 *The Annual Register, or a View of the History and Politics of the Year 1852* (London: Woodfall and Kinder, 1853): 456.

15 Nicholas A. H. Stacey, *English Accountancy: A Study in Social and Economic History, 1800–1954* (London: Gee, 1954): 13, 19, 36, 18.

16 From archivist Jesse Campbell, Barclay's Bank: jessecampbell@barclays.co.uk, Friday, 6 June 2003, 16:09:37.

17 *A Banker's Daughter* (London: Macmillan, 1864). Edited and encoded by Perry Willett for Library Electronic Text Resource Service (Bloomington: Indiana University, 1997). I want to express appreciation to Sally Mitchell for generously sharing this document with the Victoria website.

18 Charlotte Brontë (CB), letter to William Smith Williams, 3 April 1852, HM 24401. This item and all subsequent items labeled HM are reproduced by permission of The Huntington Library, San Marino, California.

19 CB, letter to Ellen Nussey, 2 April 1845, HM 24437.

20 CB, letter to Ellen Nussey, 24 April 1845, in *The Letters of Charlotte Brontë*, ed. Margaret Smith (Oxford: Clarendon Press, 1995) I: 391; CB, letter to Ellen Nussey, 14 November 1844, in *ibid.*, I: 373.

21 CB, letter to Ellen Nussey, 9 August 1846, in *ibid.*, I: 491.

22 CB, letter to Ellen Nussey, 18 June 1845, HM 24440.

23 CB, letter to Ellen Nussey, 26 February 1848, in *The Letters of Charlotte Brontë*, II: 34.

24 See also George Drummond Charles, *The Theory of Money in Connection with Some of the Prominent Doctrines of Political Economy* (Edinburgh: William P. Nimmo, 1868) for detailed discussion of the ledger recording.

25 Charlotte Brontë, *Villette*, ed. Mark Lilly (1853; Harmondsworth: Penguin, 1986): 94–95. All further citations will be to this edition and will be noted in the text. Studies of the supernatural or Gothic aspects of the story include: Toni Wein, "Gothic Desire in Charlotte Brontë's *Villette*," *SEL: Studies in English Literature 1500–1900*, 39 (Autumn 1999): 733–46; Christina Crosby, "Charlotte Brontë's Haunted Text," *SEL: Studies in English Literature 1500–1900*, 24 (1984): 701–15; E. D. H. Johnson, "'Daring the Dread Glance': Charlotte Brontë's Treatment of the Supernatural in *Villette*," *Nineteenth-Century Fiction*, 20 (1965–66): 325–36; Mary Jacobus, "The Buried Letter: *Villette*," in *Reading Woman: Essays in Feminist Criticism* (New York: Columbia University Press, 1986): 41–61; Sandra Gilbert and Susan Gubar's "The Buried Life of Lucy Snowe," in *Madwoman in the Attic: The Woman Writer and Nineteenth-Century Literary Imagination* (1979; New Haven: Yale University Press, 1984): 399–440; Sally Minogue, "Gender and Class in *Villette* and *North and South*," in *Problems for Feminist Criticism*

(London: Routledge, 1990): 70–108; Robert Heilman, "Charlotte Brontë's 'New' Gothic," in *The Brontës*, ed. I. Gregor (Englewood Cliffs, NJ: Prentice Hall, 1970).

26 Margit Stange, *Personal Property: Wives, White Slaves, and the Market in Women* (Baltimore: Johns Hopkins University Press, 1998): 7.

27 Jan Cohn, *Romance and the Erotics of Property: Mass-Market Fiction for Women* (Durham, NC: Duke University Press, 1988): 131.

28 James Robinson, *The National Distress, and its Remedy* (London: Simpkin, Marshall, 1843): 6, 7, 8, UL [Gold] [G. L.] B.844.

29 CB, letter to Margaret Wooler, 23 April 1845, in *The Letters of Charlotte Brontë*, I: 389–90.

30 CB, letter to Margaret Wooler, 30 January 1846, in *ibid.*, I: 447–49.

31 CB, letter to Eliza Kingston, 3? March 1846, in *ibid.*, I: 456–57.

32 CB, letter to Eliza Kingston, 8 May 1846, in *ibid.*, I: 472.

33 CB, letter to Margaret Wooler, 23 April 1845, in *ibid.*, I: 389–90; 390.

34 CB, letter to George Smith, 4 October 1849; cited in Juliet Barker, *The Brontës* (New York: St. Martin's Press, 1994): 617.

35 "Investments for Women," *Beeton's Guide to Investing Money with Safety & Profit* (London: Ward, Lock & Tyler, n. d.): 53–54.

36 CB, letter to Margaret Wooler, 23 April 1845, in *The Letters of Charlotte Brontë*, I: 389–90; 390; Michael Freeman, *Railways and the Victorian Imagination* (New Haven: Yale University Press, 1999): 100.

37 Paddy Ireland, "Capitalism Without the Capitalist: The Joint Stock Company Share and the Emergence of the Modern Doctrine of Separate Corporate Personality," *Legal History*, 17 (April 1996): 41–73; 66.

38 *The Railway Investment Guide: How to Make Money by Railway Shares; Being a Series of Hints and Advice to Parties Speculating in the Shares of British, Colonial, and Foreign Railways* (London: G. Mann, n. d.): 2, 4, UL I1.845. (3).

39 Hyde Clarke, *Theory of Investment in Railway Companies* (London: John Weale, 1846): 17, 9, UL 34780.5.

40 Mary Poovey, *A History of the Modern Fact: Problems of Knowledge in the Sciences of Wealth and Society* (Chicago: University of Chicago Press, 1998): 36.

41 *A Banker's Daughter.*

42 Patrick Brontë's account book. Brontë Parsonage Library.

43 *Ibid.*

44 *Ibid.*

45 Charlotte Brontë's account book, Brontë Parsonage Library.

46 *A Banker's Daughter.*

47 Fredric Jameson, "Marx's Purloined Letter," in *Ghostly Demarcations: A Symposium on Jacques Derrida's "Specters of Marx"* (London: Verso, 1999): 26–67; 49; Fredric Jameson, *The Political Unconscious: Narrative as a Socially Symbolic Act* (Ithaca: Cornell University Press, 1981): 228.

48 Linda J. Nicholson, *Gender and History: The Limits of Social Theory in the Age of the Family* (New York: Columbia University Press, 1986). See also Ann

L. Jennings, "Public or Private? Institutional Economics and Feminism," in *Beyond Economic Man: Feminist Theory and Economics*, ed. Marianne A. Ferber and Julie A. Nelson (Chicago: University of Chicago Press, 1993): 111–29.

49 Alison Milbank, "The Victorian Gothic in English Novels and Stories, 1830–1880," in *The Cambridge Companion to Gothic Fiction*, ed. Jerrold E. Hogle (Cambridge: Cambridge University Press, 2002): 145–65; 152.

50 Jennings, "Public or Private?," 125; Nancy Folbre and Heidi Hartmann, "The Rhetoric of Self-Interest: The Ideology of Gender in Economic Theory," in *The Consequences of Economic Rhetoric*, ed. Arlo Klamer, Donald N. McCloskey, and Robert M. Solow (Cambridge: Cambridge University Press, 1988): 184–206; 197.

51 Terry Eagleton, "Villette," in *Myths of Power: A Marxist Study of the Brontës* (London: Macmillan, 1975): 61–73; 64.

52 CB, letter to Ellen Nussey, 19 January 1853, in *The Letters of Charlotte Brontë* III: 108.

53 David Punter, *Gothic Pathologies: The Text, the Body and the Law* (Houndsmills, Basingstoke: Macmillan, 1998): 129.

54 See Göran Therborn, *The Ideology of Power and the Power of Ideology* (London: Verso, 1980): 18.

55 John Kucich, *Repression in Victorian Fiction: Charlotte Brontë, George Eliot, Charles Dickens* (Berkeley: University of California Press, 1987): 78–113.

4 "THE WHOLE DUTY OF MAN": CIRCULATING CIRCULATION IN
DICKENS'S *LITTLE DORRIT*

1 Georg Simmel, *The Philosophy of Money*, trans. Tom Bottomore and David Frisby (1900; 2nd enlarged ed., London: Routledge, 1990): 510. Reproduced by permission of Routledge/Taylor & Francis Books, Inc.

2 Charles Dickens, *Little Dorrit*, ed. Harvey Peter Sucksmith (Oxford: Clarendon Press, 1979): 384. Further citations will refer to this edition and will be noted in the text. Reproduced by permission of Oxford University Press.

3 C. P. Hill, *British Economic and Social History 1700–1939* (1957; London: Edward Arnold, 1985): 104.

4 Charles P. Kindleberger, *Manias, Panics and Crashes: A History of Financial Crises* (New York: Basic Books, 1978): 60.

5 S. G. Checkland, *The Rise of Industrial Society in England, 1815–1885* (London: Longman, 1964): 39–40.

6 D. Morier Evans, *The History of the Commercial Crisis, 1857–1858, and the Stock Exchange Panic of 1859* (1859; New York: Burt Franklin, 1969): 13.

7 *The Annual Register, or a view of the History and Politics of the Year 1857* (London: Woodfall and Kinder, 1858): 218, 219.

8 *Ibid.*, 217; John Clapham, *The Bank of England: A History* (Cambridge: Cambridge University Press, 1945): II: 226.

9 *Annual Register* 1857, 219.

10 Henry Warren, *The Story of the Bank of England* (London: Jordan & Sons, 1903): 185.

11 *Annual Register* 1857, 220.

12 G. W. Norman, letter to Overstone, 9 November 1857, in *The Correspondence of Lord Overstone*, ed. D. P. O'Brien (Cambridge: Cambridge University Press, 1971): II: 776–77; 776.

13 Letter to Overstone, 20 November 1857, in *ibid.*, II: 813–16; 815.

14 Letter to Overstone, in *ibid.*, II: 812.

15 Evans, *History of the Commercial Crisis*, 11.

16 Edmund Saul Dixon, "Banking," *Household Words*, 13 (17 May 1856): 427–32; 430.

17 *Ibid.*, 429.

18 Henry Dunning Macleod, *Theory and Practice of Banking: with the Elementary Principles of Currency; Prices; Credit; and Exchanges* (London: Longman, Brown, Green & Longmans, 1855): II: xlvii; I: 51–52.

19 *Ibid.*, I: 51–52; II: 408.

20 Robert Ewen, "British Progress and Free Banking," *The Westminster Review*, 148 (October 1897): 389–95; 392.

21 Macleod, *Theory and Practice*, II: 52.

22 Mary Poovey, *A History of the Modern Fact: Problems of Knowledge in the Sciences of Wealth and Society* (Chicago: University of Chicago Press, 1998): 275.

23 M. Neil Browne and J. Kevin Quinn, "Dominant Economic Metaphors and the Postmodern Subversion of the Subject," in *The New Economic Criticism: Studies at the Intersection of Literature and Economics*, ed. Martha Woodmansee and Mark Osteen (London: Routledge, 1999): 131–49; 135.

24 Philip Mirowski and Pamela Cook, "Walras' 'Economics and Mechanics': Translation, Commentary, Context," in *Economics as Discourse: An Analysis of the Language of Economists*, ed. Warren J. Samuels (Boston: Kluwer Academic Publishers, 1990): 189–224; 191.

25 Philip Mirowski, "Physics and the Marginalist Revolution," *Cambridge Journal of Economics*, 8 (December 1984): 361–79; 366.

26 Mirowski and Cook, "Walras' 'Economics and Mechanics,'"193.

27 Philip Mirowski and Pamela Cook, "Shall I Compare Thee to a Mirowski–Ricardo–Leontief–Metzler Matrix of the Mosak-Hicks Type?," in *The Consequences of Economic Rhetoric*, ed. Arjo Klamer, Donald N. McCloskey, Robert M. Solow (Cambridge: Cambridge University Press, 1988): 117–45; 133. See also *The Second Law of Thermodynamics: Memoirs by Carnot, Clausius and Thomson*, ed. W. F. Magie (New York: Harper & Brothers, 1899).

28 J. H. Macdonald, *The Errors and Evils of the Bank Charter Act of 1844* (London: Richardson Brothers, 1855): 8, UL [G. L.] E.855).

29 Mirowski, "Physics and the Marginalist Revolution," 370.

30 Friedrich Engels, "The Principles of Communism," in *The Communist Manifesto, Principles of Communism, The Communist Manifesto After 100 Years* (New York: Monthly Review): I: 72, 73.

31 The following include some of the myriad Victorian descriptions of economics as machine: "Social Aspect of Banking," *The Bankers' Magazine* (London: Waterlow & Sons, 1886), 46: 102–03; Henry Warren, *The Story of the Bank of England* (London: Jordan & Sons, 1903): 201–02; Mikhail I. Tugan-Baranovsky, "The Causes of Crises in the Capitalist Economies," in *Studies in the Theory and History of Commercial Crises in England*, in *Business Cycle Theory: Selected Texts 1860–1939*, ed. Harald Hagemann (London: Pickering & Chatto, 2002): III: 42–43.

32 See his letter to Emile de la Rue, 25 November 1853 (*The Pilgrim Edition, The Letters of Charles Dickens 1853–1855*, ed. Graham Storey, Kathleen Tillotson, Angus Easson [Oxford: Clarendon Press, 1993]: VII: 207).

33 See the following letters: 5 October 1852 to W. H. Wills (HM 18098 Dickens Papers. This item and all subsequent items labeled HM are reproduced by permission of The Huntington Library, San Marino, California.); 7 October 1852 to Wills (HM 18100); 12 July 1855 to Wills (HM 18184); 26 December 1855 to Wills (HM 18204); 26 September 1857 to Wills (HM 18249); 20 December 1841 to Messrs. Coutts and Co. (*The Pilgrim Edition, The Letters of Charles Dickens*, VII: 837).

34 See letter to W. H. Wills, 23 August 1854, in *ibid.*, VII: 404.

35 See Dickens's letter to his wife on 19 July 1854, *ibid.*, VII: 372.

36 The following letters include fiscal concerns Dickens refers to during the time of writing *Little Dorrit*: letter to Wills 10 June 1855 (HM 18181); letter to Wills 12 June 1855 (HM 18182).

37 Cited in Christina Crosby, "'A Taste for More': Trollope's Addictive Realism," in *New Economic Criticism*, 293–306; 299.

38 Raymond Williams, *The Long Revolution*, cited in Crosby, "'A Taste for More,'" 302.

39 *Ibid.*, 294.

40 *The Pilgrim Edition, The Letters of Charles Dickens*, VII: 192.

41 *The Pilgrim Edition, The Letters of Charles Dickens 1855–1857*, ed. Graham Storey and Kathleen Tillotson (Oxford: Clarendon Press, 1995): VIII: 17.

42 *Ibid.*, VIII: 145.

43 *The Pilgrim Edition, The Letters of Charles Dickens*, VII: 609.

44 *Ibid.*, VII: 626–27.

45 *Ibid.*, VII: 629.

46 *Ibid.*, VIII: 61.

47 *Ibid.*, VII: 714–15.

48 Edward D. Jones, *Economic Crises* (New York: Macmillan, 1900): 25.

49 Simmel, *The Philosophy of Money*, 175; Jean-Joseph Goux, *Symbolic Economies After Marx and Freud* (Ithaca: Cornell University Press, 1990): 48.

50 John Guillory, *Cultural Capital: The Problem of Literary Canon Formation* (Chicago: University of Chicago Press, 1993): 282.

51 Crosby, "'A Taste for More,'" 294.

52 Jacques Derrida, *Specters of Marx: the State of the Debt, the Work of Mourning, and the New International* (New York: Routledge, 1994): 10, 144, 145, 146.

53 Georg Lukács, *History and Class Consciousness: Studies in Marxist Dialectics* (Cambridge, MA: MIT Press, 1971): 83.

54 Alison Milbank, "The Victorian Gothic in English Novels and Stories, 1830–1880," in *The Cambridge Companion to Gothic Fiction*, ed. Jerrold E. Hogle (Cambridge: Cambridge University Press, 2002): 145–65; 159.

55 Dixon, "Banking," 432.

56 W. Haig Miller writes in *On the Bank's Threshold; or, The Young Banker* (London: S. W. Partridge, 1890): 70, UL E.890: "A banker promotes his deposits, to a certain extent, by having a good building in a leading part of his town … As a rule, the current of public opinion now sets in favour of banks that have commodious premises and architectural embellishment."

5 "BANKRUPTCY AT MY HEELS": DR. JEKYLL, MR. HYDE, AND THE
BANKERIZATION OF IDENTITY

1 *The Letters of Robert Louis Stevenson, July 1884–August 1887*, ed. Bradford A. Booth and Ernest Mehew (New Haven: Yale University Press, 1995): V: 412, 128, 152, 135.

2 François Crouzet, *The Victorian Economy* (New York: Columbia University Press, 1982): 65.

3 See A. E. Musson, "The Great Depression in Britain, 1873–1896: A Reappraisal," *Journal of Economic History*, 19 (June 1959): 199–228; 200; S. G. Checkland, *The Rise of Industrial Society in England 1815–1885* (London: Longman, 1964): 52, 53; C. P. Hill, *British Economic and Social History 1700–1939* (1957; London: Edward Arnold, 1985): 100–01.

4 Hill, *British Economic and Social History*, 113; Checkland, *Rise of Industrial Society*, 53.

5 Henry Warren, *The Story of the Bank of England* (London: Jordan & Sons, 1903): 187–97.

6 Dieter Ziegler, "The Banking Crisis of 1878: Some Remarks," *Economic History Review*, n. s. 45 (February 1992): 137–44; 138.

7 Michael Collins, "The Banking Crisis of 1878," *Economic History Review*, n. s. 42 (November 1989): 504–27; 506.

8 Warren, *Story of the Bank*, 205.

9 J. C. Fieldes in *British Parliamentary Papers: Second and Final Reports From the Royal Commission on the Recent Changes in the Relative Values of Precious Metals with Minutes of Evidence, Appendices and Index 1888* (Shannon, Ireland: Irish University Press, 1969): V: 131.

10 Checkland, *Rise of Industrial Society*, 54.

11 Bertram W. Currie, evidence to Parliament, 8 July 1887, in *British Parliamentary Papers*, V: 47.

12 H. D. Macleod, evidence to Parliament, 18 July 1887, in *ibid.*, V: 73; 233–34.

13 Ellis T. Powell, *The Evolution of The Money Market 1385–1915* (1915; New York: Augustus M. Kelley, 1966): 319.

14 Checkland, *Rise of Industrial Society*, 192.

15 Walter Bagehot, "The Money Market No. I: What the Money Market Is, and Why It Is So Changeable," *The Economist*, 22 (3 September 1864), in *The Collected Works of Walter Bagehot*, ed. Norman St. John-Stevas (London: The Economist, 1978): IX: 421–26; 421.

16 Powell, *Evolution of the Money Market*, 521.

17 HM 2490. This item is reproduced by permission of The Huntington Library, San Marino, California.

18 R. L. Stevenson, "A Chapter on Dreams," *Scribner's Magazine*, 3 (January–June 1888): 122–28; 124, 127. See also Richard Dury's "Introduction" to *The Strange Case of Dr. Jekyll and Mr. Hyde*, ed. Dury (Edinburgh: Edinburgh University Press, 2004).

19 Stevenson, "A Chapter on Dreams," 127.

20 Jenni Calder, "Introduction," in Robert Louis Stevenson, *The Strange Case of Dr. Jekyll and Mr. Hyde and Other Stories*, ed. Jenni Calder (London: Penguin, 1979): 7–23; 7. Further citations from the text of *Dr. Jekyll and Mr. Hyde* will be to this edition and will be noted in the text.

21 Malcolm Elwin, *The Strange Case of Robert Louis Stevenson* (London: Macdonald, 1950), 76; cited in Frank McLynn, *Robert Louis Stevenson: A Biography* (New York: Random House, 1993): 78–79. Stevenson's (RLS) letters during the time of writing *Dr. Jekyll and Mr. Hyde* that indicate his financial lapses include the following: to Charles Baxter, 18 March 1885 (*Letters Stevenson*, V: 93); to his wife, March 1885 (*ibid.*, V: 96); to William Archer, 28 October 1885 (*ibid.*, V: 141) to his parents, late July 1886 (*ibid.*, V: 297); to Messrs. Charles Scribner's Sons, 12 February 1886 [1887] (*ibid.*, V: 357). Even after the publication of *Dr. Jekyll and Mr. Hyde*, Stevenson's bank account went into arrears: for example, in May/June 1886 in his account book he shows £361.6.7 of debit and only £347.1 income (RLS Bank Book, Wilts & Dorset Banking Co., Ltd., Bournemouth Bank Book, Beinecke Library, no. 7375).

22 Sigmund Freud, "The Psychology of the Dream Processes," in *The Standard Edition of the Complete Psychological Works of Sigmund Freud*, ed. James Strachey (London: Hogarth Press, 1953): V: 509–621; 561.

23 See Alexander Welsh's critique of Freud in *Freud's Wishful Dream Book* (Princeton: Princeton University Press, 1994).

24 William Veeder, "Children of the Night: Stevenson and Patriarchy," in *Dr. Jekyll and Mr. Hyde after One Hundred Years*, ed. William Veeder and Gordon Hirsch (Chicago: University of Chicago Press, 1988), 107–60, and Alan Sandison, *Robert Louis Stevenson and the Appearance of Modernism* (Houndsmills, Basingstoke: Macmillan, 1996): 242, 244, 264 also see Hyde as Lanyon and Utterson's alter ego.

25 Philippe Forest, "Jean-Joseph Goux – Money Signs," *Art Press*, 261 (2000): 20–25.

26 Jean-Joseph Goux, "Banking on Signs," *Diacritics*, 18 (Summer 1988): 15–25.

27 Forest, "Jean-Joseph Goux – Money Signs," 20–25.

28 Edmund Saul Dixon, "Banking," *Household Words*, 13 (17 May 1856): 427–32; 432.

29 Walter Bagehot; cited in David Cannadine, "Aristocratic Indebtedness in the Nineteenth Century: The Case Re-Opened," *The Economic History Review*, n.s. 30 (November 1977): 624–50; 635–36.

30 Macleod, evidence to Parliament, 18 July 1887, in *Parliamentary Papers*, V: 72–82, Appendix 3, 226–49.

31 Bagehot, *Evidence Before the Select Committee*, 22 July 1875, in *The Collected Works of Walter Bagehot*, XI: 105–55; 107.

32 J. W. Gilbart, *The Elements of Banking; with Ten Minutes Advice About Keeping a Banker* (London: Longman, Brown, Green, and Longmans, 1854): 10, UL E. 854.3.10.

33 Dixon, "Banking," 430.

34 Henry Sidgwick, *The Principles of Political Economy* (London: Macmillan, 1883): 239.

35 Cited in Elaine Showalter, "Dr. Jekyll's Closet," in *The Haunted Mind: The Supernatural in Victorian Literature*, ed. Elton E. Smith and Robert Haas (Lanham, MD: Scarecrow Press, 1999): 67–88; 71; see also Sandison, *Robert Louis Stevenson*, and Veeder, *Dr. Jekyll*.

36 Bagehot, "General View of Lombard"; cited in *The Collected Works of Walter Bagehot*, IX: 78.

37 Cited in T. E. Gregory, *Select Statutes: Documents and Reports Relating to Banking 1832–1928* (1929; New York: Augustus M. Kelley, 1964), I: 39.

38 Sanuel Jones Loyd (Lord Overstone), *Remarks on the Management of the Circulation; and on the Condition and Conduct of the Bank of England and of The Country Issuers, During the Year 1839* (London: Pelham Richardson, 1840): 25, HM 280948.

39 Gordon Bigelow, "Market Indicators: Banking and Domesticity in Dickens's *Bleak House*," *ELH*, 67 (2000): 589–615.

40 Ann L. Jennings, "Public or Private? Institutional Economics and Feminism," in *Beyond Economic Man: Feminist Theory and Economics*, ed. Marianne A. Ferber and Julie A. Nelson (Chicago: University of Chicago Press, 1993): 111–29; 120.

41 *Ibid.*, 121.

42 *Ibid.*, 124.

43 Rondo Cameron, *Banking in the Early Stages of Industrialization: A Study in Comparative Economic History* (New York: Oxford University Press, 1967): 7.

44 Used by banks to call in transactions made upon them by other banking facilities, the Victorian clearinghouse had the authority to clear and return checks to the bank of origin. The Bank of England was viewed as the world's clearinghouse.

45 H. D. Macleod, *The History of Economics* (London: Bliss, Sands, 1896): 203.

46 Cited in *ibid.*, 218.

47 Allen Hoey, "The Name on the Coin: Metaphor, Metonymy, and Money," *Diacritics*, 18.2 (Summer 1988): 26–37; 30.

48 *Ibid.*, 30; Karl Marx, *Capital: A Critique of Political Economy* (Chicago: Charles H. Kerr, 1926): I: 128–62; see also Robbie B. H. Goh's "Stevenson's Financial Gothic: Money, Commerce, Language, and the Horror of Modernity in 'The Isle of Voices'," forthcoming in *Gothic Studies*.

49 RLS enjoyed playing with this formula; in a letter to Sidney Colvin September/October 1885, he writes about his book, "they call it Doctor Jekyll, but they also call it Mr. Hyde, Mr. Hyde, but they also, also call it Mr. Hyde" (*The Letters*, V: 128).

50 Cited in Hoey, "The Name on the Coin," 35.

51 Letter to Andrew Lang, December 1885, *Letters*, V : 158.

6 BANKERIZATION PANIC AND THE CORPORATE PERSONALITY IN *DRACULA*

1 C. P. Hill, *British Economic and Social History 1700–1939* (London: Edward Arnold, 1961): 189, 193; Peter Mathias, *The First Industrial Nation: An Economic History of Britain 1700–1914* (London: Methuen, 1969): 272, 287.

2 Charles Woolley, *Phases of Panic: A Brief Historical Review* (London: Henry Good, 1896): 54.

3 S. G. Checkland, *The Rise of Industrial Society in England 1815–1885* (New York: St. Martin's Press, 1964): 55–56. *The Times*, 15 November 1890, "Leading Article," cited in T. E. Gregory, *Select Statutes, Documents & Reports Relating to British Banking 1832–1928* (1929; New York: Augustus M. Kelley, 1964): II: 188.

4 Cited in G. H. Pownall, "The Insufficiency of Our Cash Reserves and of Our Central Stock of Gold," in *The Economic Journal*, ed. F. Y. Edgeworth (1892; London: Wm. Dawson & Sons, 1966): II: 530–43; 533.

5 George Bartrick Baker, "The Crisis on the Stock Exchange: Its Causes and Effects," *Contemporary Review*, 58 (November 1890): 680–92; 680–81.

6 L. S. Presnell, "The Sterling System and Financial Crises Before 1914," in *Financial Crises: Theory, History, and Policy*, ed. Charles P. Kindleberger and Jean-Pierre Laffargue (Cambridge: Cambridge University Press, 1982): 148–64; 160.

7 "Banks and Their Customers" (London: Effingham Wilson, Royal Exchange, 1899): 7.

8 *Ibid.*, 8, 9.

9 L. S. Presnell, "Gold Reserves, Banking Reserves, and the Baring Crisis of 1890," in *Essays in Money and Banking, In Honour of R. S. Sayers*, ed. C. R. Whittlesey and J. S. G. Wilson (Oxford: Clarendon Press, 1968): 167–228; 167.

10 Robert Ewen, "Banking Revolution," *The Westminster Review*, 150 (December 1898): 641–46; 641.

11 Joseph Sykes, *The Amalgamation Movement in English Banking, 1825–1924* (London: P. S. King, 1926): 18, 30.

12 John Clapham, *An Economic History of Modern Britain: Machine and National Rivalries* (Cambridge: Cambridge University Press, 1968): III: 278–79.

13 *Ibid.*, III : 282.

14 F. E. Steele, "Bank Amalgamations," in *The Economic Journal*, ed. F. Y. Edgeworth and Henry Higgs (London: Macmillan, 1896): VI: 535–41; 535.

15 Clapham, *An Economic History*, III: 293.

16 Cited in John Clapham, *The Bank of England: A History* (Cambridge: Cambridge University Press, 1945): II: 354.

17 Cited in Frederick Hallis, *Corporate Personality: A Study in Jurisprudence* (Oxford: Oxford University Press, 1930): xliii.

18 Cited in *ibid.*, xliii. In "Capitalism Without the Capitalist: The Joint Stock Company Share and the Emergence of the Modern Doctrine of Separate Corporate Personality," *Legal History*, 17 (April 1996): 40–72, Paddy Ireland points out that the 1862 Companies Act moved from metaphorically referring to a company or corporation as formed "*of*" people to being viewed as "*by*" shareholders, as in a chair or table being "made by a carpenter" (47).

19 William Blackstone, *Commentaries on the Laws of England* (London: John Murray, 1857): I: 497, 498.

20 *Ibid.*, 499. See, for further discussion, Ireland, "Capitalism Without the Capitalist"; Phillip I. Blumberg, *The Multinational Challenge to Corporation Law: The Search for a New Corporate Personality* (New York: Oxford University Press, 1993); *Corporate Personality in the 20th Century*, ed. Charles E. F. Rickett and Ross B. Grantham (Oxford: Hart Publishing, 1998); Frederic William Maitland, *The Collected Papers of Frederic William Maitland*, ed. H. A. L. Fisher (Buffalo: William S. Hein, 1981), vol. III; Frederic William Maitland, "Introduction," in Otto Gierke, *Political Theories of the Middle Age* (1900; Boston: Beacon Hill, 1958); O. Kahn-Freund, "Some Reflections on Company Law Reform," *Modern Law Review*, 7 (April 1944): 54–66.

21 Hallis, *Corporate Personality*, xlii.

22 *Ibid.*

23 Peter Stein, "Nineteenth Century English Company Law and Theories of Legal Personality," *Quaderni Fiorentini*, 11/12 (1982/83): 503–19; 511.

24 Hallis, *Corporate Personality*, xliii.

25 Charles E. F. Rickett and Ross Grantham, "The Bootmaker's Legacy to Company Law Doctrine," in Rickett and Grantham, *Corporate Personality*, 1–10; 1.

26 *Ibid.*, 6.

27 Maitland, *Collected Papers*, III: 241; Maitland, "Introduction," xi–xii.

28 Dillon, *Municipal Corporations*, 37a, cited in Maitland, "Introduction" xi–xii.

29 Stein, "Nineteenth Century English Company Law," 509.

30 Maitland, "Introduction," xi, xii.

31 Maitland, *Collected Papers*, III: 229; Ireland, "Capitalism Without the Capitalist," 47.

32 L. H. Jenks, *The Migration of British Capital to 1875* (1927): 131, cited in Ireland, "Capitalism Without the Capitalist," 67.

33 *Ibid.*, 69.

34 Georg Simmel, *The Philosophy of Money* (1900; London: Routledge & Kegan Paul, 1978): 216.

35 Blumberg, *The Multinational Challenge to Corporation Law*, 5; Maitland, "Introduction," xx.

36 Steele, "Bank Amalgamations," 541, 539, emphasis added.

37 Henry Warren, *The Story of the Bank of England* (London: Jordan & Sons, 1903): 236–37.

38 The novel also has produced an amalgamation of rich and diverse criticism, including feminist, queer theory, and post-colonial.

39 Henry Dunning Macleod, *The Elements of Political Economy* (London: Longman, Brown, Green, Longmans, and Roberts, 1858): 251.

40 Ellis T. Powell, *The Evolution of The Money Market 1385–1915* (1915; New York: Augustus M. Kelley, 1966): 692.

41 I say overdetermined, because clearly there are negative, racist Victorian associations of banking with Jews and usury, but as will be apparent further in this chapter, banking also is seen in very idealistic, benevolent terms, the ambiguities of such disparate views the focus of future study for our field.

42 Simmel, *Philosophy of Money*, 469.

43 Arthur Crump, "The Baring Financial Crisis," in *The Economic Journal*, ed. F. Y. Edgeworth (1891; London: Wm. Dawson & Sons, 1966): I: 388–94; 391.

44 Macleod, *Elements of Political Economy*, 251.

45 George H. Pownall, "Bank Reserves," *The Economic Journal*, ed. F.Y. Edgeworth and Henry Higgs (London: Wm. Macmillan, 1899): IX: 394–410; 403; Robert Ewen, "The Surprise Rise in the Bank Rate," *The Westminster Review*, 146 (July–December 1896): 527–31; 528.

46 Robert Ewen, "British Progress and Free Banking," *The Westminster Review*, 148 (October 1897): 389–95; 392.

47 Robert Ewen, "Cheap and Good Money," *The Westminster Review*, 149 (February 1898): 214–17; 216; see also Robert Ewen, "Better Times Beginning," *The Westminster Review*, 151 (June 1899): 630–34; 632.

48 Karl Marx, *Capital: A Critique of Political Economy* (Chicago: Charles H. Kerr, 1926): I: 257. See also Jules Zanger, "A Sympathetic Vibration: Dracula and the Jews," ELT, 34.1 (1991): 33–44; and Judith Halberstam, "Technologies of Monstrosity: Bram Stoker's *Dracula*," *Victorian Studies*, 36 (Spring 1993): 333–52.

49 Edmund Saul Dixon, "Banking," *Household Words*, 13 (17 May 1856): 427–32; 432.

50 George C. S. Churchill, "Vampire Gold," *The Fortnightly Review*, 48, o.s. (42 n. s). (1887): 77–90; 77.

51 Mikhail I. Tugan-Baranovsky, "The Causes of Crises in the Capitalist Economy," in *Studies in the Theory and History of Commercial Crises in England*, in *Business Cycle Theory: Selected Texts 1860–1939*, ed. Harald Hagemann (London: Pickering & Chatto, 2002): III: 3–44; 39, 40.

52 Ewen, "Cheap and Good Money," 216.

53 Bram Stoker, *Dracula*, ed. Nina Auerbach and David J. Skal (New York: W. W. Norton, 1997): 36. Further citations are to this edition and will be noted in the text.

54 Fred Botting, "Aftergothic: Consumption, Machines, and Black Holes," in *The Cambridge Companion to Gothic Fiction*, ed. Jerrold Hogle (Cambridge: Cambridge University Press, 2002): 277–300; 294.

55 Henry Mayhew, *London Labour and the London Poor* (New York: Dover, 1968): I: 43.

56 Yves Guyot, *Principles of Social Economy*, III: 239; cited in Edward D. Jones, *Economic Crises* (New York: Macmillan, 1900): 181.

57 John Mills, "On Credit Cycles and the Origin of Commercial Panics," in *Transactions of the Manchester Statistical Society* (1868): 11–40, in *Business Cycle Theory: Selected Texts 1860–1939*, I: 57–88.

58 N. C. Frederickson, "Periodicity of Crises, Liquidations and Expanding Periods," *Bankers' Magazine*, 53 (January 1892): 189–98; 197, 198.

59 Jones, *Economic Crises*, 215, 204, 205.

60 Powell, *Evolution of The Money Market*, 259, 220–21, 684–685.

61 *Ibid.*, 684, 258, 259, 694, 689.

62 Pownall, *English Banking*, 50, cited in *ibid.*, 691, 692.

63 Powell, *Evolution of The Money Market*, 693.

64 *Ibid.*, 222, 439, 296–97.

65 *Ibid.*, 693; Sir Edward Holden, cited in *ibid.*, 689.

66 James William Gilbart, *A Practical Treatise on Banking* (Philadelphia: Henry Carey Baird, 1860): 390.

67 Blumberg, *The Multinational Challenge to Corporation Law*, 5; Maitland, "Introduction," xx.

68 Powell, *Evolution of The Money Market*, 694.

69 Gordon Bigelow, "Market Indicators: Banking and Domesticity in Dickens's *Bleak House*," *ELH*, 67 (2000): 589–615; 593.

70 Clapham, *An Economic History of Modern Britain*, III: 293.

71 See Patrick Brantlinger, *Rule of Darkness: British Literature and Imperialism, 1830–1914* (Ithaca: Cornell University Press, 1988) and Stephen D. Arata, "The Occidental Tourist: *Dracula* and the Anxiety of Reverse Colonization," in *Bram Stoker's Dracula*, ed. Auerbach and Skal, 462–70.

72 In *The Literature of Terror: A History of Gothic Fictions from 1765 to the Present Day* (London: Longman, 1980): 258, David Punter remarks that the legends about Dracula explained, in part, the ideological axiom of the immortality of the aristocracy. As he explains, to the peasant class the feudal aristocrat "*was* immortal," for even if the individual aristocrat did not live forever, the peasantry knew that the "life and title persisted, at the expense, of course, of peasant blood, in the literal sense of blood shed in battle and cruelty."

73 Cited in Carol A. Senf, *Science and Social Science in Bram Stoker's Fiction* (Westport, CT: Greenwood Press, 2002): 55.

74 Bram Stoker, *Personal Reminiscences of Henry Irving* (New York: Macmillan, 1906): II: 304, 305.

75 Cited in Leonard Wolf, *The Annotated Dracula: With Introduction, Notes, and Bibliography* (New York: Clarkson N. Potter, 1975): xvii.

76 *The Duties of Clerks of Petty Sessions in Ireland* (Dublin: John Falconer, 1879): v, vi, BL C.S.a 26.19. Stoker provides a form to keep meticulous track of all of these duties. He insists that, when filling out the money columns, "ticks" should be used where there are blank spaces instead of the traditional O (*Petty Sessions*, 92). The "tick" instead of the "O" to fill blank spaces or gaps in the

record cannot help but draw our attention back to Adam Smith filling the space with narrative. It might also be associated with Marx's diacritical mark that, like money, obtains more power and meaning than the commodity.

77 *Ibid.*, v–vi, 27–28.
78 In *The Stenographic Expert* (New York: n. p., n. d.): 116, Willard B. Bottome also endorses "intelligent editing," because, "Let the subject be what it may, there is always room for improvement in style and diction. In the heat of argument or in the earnestness of discourse the speaker sometimes forgets himself and uses language he would not like to see reproduced verbatim. To me there is no greater pleasure than taking a speech in the rough, rounding off the ragged edges, and making it a polished article" (116). In *The Rapid Shorthand Writer* (Leicester: M. A. Roberts, 1882): 14, Francis John Lock problematizes the meaning of "verbatim"; he notes that "The genuine *verbatim* shorthand writer is a *rara avis.*"
79 Cited in Mary Poovey, *A History of the Modern Fact: Problems of Knowledge in the Sciences of Wealth and Society* (Chicago: University of Chicago Press, 1998): 245; emphasis added.
80 Powell, *Evolution of The Money Market*; Jenks, *Migration of British Capital*, 67, cited in Ireland, "Capitalism Without the Capitalist."
81 Blumberg, *The Multinational Challenge to Corporation Law*, 5; Maitland, "Introduction," xx. This discussion, of course, brings up the whole issue of limited and unlimited liability – which was an ongoing issue in the Victorian period; see David Goddard's buoyant view that corporations must be shielded from unlimited liability as laid out in "Corporate Personality – Limited Recourse and its Limits," in *Corporate Personality in the 20th Century*, 11, 11–64.

Index

158

CAMBRIDGE STUDIES IN NINETEENTH-CENTURY
LITERATURE AND CULTURE

General Editor
Gillian Beer, University of Cambridge

Titles Published